Pronto!

LET'S COOK ITALIAN IN **20** MINUTES

GINO
D'ACAMPO

To all my Twitter and Facebook followers for all your support over the years

 facebook.com/ginodacampo

 @ginofantastico

First published in Great Britain in 2017 by Kyle Books,
an imprint of Kyle Cathie Ltd.
192–198 Vauxhall Bridge Road
London SW1V 1DX
general.enquiries@kylebooks.com
www.kylebooks.co.uk

10 9 8 7 6 5 4 3 2 1

ISBN: 978 0 85783 450 8

A CIP catalogue record for this title is available from
the British Library

Gino D'Acampo is hereby identified as the author of
this work in accordance with Section 77 of the Copyright,
Designs and Patents Act 1988.

'Pronto! first published in Great Britain in 2014

Text © Gino D'Acampo 2014
Photographs © Matt Russell 2014
Design © Kyle Books 2014

Editor: Vicky Orchard
Design: Nicky Collings
Photography: Matt Russell
Food Styling: Gee Charman
Props Styling: Jo Harris
Production: David Hearn and Nic Jones

Colour reproduction by ALTA London
Printed and bound in China by C&C Offset Printing
Company Ltd

'Fantastico!' first published in Great Britain in 2007

Text © 2007 Gino D'Acampo
Photography © 2007 Kate Whitaker
Book design © 2007 Kyle Cathie Limited

Editorial Director: Muna Reyal
Designer: Carl Hodson
Photographer: Kate Whitaker
Home economist: Annie Nichols
Styling: Penny Markham
Copyeditor: Stephanie Evans
Production: Sha Huxtable and Alice Holloway

A Cataloguing In Publication record for this title is available
from the British Library.

Colour reproduction by Chromagraphic
Printed in China by C&C Offset Printing Co., Ltd.

CONTENTS

INTRODUCTION

My grandfather (nonno Giovanni) always used to say to me that a great cook should spend more time getting the right ingredients than spending hours in the kitchen trying to prepare a tasty meal. Cooking a good Italian recipe should be quick and easy and – with the right ingredients and equipment – everybody can do it. Millions of you have bought my cookery books in the past 10 years, and I thank you from the bottom of my heart, but lately I have had lots of requests for fast and tasty recipes and I feel it is my responsibility as a cook to push myself and give you what you need: quick, tasty and affordable recipes that anyone can give a go, even during the working week when we're all tired and want food… fast!

When it comes to cooking, the excuse that everybody makes is: I'm too busy. Well, that goes for just about all of us and I understand that with today's hectic lifestyles there never seem to be enough hours in the day BUT we still need to eat. In this book, I am going to show you how to create something fantastic in just 20 minutes that won't overstretch the weekly food budget and that you, your family and friends will love to share and enjoy eating again and again. Let's be honest, it will take you 20 minutes to warm up a ready-meal in the oven or pick up a takeaway, so there's no excuse – just get on with it! Use my 'Italian in 20 minutes' as a frame of mind; when you enter the kitchen relax, put on a bit of music and, if you fancy, have a little glass of wine to make the experience more enjoyable. The first couple of times you cook my recipes it might take you a little longer, but don't worry, remember this is not a competition.

TOOLS

of the

TRADE

- hand blender · food processor
- kettle · microwave · griddle pan
- frying pans (small, medium, large)
- baking trays (small, medium, large)
- lidded saucepans (small, medium, large) · large chopping (cook's) knife
- small peeling knife · long, thin-bladed knife · bread knife · a nice chunky wooden chopping board
- measuring jugs · mixing bowls (small, medium, large) · sieve
- colander · pastry brush

- wooden spoons · tongs
- spatula · fish slice · slotted spoon
- potato masher · potato peeler
- scales · tin opener · box grater
- rolling pin · meat hammer
- large serving plates and bowls

The key to cooking at speed is good organisation. The first thing you need to sort out is your equipment: go round your kitchen and pull out all the utensils you have in your cupboards and ask yourself: how many times have I used this? I am sure you will come across lots of fancy kitchen gadgets that you probably use only once a year. Get rid of them or store them out of your way. To be able to cook my 20-minute recipes you need only the items listed opposite.

As with ingredients, I think it's worth spending a little more and getting something that is good quality: it will cook better and last longer. If you are buying a new set of frying pans, make sure you invest in non-stick ones; they're infinitely easier to cook in and to clean afterwards. Always be careful not to use metal spoons in non-stick frying pans otherwise they will scratch and lose the non-stick coating. I suggest using wooden spoons or plastic-coated spatulas (the silicone ones are great). It is really important to keep your knives in good condition. The biggest mistake that people make is never to sharpen their knives. A good sharp knife will help you to slice and chop quicker instead of wasting lots of time with a blunt one. If you can stretch your budget I would suggest to buying a good knife steel sharpener. Also, tools such as vegetable peelers and graters become blunt with use – it's worth replacing these as soon you notice they are not doing their job.

INGREDIENTS
in your
CUPBOARD

Getting the right ingredients is a must, especially when it comes to store cupboard items, so I have created a very simple list of things you should always have in your cupboard.

-Tinned Ingredients-

chopped tomatoes, plum tomatoes, cherry tomatoes, tomato concentrate, chickpeas, cannellini beans, red kidney beans, borlotti beans, butter beans, anchovy fillets in oil, tuna chunks in oil and pineapple chunks

-Jarred Ingredients-

sun-dried tomatoes in oil, roasted peppers in oil, artichokes hearts in oil, salted capers, English mustard, wholegrain mustard, runny honey, Nutella chocolate spread, strawberry jam and mayonnaise

-Bottled Ingredients-

extra virgin olive oil, olive oil, balsamic vinegar, balsamic glaze, passata, white wine vinegar, red wine vinegar and tomato ketchup

-Dried Pasta and Rice-

penne rigate, rigatoni, spaghetti, linguine, farfalle, fusilli, conchigliette (small shells), orecchiette, short grain (Arborio or risotto) rice, long grain (basmati) rice, microwaveable rice, couscous, bulgar wheat and ready-made polenta

-Baking Ingredients-

plain flour, self-raising flour, cornflour, cocoa powder, baking powder, caster sugar, brown sugar and vanilla extract

-Herbs and Spices-

I am not a big fan of dried herbs or spices; I strongly believe that fresh herbs are much better in flavour and texture but there are a few I find very useful and good in taste: dried oregano, dried chilli flakes, cayenne pepper, smoked paprika, fennel seeds, saffron and nutmeg

-Miscellaneous-

chicken/vegetable/beef stock powder, almonds, hazelnuts, walnuts, pine nuts, pistachio nuts, toasted fine breadcrumbs and dried porcini mushrooms and fresh eggs.

To cook quick but super tasty Italian dishes also requires you to organise your fresh ingredients in the fridge. When reading my recipes you will find that I often use the following fresh ingredients and they are therefore part of my weekly shopping list: eggs, mozzarella balls, block of Parmesan cheese, tub of mascarpone cheese, salted butter, cooked ham, Parma ham, sliced salami, diced pancetta, fresh egg tagliatelle, lasagne sheets, cherry tomatoes, rocket leaves, double cream, creme fraîche and full-fat milk.

SHORTCUTS

to make your

LIFE EASIER AROUND
THE KITCHEN

Chopping and slicing ingredients is where everyone wastes the most time when preparing a recipe. Here are a few things you can do to make your life a little easier:

• Finely slice or chop your onions, roll in clingfilm and freeze. They will last frozen for up to 2 months and you can use them straight from the freezer.

• Slice or chop your garlic and put in a clean jam jar. Cover with olive oil and refrigerate. It will last for 10 days.

• Remember you can always prepare ahead big batches of onions and garlic by chopping and slicing using a food processor.

When cooking Italian food fresh herbs are a must; nowadays you can buy those beautiful little growing plants that you can easily keep on your windowsill and they last for weeks. Basil, flatleaf parsley, rosemary and chives are very easy to look after and remember, especially if you have a supply in your garden or allotment, that you can always pick off the leaves, roll them in clingfilm and freeze them ready to be used straight from the freezer. Chop fresh herbs on a large chopping board and use the biggest knife you have to make the job faster.

Once a week, collect all your stale bread and cut into small chunks. Put on a baking tray and cook in the oven at 110°C/gas 1 for 2 hours. Turn off the heat and leave the bread to cool down in the oven. Blitz in a food processor until you have fine crumbs with a sand-like texture. Store in an airtight container for 1 month.

Make up a big batch of tomato sauce, allow it to cool to room temperature, pour it into containers, seal and freeze for up to 2 months. Please defrost before using.

GINO'S TOP TIPS

to become

FASTER AND MORE CONFIDENT

-1-
Pour yourself a glass of wine.

-2-
Switch on the music; I find Dean Martin always helps!

-3-
Before you start, read and understand the recipe, what equipment you will need and what ingredients. You'll get a good idea of what you need to do when and won't have to waste lots of time referring back to the recipe when you could be chopping or cooking.

-4-
Arrange your equipment and ingredients to hand around the working space.

-5-
Don't forget to sip the wine from time to time.

-6-
Make room around you: get kids' toys, magazines, bills, etc. out of the way; only cooking equipment should be on your work surface.

-7-
Clean and clear up as you go along.

-8-
Don't have an argument with your partner: a sad cook doesn't produce good food.

-9-
Don't rush things, 20 minutes is plenty of time to make a good dish. If you feel hurried you are more likely to make a mistake and may have to start again.

-10-
Use local ingredients that are in season, they will be fresher and therefore require less cooking or marinating time.

SOUPS & SMALL PLATES

Zuppe e piatti piccoli

This chapter is full of dishes great for a light dinner, lunch or even for a starter if you're having a dinner party. People often think that soups take a long time to cook but my fast recipes included here preserve the freshness and flavour of the ingredients.

Italian classics such as Carpaccio and bruschetta are easy to make in 20 minutes and perfect dishes if you are pushed for time. These simple recipes require only a handful of ingredients but it's this simplicity that makes them so timeless.

SPEEDY VEGETABLE

and

CANNELLINI BEAN SOUP

Some soups taste best if they're allowed to bubble away long and slow, but this one, with its super-fast cooking time, allows you to preserve the freshness of the vegetables. There isn't actually a set recipe for minestrone, the classic Italian soup – its pedigree goes back to the times before the Romans – as it's usually made using whatever vegetables are in season, but it almost always contains beans, pasta or rice. I've chosen cannellini beans as they are full of flavour, incredibly good for you and one of my favourite pulses.

Minestrone velocissimo

serves 6

6 tablespoons extra virgin
olive oil
1 red onion, roughly chopped
2 large carrots, peeled and cut
into 1cm cubes
2 celery stalks, washed and
cut into 1cm cubes
150g curly Savoy cabbage,
roughly chopped
1.5 litres hot vegetable stock
6 slices of rustic country-style
bread
1 garlic clove, peeled
1 x 400g can cannellini beans,
drained and rinsed
4 tablespoons chopped
flatleaf parsley
100g freshly grated Parmesan
cheese
Salt and white pepper, to taste

1 Preheat a griddle pan.

2 Heat the oil in a large saucepan and fry the onion, carrots, celery and cabbage for 3 minutes. Stir occasionally with a wooden spoon. Pour in the vegetable stock, bring to the boil and cook for 10 minutes. Stir occasionally.

3 Meanwhile, toast the bread on the preheated griddle pan for about 2 minutes on each side until golden and crispy. Immediately lightly rub with the clove of garlic on one side only. Set aside.

4 Reduce the heat under the saucepan to medium and add the beans and parsley to the vegetables. Season with salt and pepper and continue to cook for a further 3 minutes.

5 To serve, place a slice of bread in each serving bowl and pour over the soup. Sprinkle over some Parmesan and serve immediately.

ROASTED RED PEPPER
and
TOMATO SOUP

A friend of mine was complaining that she found it impossible to make a tasty tomato soup. She said that it always came out too watery or lacked flavour. I created this for her; the sweetness of the roasted red peppers adds that little extra something and this soup will leave you feeling satisfied.

Zuppa di pomodori e peperoni

serves 4

3 tablespoons extra virgin olive oil, plus extra for drizzling
1 medium red onion, peeled and roughly chopped
6 large ripe plum tomatoes, roughly chopped
600ml hot vegetable stock
10 basil leaves, plus extra to garnish
200g roasted red peppers in brine, drained and roughly chopped
Double cream, for drizzling
Salt and white pepper, to taste

1 Heat the oil in a medium saucepan and fry the onion over a medium heat for 2 minutes. Stir occasionally with a wooden spoon. Add in the tomatoes and continue to cook for a further 2 minutes. Keep stirring.

2 Pour in the vegetable stock, add the basil leaves and chopped, roasted peppers and bring to the boil. Reduce the heat and simmer for 10 minutes. Stir occasionally.

3 Remove the saucepan from the heat and use a hand blender to blitz into a smooth soup.

4 Season with salt and pepper and serve in warmed bowls, garnished with a few basil leaves, a drizzle of cream and some extra virgin olive oil. I like to serve this with Italian breadsticks on the side.

PUMPKIN

and

SUN-DRIED TOMATO SOUP

I come up with a new pumpkin recipe every Halloween. I refuse to make faces out of the tough shell and not use the lovely squash itself. Pumpkins are really versatile – they give us oil, seeds and delicious-tasting flesh. There are many different squashes that you could also use for this soup at different times of the year but, come autumn, it's hard to resist buying the huge, smooth, slightly ribbed orange pumpkins that you see everywhere.

Zuppa di zucca e pomodori secchi

serves 4

50g salted butter
500g pumpkin flesh, cut into 1cm cubes
2 celery stalks, roughly chopped
2 garlic cloves, peeled and chopped
100g sun-dried tomatoes in oil, drained and roughly chopped
800ml hot vegetable stock
200ml double cream
2 tablespoons pumpkin seeds
Salt and black pepper, to taste

1 Melt the butter in a large saucepan over a medium heat and fry the pumpkin, celery and garlic for 2 minutes. Stir occasionally with a wooden spoon. Add the sun-dried tomatoes and continue to cook for a further 2 minutes. Keep stirring.

2 Pour in the stock and bring to the boil. Reduce the heat and simmer for 12 minutes. Stir occasionally.

3 Remove the saucepan from the heat and use a hand blender to blitz into a smooth, creamy soup.

4 Pour in the cream, season with salt and pepper and heat through without boiling.

5 Serve in warmed bowls, garnished with pumpkin seeds. Perfect with warm ciabatta.

COLD SUMMER TOMATO SOUP

My children still don't understand why you would choose to have cold soup and yet every time I make this recipe, they are the first to finish. It's one of those unusual recipes that you are just not sure about until you try it. Why give up soup during the warm months? The flavours of these quintessentially Mediterranean ingredients are amazing as they haven't been boiled away, the amount of goodness in one bowl is incredible and its vibrant colour looks great.

Passata fredda di pomodori

serves 6

1 yellow pepper, deseeded
and roughly chopped
1 red pepper, deseeded
and roughly chopped
½ cucumber, roughly chopped
1 medium red onion, peeled
and finely chopped
1 fresh red chilli, deseeded
and roughly chopped
600g ripe plum tomatoes, roughly
chopped
1 x 700ml bottle of passata
2 tablespoons red wine vinegar
2 tablespoons extra virgin
olive oil
10 basil leaves
1 tablespoon caster sugar
Salt and white pepper, to taste

1   Separate out a quarter of the prepared yellow and red pepper, cucumber and red onion. Chop very finely and set aside for the garnish.

2   Put all the remaining ingredients in a blender or food processor and blitz until smooth. You may need to do this in 2 batches.

3   Pass the blitzed soup through a sieve into a large clean bowl, pushing it through with a tablespoon to extract the maximum amount of flavour.

4   Season with salt and pepper and transfer to the fridge to rest for 5 minutes.

5   To serve, ladle into bowls and garnish with the reserved chopped vegetables scattered on top.

FRESH PEA

and

BASIL SOUP

We often have peas in the D'Acampo home and I must admit I created this recipe when I was just about to go on holiday and literally the only thing in my fridge was peas. It was pouring with rain outside and I wanted something warm and comforting. And this is what I created – an amazing pea soup made in minutes. Peas are starchy, which gives great texture to the soup, and they are incredibly high in fibre, protein, vitamins and minerals. Although mint is often paired with peas, basil is what gives the soup its Italian lilt.

Zuppa di pisellini

serves 4

2 tablespoons salted butter
2 tablespoons olive oil
**1 medium white onion, peeled
and finely chopped**
600g fresh peas, podded weight
600ml boiling water
15 basil leaves
1 vegetable stock cube
**100ml double cream, plus a little
extra to garnish**
Salt and white pepper, to taste

1 Melt the butter in a large saucepan with the oil and fry the onion over a medium heat for 2 minutes. Stir occasionally with a wooden spoon. Add the peas and continue to cook for a further 2 minutes. Keep stirring.

2 Pour in the water, add the basil leaves and stock cube and bring to the boil. Reduce the heat and simmer for 12 minutes. Stir occasionally.

3 Remove the saucepan from the heat and use a hand blender to blitz into a smooth, creamy soup.

4 Pour in the cream, season with salt and pepper and heat through without boiling.

5 Serve in warmed bowls, garnished with a drizzle of cream. Perfect served with warm, crusty bread.

SPICY FISH SOUP

with

ROASTED RED PEPPERS

Every region of Italy with a coastline has its own take on fish soup. This version is characteristic of the Campania region where I'm from originally. This recipe is so easy and being cooked in just one pot gives it extra appeal to busy people. You can use sustainably caught cod instead of haddock if you prefer, and please ensure the fish is extremely fresh. This soup can be served as a starter or a main meal; do make lots, as it will disappear really quickly.

Zuppa di pesce alla Torrese

serves 4

4 tablespoons olive oil
1 large red onion, peeled and finely chopped
1 teaspoon dried chilli flakes
200g roasted red peppers in brine from a jar, drained and sliced
150ml white wine
400ml hot fish stock
1 x 400g can chopped tomatoes
300g skinless haddock, cut into 5cm chunks
250g skinless red mullet, cut into 5cm chunks
16 large uncooked prawns, peeled
4 tablespoons freshly chopped flatleaf parsley
Salt, to taste

1 Heat the oil in a large saucepan over a medium heat and fry the onion, chilli and peppers for 2 minutes. Stir occasionally with a wooden spoon.

2 Pour in the wine and continue to cook for a further 2 minutes, allowing the alcohol to evaporate.

3 Pour in the fish stock, add the chopped tomatoes and season with salt. Bring to the boil, reduce the heat to low and simmer for 10 minutes, uncovered.

4 Add the fish and prawns, stir together and continue to cook for 4 minutes.

5 Stir in the parsley, check the seasoning and serve immediately with lots of crusty bread.

CARROTS AND ALMONDS

with

FRESH MINT AND CHILLI

There is almost nothing better than really fresh vegetables steamed or boiled al dente served with just a little salt and olive oil but, I must admit to occasionally getting a little bored of the same thing and have to create something with a bit of a twist – if it works, it gets to be in the next book, like this tasty carrot dish. Its flavours and textures are incredible together – try it as an accompaniment to any meat or fish.

Carote e mandorle alla menta

serves 4

6 large carrots
15 mint leaves, finely sliced
1 teaspoon dried chilli flakes
100g flaked almonds
8 tablespoons extra virgin olive oil
6 tablespoons white wine vinegar
Salt, to taste

Crispy salad leaves, to serve

1   Fill a medium saucepan with water and bring to the boil with 1 teaspoon of salt.

2   Peel the carrots and cut into 1cm rounds. Drop the carrots into the boiling water and cook for 3 minutes; drain well and place in a large bowl.

3   While the carrots are still hot, add the remaining ingredients to the bowl. Season with a little salt and gently mix together.

4   Set aside at room temperature for 10 minutes, allowing the flavours to combine beautifully. Gently stir every 2 minutes.

5   To serve, simply mix the marinated carrots into your favourite crispy salad.

SUPER-FAST OMELETTE

with

PARMA HAM

Breakfast, lunch or dinner – a tasty omelette is always a winner. This is one of the easiest, quickest recipes in the book yet it doesn't compromise on flavour. I love the combination of Parma ham and Parmesan cheese, which transports me back home to Italy, but there are numerous different variations that you can try such as cooked ham and Pecorino cheese or salami and Cheddar.

Frittatina al prosciutto

serves 1

2 large eggs
1 tablespoon freshly grated Parmesan cheese
1 teaspoon salted butter
1 teaspoon olive oil
2 slices of Parma ham
Salt and white pepper, to taste

1   Break the eggs into a medium bowl and season with salt and pepper. Use a fork to gently whisk the eggs for 10 seconds. Add the Parmesan cheese and whisk for another 10 seconds.

2   Melt the butter with the oil in a 15cm frying pan over a medium heat. Tilt the pan so that the base and the sides are well greased. Increase the heat to its highest setting and, when the butter is foaming, pour in the eggs. Tilt the pan to spread the eggs evenly over the base. Leave it over the heat without moving and count to six.

3   Tilt the pan to 45 degrees and, using a tablespoon, draw the edges of the omelette into the centre. Tip the pan the other way and do the same thing.

4   Put the Parma ham slices in the middle of the omelette. Tilt the pan again and flip one side of the omelette into the centre then fold again.

5   Take the pan across to a warm serving plate and make the last fold when you tip the omelette onto the serving plate.

6   Serve immediately with warm crusty bread.

POACHED EGGS

with

CRISPY PANCETTA ON TOASTED CIABATTA

I made this for my best friend Marco years ago after a heavy night out – we still laugh about it today. I was explaining to him how I make crispy pancetta with soft poached eggs etc. He took a bite and said it was heaven but then proceeded to say that I could have just shut up while he had a sore head and served him his usual bacon and egg sandwich… OK, it is kind of a bacon and egg sandwich, but I am steadfast in my opinion that this is the ultimate Italian bacon and egg concoction and I'm not sure it can be compared to one from a greasy spoon: you tell me…

Uova e pancetta

serves 4

2 large round tomatoes
12 slices of pancetta
3 tablespoons white wine vinegar
8 large fresh eggs
8 slices of ciabatta bread,
1cm thick
4 teaspoons mayonnaise
Salt and black pepper, to taste

1 Preheat the grill to medium.

2 Cut the tomatoes into eight thick slices and spread out on a sheet of kitchen foil with the pancetta. Put on a baking tray and set aside.

3 Place 8 poaching rings in one or two frying pans (depending on their size) and pour in enough water to cover the base of the pan, at least 1cm deep. Pour in the vinegar and bring to the boil: reduce the heat so that the water starts to simmer. Gently break one egg into each ring and poach for 4 minutes until set.

4 Meanwhile, cook the tomatoes and pancetta under the grill for 2 minutes on each side.

5 Toast the ciabatta bread.

6 Place 2 slices of bread in the middle of each serving plate and spread the mayonnaise on the top side only. Arrange 2 slices of tomato on each slice of the ciabatta and top each one with 3 slices of pancetta.

7 Carefully place the poached eggs on top of the pancetta and sprinkle with a little salt and pepper. Serve immediately.

PIZZA-STYLE CIABATTA BREAD

with

OLIVES, MOZZARELLA AND ARTICHOKES

If you love pizza please try this recipe. It is quicker to make this from scratch than it is for you to pick up the phone, order a pizza and wait for it to be delivered. I know it will taste ten times better too! I have chosen olives, pesto and artichoke hearts as I think the combination is amazing – artichokes are still so underestimated but we Italians love them.

Pizzetta

serves 4

2 medium ciabattas, each about 130g, sliced in half horizontally
8 tablespoons passata
2 x 125g mozzarella balls, drained and thinly sliced
4 tablespoons green pesto
150g artichoke hearts in oil, drained and quartered
60g black pitted olives in brine or oil, drained and halved
12 cherry tomatoes, halved
Salt and black pepper, to taste

1   Preheat the oven to 200°C/gas 6.

2   Place the ciabatta slices on a baking tray, cut-side up.

3   Spread the passata evenly over each ciabatta half then top with the slices of mozzarella.

4   Spread the pesto over the mozzarella.

5   Scatter the remaining ingredients on top, season with salt and pepper and bake in the oven for 10 minutes.

6   Serve hot with a big glass of Italian cold white wine.

COUNTRY-STYLE BREAD

topped with

TOMATO AND GREEN OLIVES

Bruschetta has been around since at least the 15th century. It used to be simply a piece of bread grilled, rubbed with garlic and topped with extra virgin olive oil, salt and pepper, but nowadays the variations are numerous. One of the most popular versions outside Italy has to be tomato, basil, garlic and olive oil. However, on this occasion I've returned it to its homeland by adding in some olives – you won't be disappointed.

Bruschetta pomodoro e olive

serves 4

500g small plum tomatoes, quartered
10 basil leaves, shredded
5 tablespoons extra virgin olive oil, plus extra for brushing
150g pitted green olives in brine, drained and halved
1 loaf of country-style bread
2 garlic cloves, peeled
Salt and black pepper, to taste

1   Preheat a griddle pan over a medium heat.

2   Put the tomatoes in a large bowl. Add in three-quarters of the basil, the extra virgin olive oil and season with salt and pepper. Add the olives, mix together and cover with a tea towel. Set aside to marinate at room temperature for 5 minutes. Stir halfway through.

3   Meanwhile, cut 8 slices of bread from the loaf, each about 2cm thick. Brush a little oil on each side of the slices. Toast the bread on the griddle pan for 2 minutes on each side, until dark brown and crispy all over. Allow to cool slightly.

4   Lightly rub the garlic over both sides of the toasted bread. Top each slice with 2–3 tablespoons of the tomato mixture and arrange the bruschetta on a large serving plate.

5   Drizzle over any remaining juices from the bowl of tomatoes and sprinkle with the reserved basil.

6   Serve with a cold glass of beer as an appetiser, or as a starter.

STICKY SPICY LAMB SAUSAGES

These make a perfect little snack and are great as a simple starter. Lamb sausages make a change from the usual pork ones and, flavoured with rosemary, honey and chilli, they become irresistible little morsels: sticky and satisfying. You could remove the chilli if the kids are going to eat them; simply grind a little black pepper over the sausages instead.

Salsicciotti piccanti

serves 4

400g lamb chipolata sausages
2 tablespoons olive oil
1 tablespoon rosemary leaves,
finely chopped
1 teaspoon dried chilli flakes
2 tablespoons runny honey

1 Preheat the oven to 220°C/gas 7 and put a large ovenproof frying pan over a high heat.

2 Take each sausage and carefully twist in the middle so that you divide it into two. Cut through the twist so that you have two small cocktail sausages.

3 Pour the oil into the frying pan and add the sausages. Fry for 4 minutes, stirring occasionally with a wooden spoon.

4 Add the rosemary leaves to the frying pan with the chilli flakes. Continue to cook for 1 minute then stir in the honey.

5 Transfer the frying pan to the oven for 10 minutes.

6 Pile the little sausages in the middle of a chopping board and provide cocktail sticks for everyone. Make sure that you have plenty of cold drinks to serve with them.

BEEF CARPACCIO

with

ROCKET, BALSAMIC GLAZE AND PARMESAN

Carpaccio was created in Venice during the 20th century and has become the internationally recognised name for a dish of thinly sliced raw meat. It is said that in 1950 Countess Amalia Nani Mocenigo was advised by her doctor only to eat raw meat. Unfortunately, she didn't care for red meat, which she found tough and hard to digest. Giuseppe Cipriani, the owner of Harry's Bar in Venice, took up the challenge and created for her a dish of top-quality raw beef fillet, sliced very thinly and served with yellow mustard dressing. He named the recipe Carpaccio as the colours reminded him of the palette used by Venetian painter Vittore Carpaccio. My version uses balsamic glaze, its sweetness sharpened by the addition of capers, rather than the mustard used in the original.

Carpaccio di manzo con rucola e Parmigiano

serves 2

250g fillet of beef
4 tablespoons extra virgin olive oil
30g Parmesan shavings
2 tablespoons small capers in vinegar, drained
30g rocket leaves
3 tablespoons balsamic glaze
6 thin slices of ciabatta bread, toasted, to serve
Salt and black pepper, to taste

1 Cut the beef into very thin slices and place in a single layer between two sheets of clingfilm. Use a cooking hammer to beat the slices gently until they become very thin slivers.

2 Arrange the beef slivers in a single layer over the base of a cold large serving plate. Drizzle over the extra virgin olive oil and then sprinkle with a little salt and black pepper.

3 Scatter the Parmesan shavings and capers over the beef and pile the rocket leaves into the centre of the plate. Drizzle the balsamic glaze over the beef and rocket.

4 Serve with the toasted ciabatta.

CHICKEN

Il pollo

Chicken is probably the most popular meat and extremely versatile as you can cook it a number of ways in a variety of different dishes. Chicken breasts are great for quick meals as they are best when cooked for a short amount of time; if they are overcooked the meat tends to dry out. I've also included a few escalope recipes here as this technique of flattening the chicken breast makes the cooking time even faster.

CHICKEN AND CHORIZO SALAD

with

BEANS AND ROCKET LEAVES

Every now and then I go on a health kick and watch what I eat, especially in the evenings. However, there are only so many salads you can have before you start to get a bit bored, especially during the winter months – but this is an amazing option: filling, delicious and incredibly good for you but at the same time it won't leave you feeling hard done by, unlike some salads.

Insalata di pollo e chorizo

serves 4

100g can cannellini beans, drained and rinsed
100g can borlotti beans, drained and rinsed
20 cherry tomatoes, quartered
1 medium hot red chilli, deseeded and thinly sliced
1 garlic clove, peeled and finely sliced
2 tablespoons freshly squeezed lemon juice
8 tablespoons extra virgin olive oil
2 medium skinless, boneless chicken breasts, cut into 1cm strips
100g hot chorizo sausage, cut into thin round slices
60g rocket leaves
Salt, to taste

1 Put all the beans in a large bowl with the tomatoes, chilli and garlic. Pour over the lemon juice with half the olive oil, season with salt, toss all together and set aside.

2 Place a large frying pan over a high heat and pour in the remaining oil. Add the chicken strips and fry for 5 minutes, stirring occasionally with a wooden spoon.

3 Season with salt, add the chorizo and continue to fry for a further 2 minutes over a high heat.

4 Toss the rocket leaves through the bean salad and transfer to a large serving plate. Top with the crispy chicken and chorizo and serve immediately.

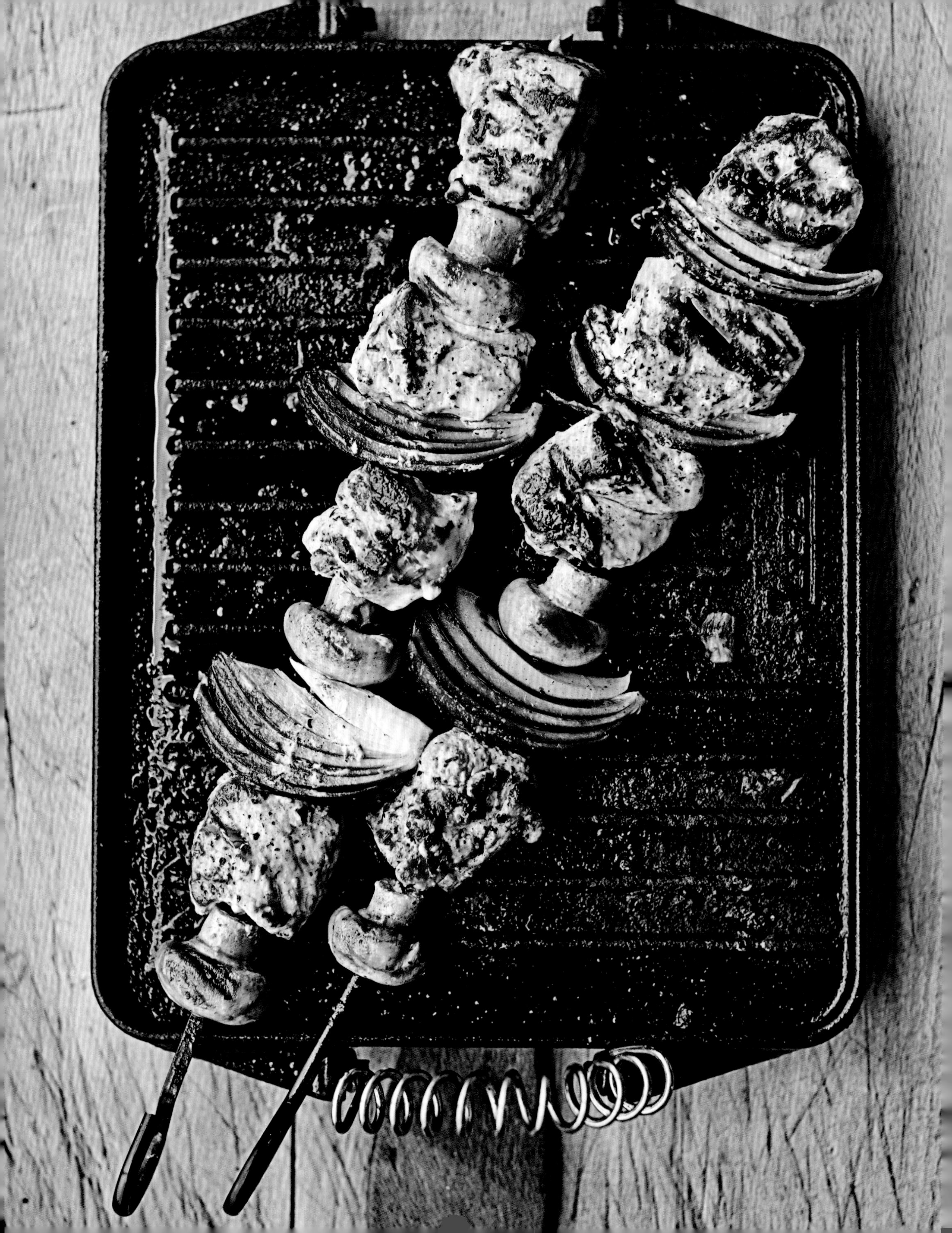

CHICKEN SKEWERS

marinated with

YOGURT AND MINT SAUCE

If it's pouring outside and you really fancy a barbecue-style dish, then these skewers are ideal. They are very light and extremely tasty, bringing a taste of summer into your life, whatever the season. Do add other vegetables like tomatoes or peppers to your skewers if you prefer.

Spiedini di pollo

serves 2

1 tablespoon ready-made mint sauce
1 tablespoon rosemary leaves, finely chopped
2 medium skinless, boneless chicken breasts, cut into 3cm chunks – ideally 8–10 big chunks
150g natural yogurt
1 large red onion, peeled and cut into 6 wedges
6 medium button mushrooms
Salt and black pepper, to taste
Crisps, to serve

1 Mix the yogurt, mint sauce and rosemary in a large bowl. Season with salt and pepper.

2 Add the chicken pieces and mix well to ensure that each piece is coated with the marinade. Leave to rest at room temperature for 8 minutes.

3 Preheat a griddle pan or a barbecue.

4 Thread the chicken onto two metal skewers (or wooden ones that have been soaked in water for at least 30 minutes), alternating each piece with onions and mushrooms.

5 Cook the skewers on the hot griddle pan or barbecue rack for 8 minutes, turning the meat to ensure that every side is coloured and cooked through.

6 Serve hot accompanied with a big bowl of your favourite crisps.

SKEWERED CHICKEN MEATBALLS
with
GARLIC YOGURT

This recipe came about one morning: the house was empty with the kids off playing football or rugby and I was in charge (as on most Sundays) of making lunch. I had every intention of making chicken meatballs in a tomato-based sauce but saw a glimpse of sun peeking through the clouds and ended up with meatball skewers instead, which was a lot quicker. They turned out to be really different and have now become a regular Sunday treat.

Polpettine di pollo

serves 4

300g minced chicken
1 large onion, finely chopped
½ teaspoon freshly ground black pepper
2 tablespoons freshly chopped mint
16 cherry tomatoes
3 tablespoons olive oil
Salt, to taste

For the garlic yogurt:
200ml natural yogurt
4 garlic cloves, peeled and crushed to a purée
1 teaspoon dried oregano
Salt, to taste

1 Preheat the grill to the highest setting.

2 Put the minced chicken in a large mixing bowl with the onion, black pepper and mint. Season with salt and mix together using your fingertips. Divide the mixture into four equal portions. Roll 5 balls from each portion to make 20 in total and set aside.

3 Thread one meatball on to a metal skewer, followed by a cherry tomato and continue until you have 5 meatballs and 4 cherry tomatoes on each skewer.

4 Transfer the skewers to a grill tray and brush with the olive oil. Cook under the grill for 10 minutes, turning the skewers regularly until browned all over.

5 Meanwhile, pour the yogurt into a bowl and add the garlic and oregano. Season with salt and mix together.

6 Put the skewered meatballs on a large serving plate and drizzle with the garlic yogurt. Serve hot with a cold beer or a glass of juice for the kids.

CHICKEN BURGERS

with

GARLIC AND THYME

I normally make this recipe with minced beef or pork but I was having friends round for lunch and their children didn't really like red meat so I made them burgers using chicken mince instead. It was such a success I decided to include it in this book. Minced chicken makes burgers that are much lighter in texture than ones made with red meat. I ended up swapping my beefburger for a chicken burger as it was so good.

Hamburger di pollo con aglio e timo

serves 4

500g minced chicken
2 teaspoons thyme leaves, finely chopped
60g fresh breadcrumbs
80g sun-dried tomatoes in oil, drained and finely sliced
1 garlic clove, peeled and finely chopped
50g freshly grated Parmesan cheese
1 egg, beaten
3 tablespoons olive oil, for greasing
4 good-quality burger baps
50g mixed salad leaves
4 tablespoons mayonnaise
Salt and black pepper, to taste

1   Use your hands to mix together the minced chicken, thyme, breadcrumbs, sun-dried tomatoes, garlic and Parmesan in a large bowl. Season with salt and pepper and pour in the beaten egg to bind the mixture. Continue to mix until well combined.

2   Preheat the oven to 150°C/gas 2 and put a griddle pan over a high heat.

3   Lightly grease the palms of your hands with olive oil and start to shape the chicken mixture into 4 large balls. Gently press each ball between your hands to create a burger patty.

4   Cook the burgers on the griddle pan for 4 minutes on each side.

5   Meanwhile, warm the baps in the oven.

6   Once the burgers are ready, cut the baps in half and put an equal layer of salad leaves on the bottom halves. Put a hot burger on top of the leaves, spread mayonnaise on the cut top half of the baps and close the burgers.

CHICKEN
in
LEMON AND PARSLEY SAUCE

This dish is actually my late grandfather's recipe. We lived near Sorrento, famous for the quality of its lemons, and he would always buy the biggest, freshest one he could find to make this recipe for us. During the hot steamy summers, this was one of our favourites as it is lovely, light and fresh on the palate. We would normally have this dish after loads of antipasti so we would have no room for more than the chicken and bread to dunk in the sauce but there's a range of serving possibilities – salad, veg or potatoes.

Pollo al limone e prezzemolo

serves 4

4 medium skinless, boneless chicken breasts
50g plain flour
4 tablespoons olive oil
80g butter
Juice of 2 lemons
50ml chicken stock
4 tablespoons freshly chopped flatleaf parsley
Salt and white pepper, to taste

1 Put the chicken breasts on a chopping board and use a sharp knife to cut each one horizontally into 2 thin slices.

2 Put the flour onto a large plate, season with salt and pepper and mix. Coat each side of the chicken breasts with the flour. Gently tap the chicken to discard any excess.

3 Heat the olive oil and half the butter in a large frying pan over a medium heat. Put the floured chicken in the pan and fry for 4 minutes on each side until it starts to brown and is cooked through. (Cook in batches if necessary.)

4 Transfer the cooked chicken slices to a large serving plate and cover with foil while you make the sauce.

5 Pour the lemon juice and the stock into the frying pan and use a wooden spoon to scrape all the brown bits from the edges and base into the sauce. Bring to the boil and stir for 1 minute. Add the chopped parsley and remaining butter and continue to stir for a further minute until it has a creamy texture.

6 To serve, place 2 slices of chicken in the middle of each serving plate and drizzle over the lemon and parsley sauce. Serve immediately with some crisp salad leaves or my warm New Potato Salad with Red Onions and Capers (see page 201).

CHICKEN BREAST
in
ROSEMARY AND ORANGE SAUCE

I'm not usually a big fan of meat with fruit but I do love this recipe. It's a simpler version of the French classic duck à l'orange but using chicken is a less fatty choice. I would normally recommend buying fruit and veg when they are in season but as this particular recipe calls for oranges, you can make it all year round. It's a classy way to serve chicken, with a subtle tangy flavour that everyone will enjoy.

Pollo in salsa di arance

serves 4

6 tablespoons olive oil
4 medium boneless chicken breasts, skin on
250g button mushrooms, cleaned and quartered
3 tablespoons rosemary leaves
½ teaspoon dried chilli flakes
Juice of 2 large oranges
1 tablespoon red wine vinegar
Salt, to taste

1 Heat the oil in a large frying pan over a medium heat and start to fry the chicken, skin-side down first, for 2 minutes on each side until browned. Remove the breasts from the pan and set aside.

2 Add the mushrooms and rosemary to the frying pan and fry for 4 minutes. Stir occasionally with a wooden spoon.

3 Sprinkle over the chilli and pour in the orange juice and the vinegar. Bring to the boil.

4 Return the chicken breasts to the pan and cook over a medium heat for 5 minutes to allow the chicken to finish cooking and the sauce to thicken. Turn the meat halfway through cooking and season with salt.

5 Serve immediately, placing the chicken breasts skin-side up surrounded by the orange sauce. Serve with a green salad.

CHICKEN BREAST
with
PINK PEPPERCORN AND GORGONZOLA SAUCE

If you are on a diet, you might want to turn to another page! The sauce I have created for this chicken is very rich and creamy but it's definitely a lovely indulgent treat. You can use a milder Dolcelatte rather than the Gorgonzola if you prefer, but don't try to make a low-calorie version of this by substituting anything lighter for the cream – you need the thickness of double cream to make the sauce work.

Petto di pollo al Gorgonzola

serves 4

50g salted butter
4 tablespoons olive oil
4 medium boneless chicken
breasts, skin on
1 tablespoon pink peppercorns in
brine, drained
100ml double cream
150g Gorgonzola cheese, cut into
small cubes

1   Place a large non-stick frying pan over a medium heat, melt the butter with the oil and cook the chicken, skin-side down first, with the peppercorns for 4 minutes on each side until golden brown all over. Do not season with salt.

2   Transfer the chicken to a plate and cover with foil to keep warm while preparing the sauce. Leave the peppercorns in the frying pan.

3   Pour the cream into the pan and cook for 1 minute, stirring constantly with a wooden spoon.

4   Add the Gorgonzola and continue to stir constantly for 3 minutes allowing the cheese to melt and create a smooth sauce.

5   Place one chicken breast, skin-side up, in the middle of each serving plate and drizzle over the Gorgonzola and peppercorn sauce.

6   Serve immediately with vegetables of your choice and some warm crusty bread to mop up the sauce.

HUNTER-STYLE CHICKEN

in

A SPICY TOMATO SAUCE

Pollo piccante alla cacciatore

Chicken thighs are often underestimated but they are a fabulous cut of chicken, with more flavour than the white meat. Cooked in a one-pot stew they remain tender and juicy. This makes a warm and tasty supper; perfect for those colder evenings.

serves 4

5 tablespoons olive oil
150g diced pancetta
1 large white onion, peeled and finely sliced
2 tablespoons rosemary leaves, chopped
1 teaspoon dried chilli flakes
800g skinless boneless chicken thighs, each cut into 4 pieces
50ml red wine
2 x 400g cans of chopped tomatoes
2 bay leaves
Salt, to taste

1   Heat the oil in a heavy-based saucepan over a medium heat and fry the pancetta with the onion for 3 minutes. Stir occasionally with a wooden spoon.

2   Add the rosemary and chilli and continue to cook for a further minute.

3   Next add the chicken, season with salt and continue to cook for a further minute.

4   Pour in the wine and let it bubble before adding the chopped tomatoes and bay leaves. Cover with a lid and allow the chicken to gently simmer for 10 minutes. Stir occasionally.

5   Remove the lid and cook over a high heat for a further 3 minutes, allowing the sauce to thicken.

6   Serve with a large glass of Italian red wine and make sure there's plenty of warm crusty bread to soak up the sauce.

STICKY HONEY CHICKEN
with
SMOKED PAPRIKA

I absolutely love the flavours of this recipe – sweet, sticky and spicy. You can serve this with potatoes, rice, couscous or roasted vegetables but I find a simple crisp salad is enough to turn it into something a little bit special. You can use the marinade for pretty much any meat.

Pollo miele e paprika

serves 4

4 medium boneless chicken breasts, skin on
4 tablespoons runny honey
2 tablespoons tomato purée
2 teaspoons smoked paprika
Juice of 1 lime
1 tablespoon olive oil
Salt, to taste
Crusty bread, to serve

for the side salad:
150g rocket leaves
3 tablespoons extra virgin olive oil
4 tablespoons balsamic vinegar
50g Parmesan shavings
Salt, to taste

1   Preheat a griddle pan to very hot or light a barbecue if you prefer.

2   Put the chicken breasts on a chopping board between two sheets of clingfilm. Use a meat hammer or a rolling pin to flatten the chicken into escalopes 1cm thick.

3   Put the honey, tomato purée, smoked paprika and 2 pinches of salt in a large bowl. Pour in the lime juice and olive oil and mix together. Add the chicken and coat the breasts in the marinade evenly.

4   Cook the chicken on the griddle pan, skin-side down first, for 6 minutes on each side.

5   Meanwhile, prepare the salad by placing the rocket leaves in a large bowl. Pour over the oil and the balsamic vinegar and season with a couple of pinches of salt. Gently use your fingertips to toss together. Transfer the salad onto a large serving plate and scatter the shaved Parmesan on top.

6   Once the sticky chicken breasts are ready, serve together with a little crusty warm bread on the side.

CHICKEN BREASTS

with

CHERRY TOMATOES, MOZZARELLA AND BASIL

I'm from Naples, the city that invented pizza, and I've been brought up with them all my life. There is nothing quite like a freshly cooked Margherita pizza. I love the flavour so much that I have copied the ingredients and added them to this chicken recipe to give me that Italian kick I sometimes crave. It is important not to use buffalo mozzarellla for this recipe as it is very milky and releases a lot of liquid when cooked.

Pollo Margherita

serves 4

4 skinless, boneless chicken breasts
6 tablespoons olive oil
4 garlic cloves, peeled and finely sliced
2 x 400g cans of cherry tomatoes
10 basil leaves, plus extra for garnish
3 x 125g mozzarella balls, drained and sliced (do not use buffalo mozzarella)
Salt and black pepper, to taste

1 Slash each chicken breast four times with a sharp knife, cutting as far as the middle of the breast.

2 Heat the olive oil in a large frying pan over a medium heat and gently fry the garlic and the chicken for 2 minutes on each side until golden all over.

3 Tip in the cherry tomatoes with the basil and season with salt and pepper. Stir all together.

4 Cook, uncovered, over a medium heat for 12 minutes. Halfway through cooking, turn over the chicken breasts.

5 Meanwhile, preheat the grill to the highest setting.

6 Remove the pan from the heat and place the mozzarella slices on top of the chicken breasts. Grind over some black pepper and put the pan under the grill for about 1 minute or until the cheese starts to melt. Protect the handle of the frying pan with foil if necessary.

7 To serve, pour some of the tomato sauce in the middle of each serving plate, place a breast of chicken on top and garnish with basil leaves. Serve with your favourite vegetables and warm crusty bread.

SPICED CHICKEN ESCALOPES

with

POTATO AND APPLE MASH

Chicken is extremely popular in our house and, for chicken fans like us, I wanted this chapter to include lots of options so that it's never bland or boring. The key to ensure your chicken dishes are appealing lies in the length of cooking (often the longer the cooking time, the drier the meat, especially the breast, becomes) and the kind of sauces you create. This one is especially light, more of a gravy than a heavy sauce, and, accompanied by my special mash, I hope my spicy escalopes will tick all your boxes.

Scaloppine speziate con patate e mele

serves 4

4 medium boneless chicken breasts, skin on
1½ tablespoons smoked paprika and ground coriander, mixed together
2 tablespoons salted butter
2 tablespoons olive oil

for the mash:
4 large potatoes, peeled and chopped into small pieces
1 tablespoon salted butter
2 cooking apples, peeled, cored and chopped into small pieces
1 tablespoon wholegrain mustard
Salt and white pepper, to taste

1 Put the potatoes in a medium saucepan and cover with boiling water from the kettle. Cook over a medium heat for 8–10 minutes until tender, drain and set aside.

2 Meanwhile, put the chicken breasts on a chopping board between two sheets of clingfilm. Use a meat hammer or a rolling pin to flatten the chicken into escalopes 1cm thick. Rub the spice mix all over both sides of the chicken breasts.

3 Melt the butter with the oil in a large non-stick frying pan over a medium heat and cook the chicken for 5 minutes on each side, skin-side down first. Remove from the pan and transfer to a warm plate, cover with foil and set aside.

4 Add 4 tablespoons of hot water to the frying pan and use a wooden spoon to move the juices around and loosen any meaty bits from the pan to make a quick gravy.

5 For the mash, melt the butter in the same saucepan used to cook the potatoes, add the apples and cook over a high heat for 3 minutes. Stir occasionally with a wooden spoon. Tip the drained potatoes into the saucepan, season with salt and pepper, add the mustard and roughly mash together.

6 Put each chicken breast on a large serving plate, surround with the mash and drizzle over the quick gravy.

CHICKEN SALTIMBOCCA

with

PARMA HAM AND MARSALA

I came up with this recipe because some friends of mine told me they were watching their weight but they loved my Pollo al Marsala dish and wished they could have a similar recipe but without the cream. Well, I got to work and here is the result (let's not tell them about the butter!). It still wows with that Marsala flavour but lets other ingredients such as the Parma ham zap your tastebuds. A really lovely recipe that can be served with anything.

Saltimbocca

serves 4

4 medium skinless, boneless chicken breasts
4 slices of Parma ham, cut in half widthways
8 large sage leaves
6 tablespoons olive oil
50g salted butter
200ml Marsala wine
Salt and black pepper, to taste

1 Put the chicken breasts on a chopping board between two sheets of clingfilm. Use a meat hammer or a rolling pin to flatten the chicken into escalopes 1cm thick.

2 Cut the escalopes in half widthways to give 8 pieces in total. Season with a little salt and pepper and lay a piece of Parma ham on each piece. Top with one sage leaf and secure with a cocktail stick.

3 Heat the oil and half the butter in a large frying pan over a medium heat. Place the saltimbocca in the pan, ham-side down. Cook for 2 minutes until browned. Turn and cook for a further 3 minutes until just cooked through. Transfer to a plate and cover with foil to keep warm.

4 Pour the Marsala wine into the hot frying pan and use a match or a lighter to flame the alcohol.

5 Once the flames die down, use a wooden spoon to deglaze the pan by scraping up the meaty bits from the bottom. Simmer over a high heat for 1 minute until slightly reduced. Stir in the remaining butter and check the seasoning.

6 Return the chicken and any juices to the pan, turning them in the sauce for 30 seconds. Remove the pan from the heat and remove the cocktail sticks from the saltimbocca.

7 Put 2 pieces of saltimbocca on each serving plate and drizzle with the Marsala sauce. Enjoy with a glass of cold medium white wine.

CHICKEN IN A MARTINI

and

SAGE SAUCE

I really like cooking with alcohol as it enhances flavours. You often find recipes with wine in the ingredients but I wanted to try something a bit different. There is always a bottle of Martini Bianco in our fridge, hence a recipe had to come about with it as the star. I think you will love this recipe and be pleasantly surprised how the sweetness of the Martini with the salt, pepper and sage create a lovely flavour.

Scaloppine al Martini e salvia

serves 4

4 medium skinless, boneless chicken breasts
6 tablespoons plain flour
100g salted butter, plus
1 tablespoon extra for the sauce
2 tablespoons olive oil
4 large sage leaves, finely sliced
200ml sweet Martini Bianco
Salt and white pepper, to taste

1. Put the chicken breasts on a chopping board between two sheets of clingfilm. Use a meat hammer or a rolling pin to flatten the chicken into escalopes 0.5cm thick.

2. Spread the flour on a flat plate and season with salt and pepper.

3. Put a large frying pan over a medium heat and start to melt the butter with the olive oil and sage.

4. Lay the chicken breasts in the seasoned flour and coat on both sides. Gently tap the chicken to discard any excess.

5. Put the chicken in the frying pan and fry for 3 minutes on one side. Turn over the meat and cook for a further minute. Pour in the Martini and use a match or a lighter to flame the alcohol. Cook for a further 2 minutes and season with salt and pepper.

6. Transfer the escalopes to a large serving plate.

7. Add the extra tablespoon of butter to the Martini sauce. Mix well over medium heat and immediately pour over the chicken breasts.

8. Serve with a simple green salad dressed with extra virgin olive oil, a squeeze of fresh lemon juice and a pinch of salt.

CHICKEN

in

A VIN SANTO SAUCE

This is my wife's favourite meal. I made it for her years ago when we first met and she was hooked. If I ever want to get in her good books or have her full attention (you know what I mean) – this is the meal I prepare. It's a lovely creamy dish and yet doesn't leave you feeling too full. I often serve this with peas and pancetta or crushed potatoes but rice, bread and couscous are also lovely side dishes.

Pollo al Vin Santo

serves 2

2 medium skinless, boneless chicken breasts
2 tablespoons plain flour, for dusting
3 tablespoons olive oil
6 tablespoons Vin Santo
150ml double cream
Salt and white pepper, to taste

1 Put the chicken breasts on a chopping board between two sheets of clingfilm. Use a meat hammer or a rolling pin to flatten the chicken into escalopes 0.5cm thick.

2 Lightly coat each chicken breast with flour. Gently tap the chicken to discard any excess.

3 Put a large frying pan over a medium heat, add the olive oil and fry the chicken breasts for 3 minutes on one side. Turn the meat over and cook for a further minute.

4 Pour in the Vin Santo and use a match or a lighter to flame the alcohol.

5 Once the flames die down, reduce the heat, pour in the cream, season with salt and pepper and cook, uncovered, for 5 minutes allowing the sauce to thicken. Stir occasionally.

6 Put a chicken breast on each serving plate and drizzle over the delicious Vin Santo sauce.

7 Serve immediately with a couscous salad (see page 194).

STUFFED CHICKEN BREAST

with

ONION MARMALADE AND GOAT'S CHEESE

Petto di pollo ripieno

I often make a goat's cheese and caramelised onion puff pastry parcel as a starter and everyone raves about it so I thought I'd incorporate those flavours into a chicken dish to serve as a main meal. Chicken can be bland and yet with a few ingredients added, it transforms into something really special. If you want a milder flavour than the goat's cheese use mozzarella – I've even used cream cheese, which also works well.

serves 4

4 medium boneless, skinless
chicken breasts
4 tablespoons red onion
marmalade
100g goat's cheese
4 tablespoons olive oil
12 thyme sprigs

for the side salad:
110g bag of mixed salad leaves
3 tablespoons extra virgin
olive oil
2 tablespoons balsamic vinegar
Salt and black pepper, to taste

1 Preheat the oven to 200°C/gas 6.

2 Place the chicken breasts on a chopping board and use a sharp knife to slice in half horizontally, making sure that you don't cut all the way through. Open out each chicken breast like a book.

3 Spread the onion marmalade evenly over the opened-out chicken breasts then crumble over the goat's cheese. Fold each breast in half and secure with a cocktail stick.

4 Place the stuffed breasts on a baking tray and brush all over with olive oil. Sprinkle the tops with salt and pepper and scatter over the thyme sprigs. Roast in the oven for 13 minutes.

5 One minute before the chicken is ready, place the salad leaves in a large bowl and toss in the extra virgin olive oil and balsamic vinegar. Season with a little salt and pepper.

6 Remove the cocktail sticks from the chicken breasts and serve immediately with the salad and warm bread on the side.

CHICKEN AND ASPARAGUS STIR-FRY

with

BALSAMIC GLAZE

I love a good stir-fry and most of the time I just make one with anything and everything I've got in the fridge. However, sometimes I like to give one ingredient the spotlight and in this recipe I've chosen asparagus. Did you know that asparagus is 93 per cent water? It is extremely low in calories and very low in sodium as well as an amazing source of calcium, magnesium, vitamin B, zinc, protein, beta-carotene, vitamin C, vitamin E, vitamin K, thiamin, riboflavin, rutin, niacin, folic acid, iron, phosphorus, potassium, copper, manganese and selenium. I'm not even sure what all these do but what an amazing vegetable!

Pollo e asparagi in padella

serves 4

200g long grain white rice
3 medium boneless and skinless chicken breasts, sliced into 5cm lengths
2 tablespoons runny honey
3 tablespoons balsamic vinegar
1 tablespoon sesame seed oil
4 tablespoons olive oil
100g chestnut mushrooms, cleaned and quartered
300g asparagus spears, cut into 5cm lengths
1 tablespoon sesame seeds
Salt and black pepper, to taste

1 Put the rice in a medium saucepan, cover with boiling water from the kettle, add a teaspoon of salt and cook until tender. Stir occasionally.

2 Meanwhile, put the sliced chicken breasts into a large bowl. Pour in the honey, balsamic vinegar and sesame seed oil. Mix well and leave to marinate for 3 minutes.

3 Heat a wok over a high heat and pour in the olive oil. Fry the mushrooms and asparagus for 2 minutes, stirring constantly with a wooden spoon.

4 Reduce the heat to medium, add the chicken and all the marinade to the wok and continue to cook for a further 10 minutes. Stir occasionally. (If the sauce gets too thick, pour in a little hot water from the kettle.)

5 Check for seasoning and sprinkle over the sesame seeds.

6 Serve immediately in the middle of a large serving plate surrounded by the cooked rice.

CRISPY CHICKEN IN BREADCRUMBS

with

TOMATO SALSA

These days many people buy ready-made chicken escalopes but I promise you, homemade ones are far superior in terms of taste and the satisfaction that comes from knowing that what you are eating is all chicken rather than 10 per cent chicken and the rest almost all bread. And I guarantee that the combination of this really crispy coating (which you wouldn't get by baking ready-made escalopes) with the fresh salsa dressing will be so worth the three extra plates you need to wash up – plus the meal will cost you less than buying escalopes from a supermarket.

Pollo alla Milanese

serves 2

8 tablespoons olive oil
2 medium skinless, boneless chicken breasts
Plain flour, for dusting
2 eggs, beaten in a bowl
70g toasted fine breadcrumbs

for the salsa:
15 yellow cherry tomatoes, quartered
80g pitted green olives
5 fresh mint leaves, sliced
3 tablespoons extra virgin olive oil

for the spinach:
2 tablespoons olive oil
250g spinach leaves
1 garlic clove, peeled and finely sliced
2 pinches of dried chilli flakes
Salt and black pepper, to taste

1 For the salsa, put the tomatoes, olives and mint leaves in a large bowl, drizzle over the extra virgin olive oil and season with salt and pepper. Mix well and set aside.

2 Put the chicken breasts on a chopping board between two sheets of clingfilm. Use a meat hammer or a rolling pin to flatten the chicken into escalopes 0.5cm thick.

3 Have ready the flour and beaten eggs and put the breadcrumbs on a large plate. Lightly dust the breasts with flour, dip in the beaten eggs and finally coat in the breadcrumbs.

4 Heat the olive oil in a large frying pan over a medium heat and gently fry the chicken for 4 minutes on each side until golden and crispy all over.

5 Meanwhile, cook the spinach. Heat the olive oil in a large frying pan over a medium heat and fry the spinach with the garlic and chilli. Season with salt and cook for about 3 minutes until wilted, stirring continuously with a wooden spoon. Remove from the heat and set aside.

6 Transfer the chicken escalopes to kitchen paper to drain any excess oil. Season with salt and pepper.

7 To serve, place each escalope in the centre of 2 serving plates, scatter the tomato salsa on top and serve immediately with the spicy spinach.

MEAT

La carne

This chapter includes recipes using pork, lamb and beef and a variety of cuts of meat. Steaks, cutlets and chops are all brilliant for fast meals but I've also included recipes using minced meat for my Italian twist on popular dishes such as burgers and cottage pie. From simple salads to hearty suppers– I've even managed to include a quick-cook pie and stew – there's a dish to satisfy every appetite and occasion.

POTTED EGGS
and
HAM

I often have this as a simple supper but it also makes a great Sunday morning brunch with the family. It's a perfect quick dish as you're cooking complete meals in individual portions so there is no serving up at the table, and little washing up afterwards. Eggs, spinach and ham is a classic Florentine combination.

Ciotoline di uova e spinaci

serves 4

3 tablespoons olive oil
800g baby spinach leaves
Pinch of ground nutmeg
8 slices of Italian cooked ham with herbs
150ml double cream
Small bunch of chives, chopped
50g freshly grated Parmesan cheese
8 eggs
8 thick slices of sourdough
Butter, to serve
Salt and black pepper, to taste

1 Preheat the oven to 190°C/gas 5 and put a large wok over a high heat.

2 Add the oil and spinach to the hot wok and allow to wilt for 5 minutes. Stir occasionally. Once it has wilted and all the water has evaporated, season with salt, black pepper and a pinch of nutmeg.

3 Line 4 individual serving dishes about 15cm in diameter (or simply use large ramekins) with 2 slices of the ham. Divide the spinach between the dishes and spread it out over the bottom.

4 Pour the cream into a large bowl and add the chopped chives and Parmesan cheese. Season with black pepper and mix.

5 Crack two eggs into each ham-lined dish and pour in the cream mixture, ensuring the chives are distributed evenly. Transfer the dishes to a baking tray and cook in the oven for 10 minutes.

6 Meanwhile, toast the sourdough.

7 Serve the potted eggs with hot buttered toast.

MARSALA PEAR SALAD

with

PARMA HAM CRISPS AND GORGONZOLA CHEESE

This is a brilliant-tasting and simple starter, one that we often serve at Christmas before the main event. It is not one you can make and plate up in advance as the warm pears quickly wilt the salad leaves. However, as you can have it prepared and cooked in 15 minutes, it's perfect for when you have a huge roast to contend with. Pears can sometimes be hard but served warm and sticky they are divine with salty Parma ham and creamy rich cheese.

Insalata di pere e prosciutto crudo

serves 4

12 slices of Parma ham
2 pears (not too ripe)
2 tablespoons salted butter
4 tablespoons runny honey
2 tablespoons fresh rosemary leaves
3 tablespoons Marsala wine
110g bag of crisp salad leaves
2 tablespoons extra virgin olive oil
Juice of ½ lemon
150g Gorgonzola cheese
Salt and black pepper, to taste

1 Preheat the oven to 180°C/gas 4.

2 Spread out the slices of Parma ham on two baking trays and cook in the oven for 8 minutes. Remove from the oven and set aside to cool and harden.

3 Quarter the pears, remove the core and cut each quarter in half.

4 Melt the butter in a medium frying pan and add the pears. Drizzle with honey and add the rosemary. Cook for 1 minute until the juices are thick and sticky.

5 Pour in the Marsala wine and continue to cook for a further 2 minutes. Stir occasionally then remove from the heat and set aside.

6 Put the salad leaves in a large bowl and dress with the olive oil and lemon juice. Season with salt and pepper and divide between 4 serving plates.

7 Break the Gorgonzola into small pieces and add them to the dressed salad leaves.

8 Top with the warm pear slices and crumble over the Parma ham crisps. Drizzle over the honey and rosemary sauce and serve immediately.

LOADED PORK TOASTIES

For me, one of the simplest pleasures in life is a mortadella sandwich. Whenever I am in Italy, a quick stop-off at the local deli and I am in heaven – thin slices of mortadella piled high in a fresh ciabatta roll. Here I've used the idea to make a tortilla toastie that's loaded with Italian hams.

Tostini di mozzarella e salumi

serves 4

4 large tortilla wraps
200g grated mozzarella cheese
12 slices salami Napoli
100g sliced mortadella
4 slices of prosciutto cotto
(cooked ham)
Salt, to taste

for the quick tomato salsa:
2 tablespoons olive oil
1 small red onion, finely sliced
250g baby plum tomatoes, halved
1 tablespoon caster sugar
1 tablespoon balsamic vinegar
Pinch of dried chilli flakes
10 basil leaves

1 First make the tomato salsa. Heat the olive oil in a medium frying pan and cook the onion for 2 minutes. Stir occasionally with a wooden spoon. Add the tomatoes, sugar, balsamic vinegar and chilli flakes. Stir everything together until the tomatoes start to burst, remove from the heat and season with salt. Stir in the basil leaves and set aside.

2 Place 2 tortillas on a chopping board and sprinkle with half the grated mozzarella. Top with the salami, mortadella and ham. Scatter over the remaining mozzarella and put the remaining 2 tortillas on top. Press down lightly.

3 Gently transfer one of the tortilla sandwiches to a large frying pan over a medium heat and cook for 1 minute or until golden and crispy. Use a fish slice to turn it over and cook the other side for a further 30 seconds. Reduce the heat if the tortilla is turning too brown before the cheese is oozing and melted.

4 Remove the tortilla sandwich from the frying pan and repeat the process with the other sandwich.

5 Cut the crispy tortillas into triangles and serve with the quick tomato salsa.

CREAMY SAUSAGE
and
BROCCOLI RAGÙ

Sausages can take a while to cook, so when you are short of time this is a great dish to make. Using sausages instead of pork mince speeds things up as they are already packed full of flavour and perfectly seasoned. If you are no fan of broccoli, you could always use peas, asparagus or some sugar snap peas.

Ragù di salsicce e broccoletti

serves 4

200g long grain rice
4 tablespoons olive oil
4 spring onions, roughly chopped
A few sprigs of thyme
6 good-quality Italian pork sausages
200g tenderstem broccoli
50ml white wine
1 tablespoon vegetable stock powder
100ml crème fraîche
30g Parmesan cheese
Salt and white pepper, to taste

1   Measure the rice into a cup and then tip into a large saucepan with a tight-fitting lid. Pour in 1½ times the amount of boiling water from the kettle and add a good pinch of salt. Put a lid on and bring to a simmer. Gently cook for 10 minutes then turn the heat off and leave to stand.

2   Heat the olive oil in a large frying pan and fry the spring onions and thyme leaves for 2 minutes. Stir occasionally with a wooden spoon.

3   Meanwhile, remove the sausagemeat from the skins and break the meat up using your fingertips. Add to the frying pan and cook for a further 5 minutes. Stir occasionally.

4   While the meat is browning, chop the broccoli into 1cm pieces. Add to the frying pan and cook for 3 minutes.

5   Pour in the white wine, stir all together and continue to cook for a further 2 minutes. Stir in the stock powder and crème fraîche. Season with salt and pepper.

6   Serve the ragù over the rice and sprinkle the top with freshly grated Parmesan.

PORK CHOPS

with

SAGE AND CANNELLINI BEANS

Italians love to cook with canned beans and will always have a good stock of them in their cupboards. They are so versatile and there is no need for long soaking and cooking; it's all done for you. Buy good-quality ones and give them a thorough rinse under cold water to remove the water that they have been canned in for freshness and flavour. White cannellini beans are an Italian staple: their mealy texture and slightly nutty flavour is great with pork.

Maiale burro e salvia

serves 4

4 tablespoons olive oil
4 x 200–250g pork loin chops
4 sprigs of thyme
2 garlic cloves, peeled
2 x 400g cans of cannellini beans, drained
50ml white wine
1 teaspoon vegetable stock powder
100ml water
100ml double cream
50g unsalted butter
16 small sage leaves
Salt and white pepper, to taste

1 Heat half the olive oil in a large frying pan and cook the chops with the thyme for 4 minutes on each side.

2 Meanwhile, pour the remaining oil into a medium frying pan. Grate in the garlic and add the beans. Stir and cook for 2 minutes. Pour the wine over the beans and cook for a further 2 minutes. Stir occasionally.

3 Sprinkle the stock powder over the beans, pour in the water and gently cook for 1 minute. Pour in the cream and continue to simmer for 3 minutes.

4 Meanwhile, transfer the pork chops to a plate. Season with salt and pepper, cover with foil and set aside.

5 Melt the butter in the pan used to cook the chops. Add 12 of the sage leaves and fry for 1 minute until crisp. Set aside.

6 Shred the remaining sage leaves and stir into the beans. Season well with salt and pepper and divide the beans between 4 serving plates.

7 Place the pork chops on top of the beans and drizzle over the sage butter. Top with the crispy sage leaves.

PORK TENDERLOIN

with

LEMON AND THYME

Tenderloin is a lean cut of pork and if it is overcooked it can become really dry. Browning it quickly and then cooking it in a sauce is a perfect way to keep it moist. If you are ever roasting it, just keep a really close eye on it or simply wrap it in bacon to help keep the moisture in.

Medaglioni di maiale al limone

serves 4

3 tablespoons plain flour
600g pork tenderloin, cut into 8 thick slices
3 tablespoons olive oil
2 unwaxed lemons, cut into 8 slices
A few sprigs of thyme
150ml white wine
100ml hot chicken stock
Salt and black pepper, to taste

1   Put the flour on a plate and season with salt and pepper.

2   Lightly dip the pork slices into the flour then shake off the excess so that they are lightly coated.

3   Heat the olive oil in a large frying pan and cook the pork slices for 1 minute on each side.

4   Transfer the pork to a plate, cover with foil and set aside.

5   Add the lemon slices to the pan along with the thyme leaves and cook for 2 minutes. Stir occasionally with a wooden spoon. Pour in the white wine and bring to a simmer. Cook for a further 2 minutes.

6   Pour in the stock, bring to the boil and return the pork to the sauce. Cook for a further 3 minutes until the sauce has slightly thickened and the pork is cooked through. Season with salt and pepper.

7   Serve the pork on a large serving plate and drizzle over the delicious lemon and thyme sauce. Accompany with the New Potato Salad with Red Onions and Capers (see page 201) if you wish.

CRISPY BREADED PORK

with

APPLE SAUCE AND WATERCRESS SALAD

Milanese di maiale con salsa di mele

It seems as if there is a universal law that if something is coated in breadcrumbs it will taste amazing, and this dish is no exception. Just remember to get your pan nice and hot so that the coating is extra crispy without the meat being overcooked. You don't need to serve anything other than a little sweet apple sauce and some peppery salad with these tasty pork steaks.

serves 2

2 x 200g boneless pork loin steaks
2 tablespoons plain flour
Pinch of smoked paprika
1 egg
100g dried fine breadcrumbs
3 tablespoons olive oil
Salt and freshly ground black pepper, to taste

for the sauce:
2 large cooking apples, peeled, quartered, cored and cut into 2cm cubes
30g salted butter
2 tablespoons water
2 tablespoons caster sugar

for the salad:
1 teaspoon honey
1 tablespoon wholegrain mustard
Juice of ½ lemon
4 tablespoons extra virgin olive oil
100g watercress
25g walnut halves

1   Put the apples for the sauce in a small saucepan with the butter, water and caster sugar. Cover with a lid and cook over a low heat for 8 minutes. Stir occasionally with a wooden spoon.

2   Meanwhile, place the pork steaks between two pieces of clingfilm and use a meat hammer or rolling pin to bash them until they are 0.5cm thick.

3   Put the flour in a shallow bowl, season with salt and pepper and a pinch of paprika. Beat the egg in a second shallow bowl. Tip the breadcrumbs into a third bowl. Dip each piece of pork first into the flour, then into the egg and finally into the breadcrumbs.

4   Heat the olive oil in a medium frying pan and cook the coated pork for 4 minutes on each side.

5   Meanwhile, make the salad dressing. Put the honey, mustard, lemon juice and extra virgin olive oil in a jam jar and season with salt and pepper. Screw on the lid and shake everything together.

6   Transfer the pork to a plate covered with kitchen paper to drain off any excess oil.

7   Put the watercress in a serving bowl with the walnuts and coat with the salad dressing.

8   Serve the breaded pork with the watercress salad and apple sauce.

PORK CHOPS AND PANCETTA

with

COURGETTE FRITTERS

These courgette fritters are a great way to get the kids to eat veg. They look like potato rösti but are much quicker to cook and once topped with pancetta and soured cream the sweet courgettes will fool even the fussiest of eaters. You can use the fritters as a side dish for any main course.

Maiale e frittatine di zucchine

serves 4

3 tablespoons olive oil
4 x 130–150g pork chops
12 slices pancetta
2 tablespoons runny honey
150ml soured cream
Cayenne pepper, to dust
Salt and black pepper, to taste

for the courgette fritters:
3 tablespoons olive oil
4 courgettes
5 tablespoons self-raising flour
50g finely grated Parmesan cheese
1 egg yolk

1 Preheat the oven to 200°C/gas 6 and put two large frying pans over a high heat. One must have a heatproof handle.

2 Heat the olive oil in the frying pan with the heatproof handle and fry the pork chops for 3 minutes on each side. Remove from the pan and set aside to rest.

3 Meanwhile, coarsely grate the courgettes into a large bowl. Stir in the flour and the Parmesan. Add the egg yolk and season well with black pepper and a little salt. Mix everything together and shape into 8 fritters.

4 Add the remaining olive oil to the preheated frying pan and fry the courgette fritters for 3 minutes on each side.

5 While the fritters are cooking on the first side, fry the pancetta for 2 minutes in the pan used for the pork. Add the chops back to the pan and drizzle over the honey. Warm through for 1 minute.

6 Meanwhile, season the soured cream with some salt and black pepper.

7 Serve the fritters with the pork chops, crispy pancetta and a good dollop of soured cream.

8 Drizzle over the sticky honey sauce from the pan and dust the top with a little cayenne pepper.

PORK MEDALLIONS

in

MARSALA AND MUSHROOM SAUCE

Tenderloin is an expensive cut of meat, so adding meaty mushrooms means that you can stretch it a little further. 'Medallion', incidentally, is simply a cook's term for the thick rounds cut from the tenderloin. Marsala, a product of Sicily, is, like port, a fortified wine, which Italians love to drink and cook with. If you don't have any Marsala in the cupboard, try using sherry or a little white wine. When wild mushrooms are in season, use those if you can get your hands on any – the flavour will be much better.

Medaglioni di maiale

serves 4

2 tablespoons olive oil
500g pork tenderloin, cut into 8 thick slices
200g chestnut mushrooms, halved
100ml Marsala wine
100ml hot chicken stock
150ml double cream
3 tablespoons chopped tarragon leaves
40g salted butter
Salt and black pepper, to taste

for the potatoes:
500g baby new potatoes
Zest of 1 unwaxed lemon
Small bunch of chives, finely chopped

1   Put the potatoes in a large saucepan, cover with boiling water from the kettle, add 2 teaspoons of salt and cook for 10 minutes.

2   Heat the oil in a large frying pan and cook the medallions of pork for 2 minutes on each side. Transfer to a plate, cover with foil and set aside.

3   Add the mushrooms to the frying pan and cook for 2 minutes. Stir occasionally with a wooden spoon.

4   Put the pork back into the frying pan with the mushrooms and pour in the Marsala. Allow to bubble for 2 minutes then add the stock and cream. Stir in the tarragon and cook for 5 minutes. Season with salt and pepper.

5   Drain the potatoes and return to the same saucepan, stir in the butter, lemon zest and chopped chives. Season with salt and pepper.

6   Put 2 pork medallions in the centre of 4 serving plates, pour over the Marsala and mushroom sauce and serve immediately with the potatoes.

GAMMON STEAKS

with

HONEY AND MUSTARD APPLES

Gammon is a great cut of pork and it is also fairly cheap to buy. Its strong salty flavour means it goes perfectly with something sweet. In this case I have chosen apples – a classic combination of ingredients that you will find in most European cuisines.

Bistecca di maiale con miele e mostarda

serves 2

2 gammon steaks
2 tablespoons olive oil
2 tablespoons runny honey
2 teaspoons Dijon mustard
1 tablespoon wholegrain mustard
1 eating apple
25g butter
1 tablespoon cider vinegar
Black pepper, to taste

1 Put a large frying pan over a high heat.

2 Snip the rind off the gammon steaks to prevent them from curling up as they cook.

3 Add the oil to the hot frying pan and cook the steaks for 3 minutes on one side until golden brown.

4 Meanwhile, combine the honey and mustards in a small bowl.

5 Turn the steaks over and continue to cook for a further 3 minutes.

6 Transfer the gammon to a plate and cover with foil to keep warm. Set aside.

7 Quarter the apple, remove the core and cut each quarter in half giving you 8 wedges.

8 Add the butter and apples to the frying pan and cook for 2 minutes. Pour in the cider vinegar and continue to cook for 1 minute, stirring with a wooden spoon.

9 Add the honey and mustard mixture and allow to bubble for a further minute. Stir together. Season with black pepper.

10 Serve the gammon with the warm sticky apples and some of the sauce poured over.

GAMMON STEAKS
with
FRUITY BULGAR WHEAT

I often make this tasty dish because I usually have raisins, dried apricots or cranberries in the cupboard along with a lone apple or pear in the fruit bowl. Bulgar wheat is readily available in supermarkets but you could also use couscous. Either way, gammon steak is an ideal meat to serve with it as the fruit and honey used here nicely balance its saltiness. So go easy on the salt when seasoning the bulgar wheat but you can load up on the black pepper.

Bistecche di maiale con miele e rosmarino

serves 2

100g bulgar wheat
1 teaspoon chicken or vegetable stock powder
3 tablespoons olive oil
2 gammon steaks
2 tablespoons fresh rosemary leaves
1 pear
2 stalks of celery
3 tablespoons honey
2 tablespoons extra virgin olive oil
Juice of 1 lemon
50g raisins (or chopped dried apricots or cranberries)
2 tablespoons chopped flatleaf parsley
Salt and black pepper, to taste

1   Tip the bulgar wheat into a bowl, sprinkle over the stock powder and pour over 150ml boiling water from the kettle. Stir, then cover the bowl with clingfilm. Set aside for 15 minutes.

2   Heat the olive oil in a medium frying pan and cook the gammon steaks with the rosemary for 5 minutes on each side.

3   Meanwhile, finely dice the pear (no need to peel; just cut around the core) and celery.

4   Transfer the gammon to a plate, cover with foil and set aside to keep warm.

5   Add the honey to the frying pan and pour in 2 tablespoons of water. Season with black pepper and stir together to create a sauce.

6   Use a fork to break up the cooked bulgar wheat and separate all the grains. Drizzle the extra virgin olive oil over the bulgar wheat with the juice of 1 lemon. Stir in the pear, celery, raisins and flatleaf parsley. Season with a little salt and plenty of black pepper.

7   Serve the gammon with the bulgar wheat and drizzle over the honey sauce.

ITALIAN SAUSAGE STEW

with

PEPPERS AND CRUNCHY CROUTONS

There is nothing more comforting than a big bowl of stew. My favourite way to eat it is with crunchy croutons that soak up all the juices and soften slightly – fantastico!

Stufato di salsicce e peperoni

serves 4

1 ciabatta, cut into 2cm cubes
6 tablespoons olive oil
4 sprigs of thyme
1 red pepper
1 yellow pepper
2 garlic cloves, peeled and sliced
2 rosemary stalks
10 Italian pork sausages
2 x 400g cans cherry tomatoes
100g pitted black olives in brine or oil, drained
5 tablespoons freshly chopped flatleaf parsley
Salt and black pepper, to taste

1 Preheat the oven to 180°C/gas 4.

2 Put the ciabatta cubes on a baking tray. Drizzle over 2 tablespoons of olive oil, season with salt and pepper and sprinkle over thyme leaves. Toss everything together and transfer to the oven for 15 minutes until crispy.

3 Meanwhile, cut the peppers in half, discard the green stem, membrane and seeds, and roughly slice.

4 Put a medium saucepan over a high heat. Pour the remaining oil into the pan, add the garlic, peppers and rosemary and fry for 3 minutes. Stir occasionally with a wooden spoon.

5 While the peppers cook, remove the sausagemeat from the skins and make 3 small meatballs per sausage. Set aside.

6 Pour the tomatoes into the saucepan with the peppers and bring to the boil. Add the sausage meatballs to the sauce, gently stir and cook for 13 minutes, uncovered. Stir occasionally.

7 Don't forget to check the croutons!

8 Once the meatballs are cooked, season with salt and pepper. Finally, stir the olives and parsley into the stew and serve immediately with the delicious croutons.

SPICY CHORIZO
and
BORLOTTI BEAN STEW WITH POLENTA

I know chorizo is Spanish but it is so good I have stolen some for this recipe! There are two different types: 'eating' chorizo, which is like a salami that can be eaten raw, and 'cooking' chorizo which is like any other sausage but it's full of spices and paprika.

Stufato piccante con polenta

serves 4

8 'cooking' chorizo sausages, sliced into 2cm-thick rounds
1 teaspoon smoked paprika
1 garlic clove, peeled and sliced
1 x 400g can borlotti beans, drained and rinsed
1 x 400g can chopped tomatoes
1 teaspoon dried chilli flakes

for the polenta:
2 teaspoons vegetable stock powder
200g quick polenta
50g salted butter
50g freshly grated Parmesan cheese
Salt and white pepper, to taste

for the garnish:
4 spring onions, finely chopped

1　Place a medium saucepan over a medium heat and cook the chorizo for 5 minutes. Stir occasionally with a wooden spoon.

2　Add the paprika and garlic and cook for a further minute. Continue to stir.

3　Pour in the borlotti beans and the tomatoes, add the chilli flakes and gently cook for 12 minutes, uncovered. Stir occasionally.

4　Meanwhile, make the polenta. Measure out 800ml of boiling water from the kettle and pour into a large saucepan. Add the stock powder and bring to the boil. Slowly sprinkle in the polenta and whisk continuously for 1 minute, until thick. Once it has boiled for 1 minute remove from the heat and stir in the butter and the Parmesan and season with salt and pepper.

5　Season the chorizo and bean stew with salt.

6　Spoon the polenta in the centre of 4 serving plates and top with the stew.

7　Scatter over the chopped spring onions.

8　Serve hot with a nice bottle of Italian red wine.

ITALIAN SAUSAGE PATTIES

with

MASH AND ONION GRAVY

This is a quick version of sausage and mash, which I love to make with Italian sausages as they are full of delicious herbs and spices such as fennel and rosemary. Using red onion marmalade makes a quick but really flavoursome gravy.

Svizzerine di salsicce

serves 4

1 beef stock cube
8 Italian pork sausages
3 tablespoons olive oil
1 tablespoon plain flour
50ml red wine
6 tablespoons caramelised red onion marmalade
Salt and white pepper, to taste

for the mash:
1kg floury potatoes, e.g. King Edward or Maris Piper, peeled and cut into 3cm chunks
80ml full-fat milk
50g salted butter

1 Preheat the oven to 180°C/gas 4. Put the potatoes in a large saucepan. Cover with boiling water from the kettle, add 2 teaspoons of salt and cook for 8 minutes.

2 Meanwhile, pour 300ml of boiling water into a measuring jug and crumble in the stock cube. Mix and set aside.

3 Remove the sausages from their skins and divide each one into two. Roll the pieces into balls and flatten into a patty.

4 Heat the olive oil in a large frying pan and cook the sausage patties for 2 minutes on each side. Remove from the pan, transfer to a baking tray and cook in the oven for 5 minutes.

5 Meanwhile, add the flour to the frying pan to soak up any fat, and cook for 1 minute. Stir occasionally with a wooden spoon. Pour in the red wine and scrape all the caramelised bits from the bottom of the pan as these add real flavour to the gravy.

6 Pour the stock into the frying pan and stir continuously to prevent lumps forming. Bring to the boil, stir in the caramelised red onion marmalade and season with black pepper. Simmer gently until ready to serve.

7 Drain the potatoes, tip back into the saucepan and mash with the milk and butter. Stir well and season with salt and pepper.

8 Serve the patties with the mashed potatoes and drizzle over the gravy.

PORK

and

APPLE MEATBALLS

Pork and apples complement each other beautifully and this speedy recipe is both comforting and delicious.

Polpette di maiale e mele

---

serves 4

750g minced pork
2 eating apples
6 sage leaves, chopped
5 tablespoons olive oil
1 tablespoon cornflour
100ml soured cream
150ml hot chicken stock
3 tablespoons chopped flatleaf parsley
Salt and black pepper, to taste

for the mash:
1kg floury potatoes, e.g. King Edward or Maris Piper, peeled and cut into 3cm chunks
60g salted butter
80ml double cream

1   Put the potatoes into a large saucepan and cover with boiling water from the kettle. Add 2 teaspoons of salt and boil for 10 minutes.

2   Meanwhile, put the minced pork in a large bowl. Grate in the apples (no need to peel them: just grate down to the core). Add the sage, season with salt and pepper and mix everything together. Roll the pork mix into 12 meatballs.

3   Heat the oil in a medium frying pan and cook the meatballs for 7 minutes, turning them regularly so they are browned all over.

4   Drain the potatoes and return to the same saucepan, stir in the butter and start to mash. Add the cream and continue to mash until smooth. Season with salt and pepper.

5   Transfer the meatballs to a plate, cover with foil and set aside.

6   Mix the cornflour in a cup with 2 tablespoons cold water.

7   Add the soured cream to the frying pan used to cook the meatballs. Pour the stock over the soured cream followed by the cornflour mixture. Keep stirring with a wooden spoon while it comes to a simmer, then remove from the heat. Stir in the parsley and season with salt and pepper.

8   Serve the meatballs with the mash and spoon over the parsley sauce.

THINLY SLICED LAMB

with

WATERCRESS AND BALSAMIC VINEGAR

Tagliata means 'cut' or 'sliced' and it is the perfect family meal for sharing. It is also a great way to make meat go a little further because slicing it thinly makes it look as if there's a whole lot more than there is – a canny Italian trick! You can make this recipe using any leftover roast beef or lamb too. I suggest keeping the meat nice and rare – you get the best flavour that way. Peppery watercress and salty Pecorino are perfect with the sweet lamb meat.

Tagliata di agnello

serves 4

2 x 200g lamb rump steaks, excess fat removed
2 tablespoons olive oil
250g baby tomatoes on the vine, in small bunches
3 tablespoons balsamic vinegar
1 tablespoon redcurrant jelly
1 tablespoon salted capers, rinsed under cold water
1 tablespoon freshly chopped flatleaf parsley
100g watercress
50g Pecorino cheese
3 tablespoons extra virgin olive oil
Salt and pepper, to taste
Crusty bread, to serve

1   Preheat the oven to 200°C/gas 6 and preheat a medium frying pan over a high heat.

2   Drizzle the lamb with the olive oil and fry for 2 minutes on each side. Remove from the pan and transfer to a roasting tray with the tomatoes. Cook in the oven for 10 minutes.

3   Return the frying pan to the heat and pour in the balsamic vinegar and redcurrant jelly. Cook for 30 seconds, stirring with a wooden spoon. Stir in the capers and parsley, and season with salt and pepper. Set aside.

4   Pile the watercress onto a large serving platter. Use a peeler to shave the Pecorino cheese on top of the watercress. Drizzle over the extra virgin olive oil and season with salt and pepper.

5   Remove the lamb from the oven, and leave to rest for 2 minutes on a plate at room temperature. Season with salt and pepper.

6   Place the roasted tomatoes around the serving platter.

7   Thinly slice the lamb, place on top of the watercress and drizzle over the balsamic and redcurrant sauce.

8   Serve immediately with crusty bread.

LAMB PITTA POCKETS

with

MASCARPONE DRESSING

Little lamb patties stuffed inside warm pitta bread and crammed full of salad make an amazing alternative to a burger. There is far less bread and they are almost easier to eat as the natural pocket shape helps keep them together. My kids love these as they can make their own, filling it up with as much or as little of each ingredient as they like. The minted mascarpone is fantastic with the lamb!

Portafogli di pane con agnello e mascarpone

serves 4

500g minced lamb
2 tablespoons sweet chilli sauce
2 tablespoons chopped chives
3 tablespoons olive oil
4 pitta breads: either white or wholemeal
110g bag of lettuce leaves
4 large plum tomatoes, sliced lengthways
Salt and white pepper, to taste

for the mascarpone dressing:
8 tablespoons mascarpone cheese
Juice of ½ lemon
1 tablespoon freshly chopped mint

1   Put the minced lamb in a large bowl with the sweet chilli sauce and chopped chives. Season with salt and pepper. Mix together and divide the mixture into 12 balls. Gently flatten the balls into patties.

2   Heat the olive oil in a large frying pan and fry the patties for 3 minutes on each side. Transfer onto some kitchen paper to absorb any excess oil and set aside.

3   Mix together the mascarpone, lemon juice and mint in a medium bowl. Add a splash of water to the mascarpone dressing to loosen it slightly so it has the consistency of mayonnaise. Set aside.

4   Heat the pitta bread in a toaster until warm; do not overheat them otherwise they will become hard and impossible to open like a pocket.

5   Carefully split open the pitta breads and fill the pocket with lettuce, tomatoes, lamb patties and mascarpone dressing.

6   Enjoy with a cold beer or a glass of juice for the kids.

LAMB KEBABS

with

TOMATO AND FETA CHEESE SALSA

I like kebabs that have a bit of texture to them and therefore diced leg of lamb is a great choice for this recipe. If you like the meat really tender you can use fillet of lamb, although this costs a lot more and is less 'lamby'. Oregano gives the meat a wonderful flavour – the taste of the Mediterranean.

Spiedini di gamba d'agnello

serves 4

600g leg of lamb, cut into 2cm chunks
2 tablespoons olive oil
1 teaspoon dried oregano
2 red onions

for the salsa:
250g cherry tomatoes
2 tablespoons mint leaves
150g feta cheese
2 tablespoons olive oil
Salt and black pepper, to taste

8 wooden skewers, soaked in cold water

1   Heat a griddle pan over a high heat.

2   Put the lamb in a large bowl, drizzle over the oil and sprinkle in the dried oregano. Season with salt and pepper, mix well and set aside.

3   Peel and cut the red onions into 8 wedges. Try to cut them through the root (the small circular non-layered part at the base of the onion), as this will hold the layers of the onion together, ensuring that each wedge maintains its shape.

4   Thread the lamb and onions onto the skewers and cook on the griddle pan for 8 minutes. Turn the skewers every 2 minutes to ensure that all sides are cooked.

5   Meanwhile, cut the cherry tomatoes in half and put in a bowl. Roughly slice the mint leaves and add to the tomatoes. Crumble over the feta cheese, drizzle with the oil and season with black pepper. Gently mix together.

6   Once the kebabs are cooked, remove from the griddle and serve with the tomato and feta cheese salsa.

SPICY LAMB MEATBALLS

with

ITALIAN FLATBREADS AND QUICK TOMATO SAUCE

The best-known flatbreads are pittas, tortillas or Turkish flatbreads that you can pick up in most supermarkets and specialist shops, but now, I'm pleased to say, you can also find lots of Italian flatbreads. They tend to be much richer than the other flatbreads as they are usually made with extra virgin olive oil. If you can't get hold of them, brush any flatbread with a little extra virgin olive oil and warm through in the oven.

Polpette piccanti con pomodorini

serves 4

500g minced lamb
2 garlic cloves, peeled
1 teaspoon dried chilli flakes
3 tablespoons olive oil, plus extra for brushing
4 large Italian flatbreads, such as piadina or schiacciata
140g bag of rocket leaves
Salt and black pepper, to taste

for the tomato sauce:
3 tablespoons olive oil
300g cherry tomatoes
3 tablespoons white wine vinegar
3 tablespoons caster sugar
10 basil leaves

1 Preheat the oven to 180°C/gas 4.

2 Put the minced lamb in a large bowl and finely grate in the garlic. Season with salt and the chilli flakes and mix together. Divide into 20 pieces and roll into small balls.

3 Pour the olive oil in a large frying pan over a medium heat. Cook the meatballs for 8 minutes, turning them regularly so that they brown all over.

4 Meanwhile, brush the flatbreads with a little olive oil (preferably extra virgin) and wrap them in a pile in foil. Put in the oven to warm through.

5 To make the sauce, heat the oil in a medium frying pan and add the tomatoes. Cook for 2 minutes, stirring occasionally with a wooden spoon. Add the vinegar and sugar and continue to cook for a further 2 minutes. Stir in the basil leaves and set aside.

6 Place the meatballs in the middle of a large serving plate surrounded by the tomato sauce and rocket leaves.

7 Serve immediately with the warm Italian flatbreads.

LAMB MEATBALLS

with

SPICY TOMATO SAUCE AND HERBY COUSCOUS

The red wine reduction in this sauce gives a warm and rich flavour which can be achieved surprisingly quickly. The chilli flakes add a subtle spice that works beautifully with the freshness of the parsley and sweetness of the apricots in the couscous.

Polpettine di agnello

serves 4

150ml red wine
500g minced lamb
1 garlic clove, peeled
1 tablespoon dried oregano
4 tablespoons olive oil
½ teaspoon dried chilli flakes
1 x 400g can chopped tomatoes

for the couscous:
200g couscous
2 tablespoons vegetable
stock powder
3 tablespoons extra virgin
olive oil
50g dried apricots, chopped
10 small basil leaves
3 tablespoons freshly chopped
flatleaf parsley
Salt and black pepper, to taste

1   Pour the red wine into a small saucepan and bring to the boil. Reduce the heat and gently simmer for 8 minutes. Stir occasionally with a wooden spoon.

2   Meanwhile, put the couscous in a large heatproof bowl, add the stock powder and pour over 500ml boiling water from the kettle. Cover with clingfilm and set aside.

3   Put the minced lamb in a large bowl and grate the garlic over the top. Add the oregano and season well with salt and pepper. Mix together and roll into 20 small balls.

4   Heat the olive oil in a large frying pan and cook the meatballs for 5 minutes, turning them regularly so that they brown all over.

5   Add the chilli flakes and tomatoes to the frying pan with the tomatoes and pour in the reduced red wine. Stir together and cook for a further 8 minutes, stirring occasionally.

6   Use a fork to loosen the couscous grains, pour in the extra virgin olive oil and carefully stir in the chopped apricots, basil and parsley. Season with salt and pepper.

7   Serve the meatballs with the spicy sauce on a bed of herby couscous.

LAMB CHOPS

with

ROASTED VEGETABLES AND HOMEMADE MINT SAUCE

Lamb and mint are a match made in culinary heaven, and to make my mint sauce Italian I use balsamic instead of malt or white wine vinegar, as it cuts through the fattiness of the lamb chops perfectly. If you want to achieve this in 20 minutes, don't worry about cutting the vegetables precisely – they can be nice and rustic.

Costolette d'agnello con salsa alla menta

serves 4

200g cherry tomatoes on the vine
2 courgettes, cut into 1cm rounds
2 yellow peppers, halved, deseeded and cut into 1cm slices
Bunch of spring onions, trimmed and roughly sliced
5 tablespoons olive oil
4 sprigs of rosemary
8 lamb chops

for the mint sauce:
2 tablespoons balsamic vinegar
1 tablespoon caster sugar
3 tablespoons olive oil
10 mint leaves
Salt and black pepper, to taste

1 Preheat the oven to 220°C/gas 7.

2 Cut the tomatoes into small bunches and place on a large baking tray along with all the veg. Drizzle over 3 tablespoons of olive oil, add the rosemary sprigs and season with salt and pepper. Cook in the oven for 15 minutes. Every 5 minutes remove the tray from the oven, stir the veg and continue to cook.

3 Meanwhile, heat 2 tablespoons of oil in a large frying pan. Cook the lamb chops for 4 minutes on each side. Transfer the chops to a plate and season with salt and pepper. Cover with foil and set aside.

4 To make the mint sauce, mix together the balsamic vinegar, sugar and the rolive oil. Finely chop the mint and stir into the sauce. Season with salt and pepper.

5 Pile the roasted vegetables in the middle of 4 serving plates and arrange the chops on top. Drizzle over the mint sauce and serve. You could also try this with my fruity bulgar wheat (see page 79).

SPICED LAMB CHOPS
with
SWEET POTATOES

Tasty lamb flavoured with thyme, lemon and paprika and served with caramelised sweet potatoes – what's not to like? You need to get a wiggle on with the prep of the potatoes for this recipe: the high natural sugar content of sweet potatoes means they cook and caramelise much faster than ordinary potatoes. Make sure you brown the edges of the potatoes to get a beautiful caramel flavour.

Costolette di agnello con patate dolci

serves 4

8 lamb chops
3 tablespoons olive oil
Juice of 1 lemon
1 teaspoon thyme leaves
½ teaspoon smoked paprika
Salt, to taste

for the sweet potatoes:
3 large sweet potatoes, washed and cut into 1cm cubes
3 tablespoons olive oil
Pinch of cayenne pepper
1 tablespoon fresh rosemary leaves

1 Preheat the oven to 220°C/gas 7.

2 Put the potatoes on a large baking tray. Drizzle over the oil and sprinkle with the cayenne pepper and salt. Add the rosemary, toss everything together and roast in the oven for 15 minutes. Shake the baking tray every 5 minutes during roasting.

3 Preheat a large frying pan over a high heat.

4 Meanwhile, place the lamb chops on a plate and drizzle over the oil. Squeeze over the lemon juice and sprinkle with thyme leaves and paprika, ensuring the chops are well coated. Cook in the frying pan for 4 minutes on each side.

5 Transfer the chops to a plate, season with salt and set aside to rest for 1 minute.

6 Serve the lamb chops with the caramelised sweet potatoes and a salad of your choice.

7 For a more substantial meal, serve with some green beans and polenta.

LAMB STEAKS

with

WARM BABY GEMS AND PEAS

Cooking lettuce may seem a little odd but many of the top restaurants have been doing it for years. Lettuces like baby gems become soft and sweet as they cook and make a perfect match for the peas and parsley.

Agnello con pisellini

serves 4

4 lamb steaks
3 tablespoons olive oil
25g salted butter, plus 1 teaspoon softened butter
1 shallot, peeled and finely sliced
4 baby gem lettuces, quartered
300ml hot chicken stock
1 teaspoon plain flour
200g frozen peas, defrosted
2 tablespoons freshly chopped flatleaf parsley
4 tablespoons crème fraîche, to serve
Salt and black pepper, to taste

1 Preheat the grill to moderate.

2 Put the lamb steaks on a grill tray and drizzle over 2 tablespoons of olive oil. Cook under the grill for 6 minutes on each side.

3 Heat the butter and the remaining oil in a medium frying pan. Cook the shallot for 2 minutes until soft and translucent. Stir occasionally with a wooden spoon.

4 Add the baby gems to the frying pan, cut-side down. Cook for 2 minutes. Pour in the stock and bring to a simmer.

5 Mix together the softened butter and flour. Whisk into the frying pan and simmer for 2 minutes. Add the peas and continue to cook for a further 2 minutes.

6 Remove the lamb from the grill and leave to rest for 2 minutes on a plate at room temperature. Season with salt and pepper.

7 Meanwhile, stir the parsley into the frying pan with the lettuce and peas.

8 Serve the peas and baby gems in deep, wide bowls with the grilled steaks on top and a spoonful of crème fraîche to garnish.

LAMB CUTLETS

with

FENNEL SALAD AND HONEY SAUCE

Lamb cutlets are my favourite cut of lamb and to my mind there is only one way to cook them: fast and medium-rare. I learned this way of serving them when I was training in catering college and I remember that I was very impressed with the smooth flavours. If you prefer, you can substitute the honey with maple syrup – it works just as well.

Costolette di agnello con miele e finocchio

serves 4

4 tablespoons olive oil
8–12 lamb cutlets, preferably French-trimmed (ask your butcher to do this for you)
3 tablespoons fresh rosemary leaves
3 tablespoons runny honey
12 thin slices of pancetta
Salt and black pepper, to taste

for the fennel salad:
100g pitted Kalamata olives in oil or brine, drained
2 large fennel bulbs, finely sliced
1 tablespoon runny honey
4 tablespoons extra virgin olive oil
Juice of ½ lemon
2 tablespoons freshly chopped flatleaf parsley

1 To make the fennel salad, halve the olives and put them in a large bowl with the fennel slices. Drizzle over the honey and extra virgin olive oil. Squeeze in the lemon juice and add the parsley. Season with salt and pepper, mix well and set aside.

2 Heat the olive oil in a large frying pan over a high heat.

3 Fry the lamb cutlets with the rosemary in the hot oil for 2 minutes on each side. Transfer to a plate, season with salt and pepper and cover with foil to keep warm.

4 Drizzle the honey into the frying pan and stir with a wooden spoon for 1 minute over a low heat. Season with black pepper and set aside.

5 Pile the fennel salad into the middle of 4 serving plates and place the slices of pancetta on top. Arrange the cutlets around the salad and drizzle over the honey dressing.

6 Serve immediately with lots of warm Italian bread or my New Potato Salad with Red Onions and Capers (see page 201).

LAMB CUTLETS

coated with

PARMA HAM AND PARMESAN

I honestly can't remember how many times I have cooked this recipe. It is one of my wife's favourites and as a good husband I was born to please her, over and over again. You can substitute the Parmesan with Pecorino if you prefer and sliced pancetta works just as well as the Parma ham.

Costolette impanate

serves 4

50g sliced Parma ham, finely chopped
80g toasted fine breadcrumbs
3 tablespoons freshly grated Parmesan cheese
12 lamb cutlets, preferably French-trimmed (ask your butcher to do this for you)
2 large eggs, beaten into a medium bowl
6 tablespoons olive oil
Warm bread, to serve

for the salad:
140g rocket leaves
20 cherry tomatoes, halved
3 tablespoons extra virgin olive oil
3 tablespoons balsamic vinegar
Salt and black pepper, to taste

1   Mix together the Parma ham with the breadcrumbs and Parmesan cheese in a large bowl. Set aside.

2   Dip each cutlet first into the beaten eggs and immediately coat with the breadcrumb mixture. Press the lamb firmly into the breadcrumb mixture so it coats the cutlets evenly.

3   Heat the oil in a large frying pan over a medium heat.

4   Cook the cutlets in the hot oil for 3 minutes on each side.

5   Transfer the cutlets to some kitchen paper to absorb any excess oil. Season with salt and pepper.

6   Meanwhile, put the rocket leaves in a large bowl with the cherry tomatoes. Drizzle over the extra virgin olive oil and balsamic vinegar. Season with salt and pepper and mix well.

7   Serve the cutlets with the beautiful rocket salad and lots of warm bread on the side. It would also go rather well with the Carrots and Almonds with Fresh Mint and Chilli (see page 23).

CANNON OF LAMB

with

CAPERS AND ROSEMARY

The cannon of lamb is the fillet; it is very low in fat, just like fillet of beef, but it is also extremely tender. You really need to serve this cut nice and pink to get the best out of it. The flavour is mild so it goes well with stronger-tasting ingredients like capers and rosemary, both favourites with Italians.

Filetto di agnello con capperi

serves 4

400g new potatoes
4 x 175g cannon of lamb fillets
2 tablespoons olive oil
200g green beans
1 tablespoon rosemary leaves
150ml white wine
2 tablespoons capers in vinegar, drained
1 tablespoon freshly chopped flatleaf parsley
30g salted butter
Juice of ½ lemon
Salt and black pepper, to taste

1 Preheat a frying pan over a high heat.

2 Put the potatoes in a medium saucepan and cover with boiling water from the kettle. Add 1 teaspoon of salt and boil for 8 minutes.

3 Roll the lamb fillets in the olive oil and cook in the frying pan for 3–4 minutes until golden brown. Turn the fillets regularly so that they brown all over. Remove the pan from the heat, transfer the lamb to a plate and set aside.

4 Use a slotted spoon to scoop the potatoes out of the boiling water and put in a large bowl to keep warm.

5 Add the beans to the boiling water and boil for 2 minutes.

6 Meanwhile, return the frying pan to the heat and add the rosemary. Cook for 2 minutes, stirring with a wooden spoon. Pour in the wine, stir and cook for a further 2 minutes, stirring continuously. Add the capers, parsley and 20g butter. Season with salt and pepper and set aside.

7 Meanwhile, drain the beans, tip them back into the same saucepan and add the remaining butter. Squeeze over the lemon juice and season with salt and pepper. Set aside.

8 Carve each piece of lamb into 1cm thick slices and serve alongside the potatoes and beans. Drizzle over the rich wine sauce and serve immediately.

LAMB MEDALLIONS

with

HAZELNUT DRESSING

Texture is so important when it comes to food – it can transform a dish from dull to amazing in minutes and nuts are a great way of achieving this. Italian cooks use hazelnuts in a vast array of dishes, savoury and sweet, from salads to desserts. If you prefer you can substitute the hazelnuts with walnuts.

Medaglioni con salsina di noci

serves 4

400g small new potatoes
4 x 175g fillets of lamb
4 tablespoons olive oil
1 teaspoon Dijon mustard
1 tablespoon white wine vinegar
2 tablespoons hazelnut oil
200g green beans, cut into 2cm lengths
50g chopped hazelnuts
1 tablespoon freshly chopped mint, to serve
Salt and black pepper, to taste

1 Preheat the oven to 200°C/gas 6.

2 Put the potatoes in a medium saucepan and cover with boiling water from the kettle. Add 1 teaspoon of salt and boil for 7 minutes.

3 Put the lamb fillet on a baking tray and drizzle over half the olive oil. Roast in the oven for 8 minutes. After 4 minutes of cooking, turn the lamb so it browns all over.

4 Whisk together the mustard, vinegar and hazelnut oil in a small bowl. Season with salt and pepper and set aside.

5 Drain the potatoes, cut in half and put in a large bowl.

6 Remove the lamb from the oven and transfer to a plate, season with salt and pepper and cover with foil to keep warm.

7 Heat the remaining olive oil in a large frying pan and add the drained potatoes. Fry for 1 minute before adding the beans. Continue to fry for a further 3 minutes until the beans are just cooked, stirring occasionally with a wooden spoon.

8 Remove the potatoes and beans from the heat, pour in the dressing and stir in the chopped hazelnuts. Slice the lamb in 2cm thick medallions. Arrange the beans and potatoes in the centre of a large serving platter and place the lamb on top. Sprinkle over the freshly chopped mint and serve.

QUICK LAMB STEW

with

BABY NEW POTATOES

Stews normally take hours to cook because the cuts of meat traditionally used are the larger muscles that the animal used most; therefore, they taste the best but are tougher, requiring long, slow cooking. This stew is a quick variation but still has all the flavour of a traditional version.

Stufato d'agnello

serves 4

400g baby new potatoes
2 carrots, peeled and cut into 1cm cubes
4 tablespoons olive oil
500g leg of lamb, cut into 2cm cubes
1 tablespoon plain flour
100ml red wine
500ml hot beef or lamb stock
2 tablespoons mint jelly
150g frozen peas, defrosted
1 tablespoon freshly chopped mint
Salt and black pepper, to taste
Warm crusty bread, to serve

1 Put the potatoes in a medium saucepan and cover with boiling water from the kettle. Add 1 teaspoon of salt and cook for 7 minutes.

2 Cook the carrots for 1 minute with the potatoes (add to the pan for the last minute of cooking time). Drain the lot and set aside.

3 Meanwhile, heat the oil in a large frying pan and fry the lamb for 8 minutes. Stir occasionally with a wooden spoon to ensure that the pieces brown all over. Remove from the frying pan and set aside.

4 Add the flour to the frying pan, stir well and cook for 1 minute. Pour in the wine and bring to the boil, still stirring. Pour in the stock and continue to cook for 3 minutes, stirring continuously.

5 Return the lamb to the frying pan with the mint jelly. Stir well and cook gently for 6 minutes, stirring occasionally.

6 Add the potatoes, carrots, peas and fresh mint. Simmer for a further minute, season with salt and pepper and serve immediately with lots of warm crusty bread to mop up the delicious sauce.

LAMB, SPINACH
and
GORGONZOLA PIE

The great thing about minced meat is that it cooks much quicker than larger cuts, so you have time to make this delicious lamb pie within 20 minutes. Rather like a Greek kotopita, it uses filo pastry, which takes a matter of minutes to cook, unlike the more traditional pie pastries such as shortcrust or puff.

Torta salata con agnello e Gorgonzola

serves 4

3 tablespoons olive oil
2 tablespoons fresh rosemary leaves, finely chopped
500g minced lamb
2 garlic cloves, peeled
400g baby spinach leaves
4 large sheets of filo pastry
50g salted butter, melted
200g Gorgonzola cheese, chilled
Salt and black pepper, to taste

1 Preheat the oven to 220°C/gas 7.

2 Heat the oil in a large frying pan with the rosemary, add the minced lamb and cook for 3 minutes. Stir occasionally with a wooden spoon to break the mince up.

3 Grate the garlic on top of the meat and cook for a further 2 minutes.

4 Add the spinach and continue to cook for 3 minutes, stirring occasionally. Season with salt and pepper and set aside.

5 Lay one sheet of filo pastry onto a chopping board. Brush with a little of the melted butter and place in a 20cm cake tin, letting the edges of the pastry hang over the sides. Repeat with the remaining sheets until the base and sides of the tin are covered and there is a lot of overhang.

6 Spoon the mince and spinach mixture into the middle of the tin and crumble over the Gorgonzola. Cover the top of the pie with the overhanging pastry.

7 Brush the top with melted butter and grind over some black pepper. Cook in the middle of the oven for 10 minutes.

8 Serve hot with your favourite salad on the side.

BUILD YOUR OWN BEEF BRUSCHETTA

Half the pleasure of food is being able to enjoy it with your friends and family. I love dishes that can be placed in the centre of the table and everybody helps themselves. It's the most social form of eating and it means I'm not stuck in the kitchen! This recipe cooks the beef from scratch, but if you have any leftover roast beef from a Sunday roast by all means use that.

Bruschetta fai da te

serves 4

300g steak, cut of your choice
3 tablespoons olive oil
1 ciabatta, cut into 2cm thick slices
200g cherry tomatoes, halved
1 garlic clove, peeled and halved
6 tablespoons extra virgin olive oil
6 basil leaves, torn
150g ricotta cheese
Small bunch of mixed herbs, such as parsley, dill or chives, finely chopped
Zest and juice of 1 unwaxed lemon
8 sun-dried tomatoes in oil, drained
80g pitted mixed olives in oil or brine, drained
50g Parmesan cheese
150g rocket leaves
Salt and black pepper, to taste

1   Preheat a griddle pan and put a frying pan over a high heat. Drizzle the steak with a little of the olive oil and cook in the hot frying pan for 2 minutes on each side. Transfer to a plate and season with salt and pepper. Cover with foil and set aside.

2   Brush the slices of ciabatta with the rest of the olive oil. Place on the griddle pan and cook until crispy and golden on both sides.

3   Put the cherry tomatoes in a bowl and finely grate over one half of the garlic. Pour in half the extra virgin olive oil, season with salt and pepper and stir in the basil leaves. Set aside.

4   Put the ricotta cheese in a separate bowl and stir in the herbs and lemon zest. Season with salt and pepper and set aside.

5   Rub the griddled bread with the remaining half garlic clove and place on a large serving board. Arrange the sun-dried tomatoes and olives around the board then use a swivel-head potato peeler to create a pile of Parmesan shavings.

6   Put the rocket leaves in a bowl and dress with the lemon juice, the remaining extra virgin olive oil, salt and pepper. Make a pile of dressed leaves on the serving board or serve separately.

7   Slice the steak thinly with a long sharp knife and pile onto the serving board.

8   Place the serving board in the centre of the table with the bowls of tomatoes and ricotta and let everybody enjoy making their own tasty bruschetta.

BEEF SALAD

with

LEMON, CHILLI AND CHIVES

This dish combines simple flavours so make sure you buy good-quality ingredients – the best you can afford. Fillet of beef is so tender it is perfect for eating 'blue' by quickly searing it on all sides in a hot pan while the centre stays beautifully rare. If, however, you are not a fan of really rare meat, preheat the oven to 200°C/gas 6, sear your steak, and then pop it into the oven for 8 minutes to cook a little more.

Insalata rustica

serves 4

300g beef fillet
4 tablespoons olive oil
1 red chilli, halved, deseeded and finely chopped
280g chargrilled artichokes in oil, drained and halved
Juice of 1 lemon
50g pine nuts
70g mixed salad leaves
2 tablespoons chopped chives
3 tablespoons extra virgin olive oil
Salt and black pepper, to taste

1   Preheat a large frying pan until very hot.

2   Put the beef on a large flat plate and drizzle over the olive oil, season with salt and pepper and make sure that it is seasoned all over. Put the beef in the frying pan and fry for 3 minutes on each side.

3   Remove the pan from the heat and transfer the meat to rest on a plate, covered with foil to keep warm.

4   Add the chilli and artichokes to the beef pan and squeeze over a little of the lemon juice. Stir and set aside.

5   Put the pine nuts in a small frying pan and toast over a medium heat until golden brown – take care as they burn really easily.

6   Use a really sharp knife to slice the beef in 0.5cm thick slices and arrange on a large serving plate.

7   Scatter over the warm artichokes and chilli then top with the salad leaves and toasted pine nuts.

8   Squeeze over the remaining lemon juice. Top with the chopped chives and finally drizzle with the extra virgin olive oil. Serve with warm crusty bread.

BRESAOLA AND QUAIL'S EGG SALAD

This is one of the fastest salads that you can throw together. It's almost cheating as lots of it is pre-cooked and bought ready-prepared, but when time is tight it's good to have a helping hand. Bresaola is an Italian speciality – salted beef that is air-dried for 2–3 months, so even if you had an hour to cook you couldn't make this yourself!

Bresaola con uova di quaglie

serves 4

12 quail's eggs
125g fine asparagus tips
2 tablespoons olive oil
150g sliced Bresaola
1 tablespoon tarragon leaves
100g mayonnaise
Juice of ½ lemon
Salt and black pepper, to taste

1 Put the quail's eggs in a small saucepan and cover with boiling water from the kettle. Boil for 5 minutes. Put the saucepan under cold running water for 2 minutes. Peel the eggs and set aside.

2 Preheat a griddle pan over a high heat.

3 Put the asparagus on a plate and drizzle over the olive oil, season with salt and pepper and mix well. Cook on the griddle pan for 3–4 minutes, turning occasionally. Transfer to a plate and set aside.

4 Arrange the Bresaola slices on 4 serving plates. Halve the quail's eggs and place on top of the meat. Share the asparagus between the plates.

5 Chop the tarragon and put into a bowl. Mix in the mayonnaise and lemon juice, adding just enough cold water to create a runny dressing. Season with salt and pepper and drizzle the dressing over the salad.

THE ULTIMATE STEAK ROLL

Nothing beats a soft ciabatta roll that is flavour-packed and filled with so many ingredients that it is difficult and messy to eat! This recipe is another great way to make a good piece of steak go a little further.

Panino fantastico

serves 2

1 x 250g rump or sirloin steak
2 tablespoons olive oil
2 individual ciabatta rolls, halved
3 tablespoons mayonnaise
2 tablespoons good-quality ready-made pesto
1 ripe avocado
2 handfuls of mixed salad leaves
4 sun-dried tomatoes in oil, drained
Salt and black pepper, to taste

1 Put a frying pan over a high heat.

2 Rub the steak with olive oil and cook in the hot frying pan for 2 minutes on each side.

3 Transfer the steak to a plate and season with salt and pepper. Cover with foil and set aside.

4 Place the ciabatta halves, cut-side down, in the pan you cooked the steaks in – as they toast they soak up all the steak juices until they start to go crispy.

5 Meanwhile, mix the mayonnaise with the pesto and season with black pepper. Halve the avocado, carefully remove the stone and skin, and cut into thick slices.

6 Remove the bread from the pan and spread both halves of each roll with the pesto mayo. Top the bottom half with salad leaves and avocado.

7 Using a sharp long knife, cut the steak into thin strips. Place the steak on top of the avocado, top each one with a couple of sun-dried tomatoes and sandwich with the ciabatta top. Enjoy hot and prepare to get messy!

BEEF LOLLIPOPS

with

SPICY TOMATO DIPPING SAUCE

Meatballs are often a main course but my kids love them without the pasta, served on little wooden skewers so that they look like lollipops – perfect for dipping into a spicy tomato sauce. They make a family-friendly starter as they are fun to eat. If you are making them for the kids, just watch the amount of chilli you add but if you like it hot, go for it!

Lecca lecca di manzo con salsa piccante

serves 6

50g fresh breadcrumbs
50ml semi-skimmed or
full-fat milk
4 tablespoons olive oil
500g minced beef
1 teaspoon fresh oregano leaves,
chopped
1 teaspoon Dijon mustard

for the spicy tomato sauce:
2 tablespoons olive oil
2 garlic cloves, peeled and sliced
300ml passata
Pinch of dried chilli flakes
1 tablespoon sweet chilli sauce
12 fresh basil leaves
Salt, to taste

1 Put the breadcrumbs in a small bowl and pour over the milk. Leave for 2 minutes for the milk to soak into the breadcrumbs. Set aside.

2 Heat 2 tablespoons of the olive oil in a medium saucepan. Add the garlic and fry for 30 seconds, pour in the passata and add the chilli flakes. Cook gently for 10 minutes. Stir occasionally with a wooden spoon.

3 Meanwhile, place the minced beef in a large bowl. Add the oregano, mustard and soaked breadcrumbs. Season with salt and mix together.

4 Roll the mix to make 24 mini meatballs.

5 Heat the remaining olive oil in a large frying pan and fry the meatballs for 7 minutes, until brown all over.

6 Add the sweet chilli sauce and basil leaves to the tomato sauce. Season with salt and stir.

7 Serve the meatballs on small wooden skewers with the spicy tomato sauce on the side. Enjoy!

ITALIAN-STYLE CHEESE BURGERS

with

COLESLAW CUPS

Burgers are a great Friday night supper, perfect for the whole family. I love using mozzarella to melt on top of the beef patties as it goes so beautifully stringy.

Svizzerine di manzo con insalatina

serves 4

500g minced beef
1 teaspoon English mustard
4 good-quality burger buns
1 x 125g mozzarella ball, drained and cut into 4 thick slices
4 tablespoons tomato chutney, to serve

for the coleslaw cups:
1 tablespoon wholegrain mustard
6 tablespoons mayonnaise
Juice of ½ lemon
2 carrots, peeled and grated
1 fennel bulb, grated
¼ red cabbage, finely chopped
2 baby gem lettuces
Salt and white pepper, to taste

1 Preheat the oven to 150°C/gas 2 and put a griddle pan over a high heat.

2 Mix the minced beef and mustard in a large bowl. Try not to crush it with your hands too much as this makes the burgers too dense. Season well with salt and pepper and divide the mix into four. Shape into burgers about 2.5cm thick. Put the burgers onto the griddle pan and cook for 4 minutes on one side.

3 Meanwhile, put the buns on a baking tray and pop them into the oven to warm through.

4 Mix together the wholegrain mustard, mayonnaise and lemon juice in a large bowl and season with salt and pepper. Add the carrots and fennel to the mayonnaise mixture. Stir everything together and set aside.

5 Turn the burgers over and top each one with a slice of mozzarella. Continue to cook for 3 minutes.

6 Mix the cabbage into the coleslaw mixture. Break the baby gem lettuce into individual leaves and fill each one with some of the coleslaw.

7 Remove the buns from the oven and cut in half. Place a burger on the bottom half of each bun, then top the melted mozzarella with some tomato chutney and serve alongside the lettuce coleslaw cups.

SPICY BEEF LETTUCE CUPS

I don't often use ready-made sauces like tomato ketchup in my cooking but this adds sweetness to a hot and spicy dish. It's fun to put everything on the table and let the family tuck in and fill their own cups.

Coppette di manzo piccanti

serves 6

4 tablespoons olive oil
6 spring onions, finely chopped
1 hot red chilli, halved, deseeded and finely chopped
1 teaspoon fennel seeds, crushed
500g minced beef
2 tablespoons tomato ketchup
50ml hot beef stock
2 tablespoons freshly chopped flatleaf parsley
2 baby gem lettuces
100ml natural yogurt
40g Pecorino cheese, grated
Salt, to taste

1 Heat the oil in a large frying pan and gently fry the spring onions, chilli and fennel seeds for 30 seconds. Stir with a wooden spoon.

2 Add the minced beef and continue to fry for 10 minutes, breaking it up with a wooden spoon as it cooks.

3 Stir in the tomato ketchup and beef stock. Season with salt.

4 Remove from the heat and stir in the parsley.

5 Break the baby gem lettuces into individual leaves and place on a large serving plate. Fill each leaf cup with a little of the mince mixture and top with a spoonful of natural yogurt and a little Pecorino cheese – or let everyone do this themselves.

6 Serve with plenty of cold beer on the side for the adults and cold soft drinks for the kids.

BALSAMIC-GLAZED BEEF SKEWERS

I always have a bottle of good-quality balsamic vinegar in the cupboard as it is perfect for salad dressings and marinades. Buy the best that you can afford, that way you will enjoy its intense flavour rather than just a strong acidity. Not only does balsamic give a wonderful flavour to this recipe, its acidity also tenderises the meat.

Spiedini di manzo

serves 4

50ml good-quality balsamic vinegar
3 tablespoons runny honey
2 garlic cloves, peeled and finely chopped
600g rump steak, cut into 2cm cubes
1 yellow pepper, halved and deseeded
1 red pepper, halved and deseeded
1 courgette

for the egg-fried rice:
40g salted butter
2 x 250g packets of ready-cooked basmati rice
2 eggs, beaten
4 tablespoons freshly chopped flatleaf parsley, plus extra to garnish
Salt and black pepper, to taste

8 wooden skewers, soaked in cold water

1   Preheat a griddle pan over a high heat.

2   In a large bowl, mix together the balsamic vinegar, honey and garlic. Add the diced beef and mix well.

3   Cut the peppers into 2cm cubes and the courgettes into 0.5cm thick rounds.

4   Thread the meat, peppers and courgettes onto the skewers in random order aiming to distribute the ingredients evenly and place them on the griddle pan.

5   Cook for 6 minutes, turning occasionally and brushing them with the marinade.

6   Transfer the skewers to a plate and season with salt and pepper. Cover with foil to keep warm.

7   Melt the butter in a wok or a large frying pan and stir in the rice. Add a splash of water and cook for 2 minutes until hot.

8   Push the rice to one side and pour in the beaten eggs. Use a wooden spoon to scramble the eggs for 30 seconds before stirring in the rice and parsley. Season with salt and pepper.

9   Divide the rice between 4 serving plates and place the beef skewers on top. Serve immediately with a little more parsley sprinkled on top.

RARE ROAST BEEF

with

MINTY POTATO SALAD

This is a delicious salad. I love the combination of the cold dressing and salad with the warm beef and potatoes. If you have any leftover beef from your Sunday roast this is a great way to use it up – you'll have a meal in moments.

Insalata di manzo e patate

serves 4

300g small waxy new potatoes
8 mint leaves
400g beef fillet
2 tablespoons olive oil
8 tablespoons mayonnaise
1 small garlic clove, peeled
1 avocado
10 radishes, quartered
175g chargrilled artichokes in oil,
drained and quartered
6 spring onions, finely chopped
Salt and white pepper, to taste

1 Preheat the oven to 200°C/gas 6. Put the potatoes and half of the mint in a medium saucepan, cover with boiling water from the kettle, add 1 teaspoon of salt and cook for 10 minutes.

2 Meanwhile, put a frying pan with an ovenproof handle over a high heat.

3 Rub the beef with the oil and put in the hot frying pan. Sear on all sides until browned, and then transfer to the oven to cook for 8 minutes.

4 Put the mayonnaise in a bowl and finely grate in the garlic clove. Chop the remaining mint leaves and add to the mayo. Add a little water to create a runny dressing and season with salt and pepper. Set aside.

5 Drain the potatoes and leave to cool.

6 Transfer the beef from the oven to a plate and season with salt and pepper. Cover with foil and set aside to rest at room temperature.

7 Meanwhile, halve the avocado and remove the stone. Peel off the skin and cut the flesh into rough chunks. Halve the cooled potatoes.

8 Use a long sharp knife to cut the beef into thin slices. Arrange them over a platter and scatter the prepared radishes, artichokes and avocado on top. Drizzle over the mayo dressing and sprinkle over the chopped spring onions.

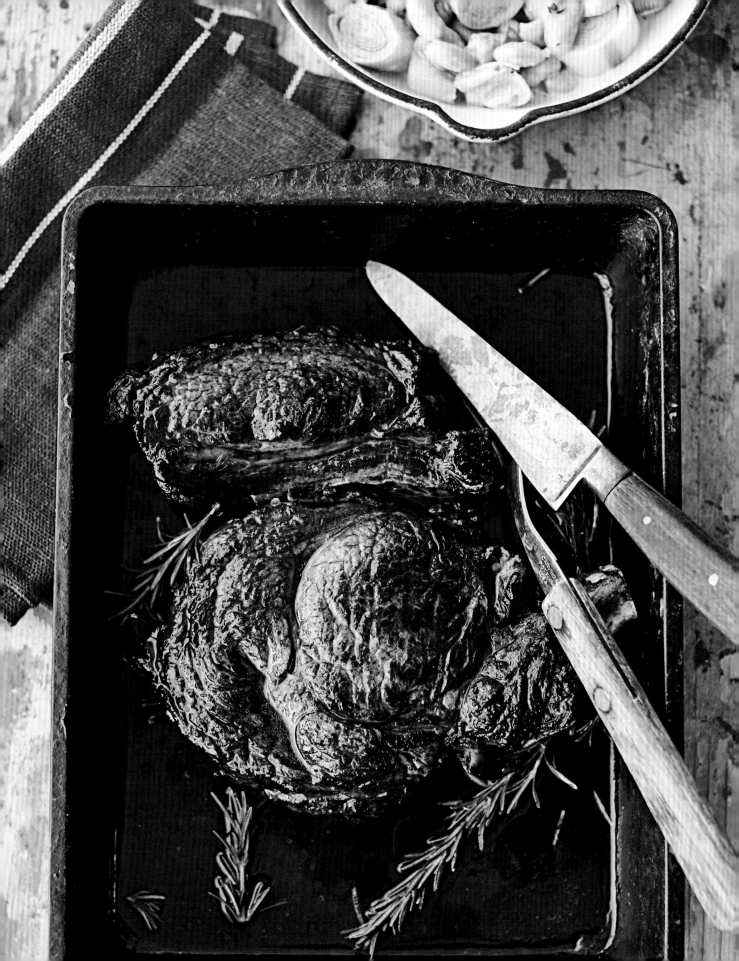

ROAST RIB OF BEEF

---

with

CREAMY LEEKS AND CANNELLINI BEANS

Roast rib of beef seems an unlikely dish to cook in 20 minutes. However, if you can get hold of single-bone ribs they are just like cooking an extra-thick steak, but with the added flavour from the bone. Rib of beef is deliciously tender meat and perfect eaten rare. It's typically Italian to use cannellini beans – I think their flavour and texture is brilliant with a juicy steak.

Bistecca con crema di porri e cannellini

---

serves 4

1 'on the bone' rib of beef, about 6cm thick
2 tablespoons olive oil
4 sprigs of rosemary
30g salted butter
2 leeks, trimmed and cut into 0.5cm rounds
1 tablespoon thyme leaves
1 garlic clove, peeled
50ml white wine
2 x 400g cans cannellini beans, drained and rinsed
200ml double cream
100ml hot chicken stock
Salt and white pepper, to taste

1   Preheat the oven to 220°C/gas 7. Put a large ovenproof frying pan over a high heat.

2   Rub the beef with half the oil and cook in the hot frying pan for 2 minutes on each side. Add the rosemary to the pan and transfer it to the oven to roast for 12 minutes.

3   Meanwhile, melt the butter with the remaining olive oil in a medium frying pan. Add the leeks and fry for 2 minutes. Stir occasionally with a wooden spoon.

4   Add the thyme leaves and grate in the garlic. Mix everything together and fry for a further minute. Pour in the white wine and continue to cook for 1 minute.

5   Add the cannellini beans to the frying pan. Stir well before pouring in the double cream and stock. Gently cook for 4 minutes and stir occasionally.

6   Remove the beef from the oven and leave to rest for 5 minutes at room temperature. Season with salt and pepper on both sides.

7   Serve the beef accompanied by the creamy leeks and cannellini beans.

CHILLI STEAK

with

ROCKET PESTO

Everybody knows traditional basil pesto but it can also be made with other herbs and green leaves. Naturally, I want you to make your own: the flavour of homemade pesto is unbeatable. Here I use peppery rocket and watercress, which work really well with beef, and the kick of chilli in this recipe gives everything an extra boost.

Tagliata di manzo piccante

serves 2

1 ciabatta, cut into 2cm chunks
4 tablespoons olive oil
2 x 300g sirloin steaks
1 red chilli, halved, deseeded and chopped
2 tablespoons extra virgin olive oil

for the rocket pesto:
75g rocket leaves
1 small garlic clove, peeled
25g pine nuts
125ml extra virgin olive oil
Juice of ½ lemon
50g Parmesan cheese
Salt, to taste

1 Preheat the oven to 200°C/gas 6. Put a large frying pan over a high heat.

2 Tip the ciabatta chunks onto a baking tray and spread out in a single layer. Drizzle with half the olive oil and season with salt. Cook in the oven for 10 minutes.

3 Rub the steaks with the remaining olive oil and cook in the frying pan for 3 minutes on each side.

4 Meanwhile, put the chilli on a large plate, pour over 2 tablespoons of extra virgin olive oil and season with salt.

5 Transfer the steaks to the plate with the chilli, oil and salt. Turn them over in the seasoned oil and cover with foil to keep warm.

6 Put the rocket leaves, garlic and pine nuts in a food processor, add half the extra virgin olive oil and blitz until smooth. Add the remaining oil and lemon juice and grate in the Parmesan cheese. Blitz once more until smooth. Season with a little salt.

7 Thinly slice the steaks and arrange on a large serving plate, drizzle over the rocket pesto and serve immediately, surrounded by the warm croûtons. Serve with my Honey Beetroot (see page 186) if you wish.

STEAK
in
A RED WINE BUTTER SAUCE

It's so easy to make herb butters for fish and steaks. This one takes a little more time but if you double the recipe, roll it into a sausage shape in clingfilm and freeze it, the next time you have a steak or simple chicken breast, you can cut off a slice and melt it in a hot pan for an instant sauce.

Bistecca al vino rosso e burro

serves 4

150g salted butter, softened
1 small onion, peeled and finely chopped
1 teaspoon thyme leaves
1 teaspoon caster sugar
300ml red wine
4 x 175g steaks, cut of your choice
2 tablespoons olive oil
Green salad leaves, to serve
Extra virgin olive oil, to taste
Juice of ½ lemon
Salt and black pepper, to taste

1   Melt 25g butter in a small saucepan and add the onion, thyme leaves and sugar. Season with a pinch of salt and cook for 2 minutes until the onions are translucent.

2   Pour in the wine and gently cook for 8 minutes. Stir occasionally with a wooden spoon.

3   Meanwhile, preheat a large frying pan over a high heat.

4   Rub the steaks with the oil and cook in the hot frying pan for 3 minutes on each side. Transfer to a plate and season with salt and pepper. Cover with foil to keep warm and set aside.

5   Put the remaining butter in a bowl and season with black pepper. Pour the wine sauce over the butter and beat together. (If you want to freeze this sauce for a later date, leave it to cool, roll in clingfilm to form a sausage-shape and pop into the freezer.)

6   Put the steaks in the middle of 4 serving plates and drizzle over the red wine butter sauce.

7   Serve with the salad leaves drizzled with extra virgin olive oil and a squeeze of lemon juice.

FILLET STEAKS

coated

IN BLACK PEPPER AND FRESH ROSEMARY

Fillet steak is the most tender of all the steaks but although it gives great texture it often lacks flavour. I think fillet needs a helping hand so a thick pepper crust works wonders bringing this cut of meat to life.

Filetto di manzo al pepe nero

---

serves 4

4 tablespoons coarse ground black pepper
4 x 175g fillet steaks
4 tablespoons olive oil
2 tablespoons fresh rosemary leaves
50ml brandy
200ml double cream
Salt, to taste

for the rice:
2 teaspoons vegetable stock powder
200g long grain white rice
200g frozen peas, defrosted

1 Measure out 600ml of boiling water from the kettle. Pour into a medium saucepan and add the stock powder and rice.

2 Cover with a lid and bring to the boil. Reduce the heat and gently cook for 10 minutes. Once all the water has been absorbed, stir in the peas, cover with the lid and remove from the heat. Leave the rice to stand.

3 Put the black pepper on a plate and use it to coat the steaks on both sides.

4 Heat the oil in a large frying pan and cook the peppered steaks, with the rosemary leaves, for 3 minutes on each side.

5 Transfer the steaks to a plate and season with salt. Cover with foil to keep warm. Set aside.

6 Pour the brandy into the frying pan and cook for 1 minute. Stir with a wooden spoon and make sure that you scrape all the bits from the bottom of the pan. Pour in the cream, stir together and cook for a further 2 minutes. Season with salt.

7 Simply arrange the rice in the middle of 4 serving plates, top with the steaks and drizzle over the beautiful brandy sauce. Buon Appetito!

BEEF STRIPS

in

PORCINI MUSHROOM SAUCE

Beef and mushrooms are a match made in heaven, whether in a pie or a stew. Fresh porcini mushrooms are really expensive so using a few dried ones gives you the depth of flavour without the expense. They are a perfect storecupboard ingredient as they last for months and once soaked in boiling water add a hit of flavour to sauces and even your Sunday roast's gravy.

Stufatino con porcini

serves 4

150g dried porcini mushrooms
300g basmati rice
450g sirloin steak
4 tablespoons olive oil
250g chestnut mushrooms, sliced
1 garlic clove, peeled
1 teaspoon thyme leaves
50ml red wine
3 tablespoons freshly chopped flatleaf parsley
150g mascarpone cheese
Salt and black pepper, to taste

1   Put the porcini mushrooms in a bowl and pour over enough boiling water from the kettle to cover. Set aside for 5 minutes.

2   Pour the rice into a measuring jug and read off how much you have, then tip the rice into a medium saucepan. Now pour 1½ times the amount of water into the saucepan. Season with ½ teaspoon of salt, cover with a lid and put over the heat. Bring to the boil and simmer for 6 minutes or until all the water has completely evaporated. Remove from the heat and leave to stand for 10 minutes with the lid on.

3   Meanwhile, cut the steak into 0.5cm strips. Heat half the oil in a large frying pan and fry the steak for 1 minute on each side just to take on a little colour. Transfer to a plate, cover with foil and set aside.

4   Pour the remaining oil into the frying pan and fry the chestnut mushrooms for 2 minutes. Stir occasionally with a wooden spoon. Grate in the garlic, add the thyme and cook for a further minute. Pour in the wine, stir together and cook for 2 minutes.

5   Meanwhile, drain the porcini mushrooms and reserve the liquid. Stir the liquid into the frying pan. Roughly chop the mushrooms and add to the sauce.

6   Stir in the parsley and mascarpone cheese then add the meat back to the frying pan. Cook gently for 2 minutes.

7   Season with salt and pepper and serve with the rice.

ITALIAN-STYLE COTTAGE PIE

with

CRUSHED POTATOES

Cottage pie normally takes a while to make: first the sauce and then you need to peel, boil and mash the potatoes – well, with this version there's far less work. Using new potatoes means there is no need to peel them as the skins are so thin, and the added bonus is that you get all the nutrients as well. Grating the onions and carrots cuts down the cooking time, so you can be serving up in 20 minutes.

Torta rustica

serves 4

600g baby new potatoes
5 tablespoons olive oil
150g diced pancetta or lardons
2 tablespoons fresh rosemary leaves, finely chopped
1 medium onion, peeled and grated
2 carrots, unpeeled and grated
500g minced beef
1 tablespoon plain flour
1 tablespoon tomato purée
200ml hot beef stock
50g freshly grated Parmesan cheese
Salt and black pepper, to taste

1 Preheat the grill to moderate.

2 Put the potatoes in a large saucepan, cover with boiling water from the kettle, add 1 teaspoon of salt and cook for 10 minutes.

3 Meanwhile, heat 3 tablespoons of the olive oil in a medium saucepan and cook the pancetta and rosemary for 2 minutes over a high heat. Stir occasionally with a wooden spoon.

4 Add the grated onion and carrots to the saucepan and cook for a further 2 minutes.

5 Add the minced beef and use a wooden spoon to break up the meat. Continue to cook for 3 minutes.

6 Stir in the flour and tomato purée and cook for 1 minute. Pour in the stock and continue to cook for 8 minutes. Stir occasionally.

7 Drain the potatoes and return to the same saucepan. Use a potato masher to crush the potatoes. Add the remaining olive oil and Parmesan cheese. Mix together and season with salt and pepper.

8 Spoon the meat sauce into an ovenproof dish and top with the crushed potatoes. Put the dish under the grill for 2 minutes until lightly browned.

9 Enjoy with a bottle of Italian red wine.

FISH & SEAFOOD

Fish and seafood such as mussels, prawns or scallops are the perfect ingredients for dinner if you haven't got much time as they can all be cooked easily within 20 minutes. This chapter features fish fillets or smaller whole fish such as red mullet and sea bream so there's no time wasted in any messy or complicated preparation. The only recipe that is a little bit trickier is the lobster, but it's such an indulgent recipe that it's certainly worth any extra effort and is perfect for celebrations or special occasions when you haven't had much time to prepare.

Pesce e frutti di mare

SCALLOPS
with
PEPPER AND TOMATO SALSA

Every single time I have prepared this dish for guests, they have been really impressed and have often commented that they have never tasted anything quite like it. The juicy scallops (try to buy big ones) are perfect combined with the tomato salsa.

Capesante e peperoni

serves 4

12 scallops, white flesh only
2 tablespoons olive oil
Juice of 1 lemon
50g salted butter
A handful of pea shoots, to serve

for the salsa:
4 tablespoons olive oil
2 garlic cloves, peeled and sliced
1 yellow pepper, cut into
0.5cm dice
4 large ripe plum tomatoes,
deseeded and diced
Salt and black pepper, to taste

1 To make the salsa, heat the olive oil in a large frying pan over a medium heat and fry the garlic for 30 seconds. Add the yellow peppers and cook for 2 minutes before stirring in the tomatoes. Warm them through for a minute before seasoning with salt and pepper. Set aside.

2 Wash the scallops under cold running water and pat dry with kitchen paper. Season with salt and pepper.

3 Add the olive oil to a large frying pan over a high heat and fry the scallops for 1 minute on each side. Squeeze over the lemon juice, remove the scallops from the pan and place on a plate.

4 Add the butter to the pan and season with salt and pepper.

5 To serve, place the salsa in the middle of each serving plate and arrange 3 scallops on top.

6 Drizzle over the lemon butter sauce and scatter with pea shoots. Serve immediately.

MUSSELS AND CLAMS STEW
in a
CREAMY PAPRIKA SAUCE

If I'm eating out, I often order seafood simply cooked with garlic and wine but I have to say I really like the creamy paprika sauce in this recipe (if I do say so myself). It makes the dish really indulgent. For me, the nicest way to serve this stew is in a large pot in the centre of the table and let everyone to dig in. Make sure you have loads of crusty bread for the sauce – you'll be fighting over the last dunk!

Cozze e vongole alla paprika

serves 4

1kg mussels
1kg clams
4 tablespoons olive oil
1 large white onion, peeled and finely sliced
100ml white wine
200ml double cream
4 tablespoons freshly chopped chives
½ teaspoon smoked paprika
Salt, to taste

1 Wash the mussels and clams under cold running water, discarding any broken ones and those that do not close when tapped firmly.

2 Heat the oil in a large saucepan and fry the onion for 3 minutes until soft. Stir with a wooden spoon.

3 Add the mussels and clams and pour over the wine. Stir well, cover the saucepan with a lid and cook over a medium heat for 4 minutes.

4 Remove the lid and pour in the cream with the chives and paprika. Season with salt, stir and continue to cook for a further 3 minutes by which time the sauce will have slightly thickened.

5 Serve the stew immediately, discarding any mussels or clams that have not fully opened.

GRILLED KING PRAWNS

with

ASPARAGUS AND WALNUTS

I wanted to come up with a dish using prawns that could be eaten hot or cold, with more of a salad feel than a main meal. You get all the nutritional benefit from the asparagus and the prawns (both extremely good for you) as they are so lightly cooked and, more importantly, the full flavour. Walnuts add taste and texture – or you could use pine nuts if you prefer.

Gamberoni alla griglia

serves 4

500g asparagus spears, trimmed
12 large raw king prawns, head and shells on
8 tablespoons extra virgin olive oil
1 unwaxed lemon, cut in half
2 tablespoons freshly chopped flatleaf parsley
100g walnuts halves
Salt and pepper, to taste

1 Preheat a griddle pan over a high heat.

2 Fill a medium saucepan with water, bring it to the boil and cook the asparagus for 1 minute. Drain and set aside to cool slightly.

3 Drizzle the asparagus and the prawns with 4 tablespoons of oil. Season with salt and pepper.

4 Cook on the preheated griddle pan for 5 minutes, turning regularly to ensure an even colouring.

5 To make the dressing, pour the remaining oil into a small bowl, squeeze in the juice of half the lemon and add the parsley together with a little salt and pepper. Whisk to combine.

6 Once the asparagus and prawns are ready, arrange on a large serving plate and drizzle over the dressing. Cut the remaining pieces of lemon into 4 wedges and serve around the dish.

7 Finally, scatter over the walnuts and serve.

KING PRAWNS

in

GARLIC AND CHILLI TOMATO SAUCE

Prawns are a big winner in the D'Acampo family and this recipe is one of my favourites. I often prepare this as a starter but also serve it for lunch as it is surprisingly filling. It gives you the kick that you would expect from the spicy sauce and yet is very light in texture. To make a much more substantial meal add cooked pasta to this – amazing!

Gamberoni arrabbiata

serves 4

6 tablespoons olive oil
6 canned anchovy fillets in oil, drained
1 teaspoon dried chilli flakes
2 garlic cloves, peeled and sliced
6 tablespoons pitted green olives in oil or brine, drained
2 tablespoons capers in salt, rinsed under cold water and drained
2 x 400g cans chopped tomatoes
4 tablespoons freshly chopped basil
16 large raw king prawns, head and shells on
Salt, to taste

1   Heat the oil in a large frying pan over a medium heat and cook the anchovies for 3 minutes until they dissolve. Add in the chilli with the garlic and continue to fry for a further minute. Stir occasionally with a wooden spoon.

2   Stir in the olives and capers. Pour in the chopped tomatoes, add the basil and season with salt – but be careful as the anchovies are already salty. Simmer for 8 minutes, uncovered. Stir occasionally.

3   Add the prawns to the sauce and continue to cook for a further 6 minutes. After the first 3 minutes, turn the prawns onto the other side.

4   To serve, divide the sauce equally between each serving plate and place 4 prawns on top. Try to cross 2 prawns together so they can sit up on the plate.

5   Enjoy my spicy prawns with warm crusty bread and a glass of cold Prosecco.

FRESH LOBSTER

with

CHILLI, GARLIC AND EXTRA VIRGIN OLIVE OIL

This recipe is a bit more extravagant, not in terms of preparation but in terms of cost. Any guests will consider themselves very lucky if you decide to make this meal for them. Once in a while this is worth indulging in – even if it's just for yourself… why not?!? There aren't many ingredients here as I want to keep things quick and simple and not take too much attention away from the lobster – that has to be the star of the show.

Aragosta aglio, olio e peperoncino

serves 4

2 large whole live lobsters (approx. 1.5kg each)
Juice of 2 lemons
8 tablespoons extra virgin olive oil
3 garlic cloves, peeled and crushed
½ teaspoon dried chilli flakes
Salt, to taste

1 Fill a very large pot with boiling water from the kettle. Add 1 tablespoon of salt and bring to the boil. Plunge the live lobsters into the boiling water and cook for 10 minutes exactly.

2 Meanwhile, prepare a very large bowl of cold water, adding in a few ice cubes if necessary. Remove the lobsters from the boiling water and drop immediately into the cold water for 3 minutes. Remove and drain.

3 Preheat the grill to the highest setting.

4 Place the lobsters on their backs on a large chopping board and, holding them steady with your free hand, use a large heavy knife to cut from the top of the head straight down to the end of the tail. Turn them over and use the same technique to cut through the shell on the back. By now you should have each lobster separated in two halves.

5 Twist the claws away from the body and use a large knife to cut the shells by holding the knife in place and banging the top of it down with the other hand. Pick out the flesh and place on top of the lobster halves.

6 Squeeze the lemon juice all over the flesh and drizzle over the oil. Spread the crushed garlic over the lobster flesh and sprinkle over the chilli flakes. Season with salt.

7 Place the prepared halves, flesh-side up, under the hot grill for 1 minute. Don't overcook the lobster otherwise it will be chewy. Serve immediately accompanied with a fresh salad of your choice.

SLICED TUNA STEAK

with

PARSLEY, LEMON AND GARLIC DRESSING

Fish is incredibly good for you and tuna is a really top superfood. A meaty tuna steak is a great source of lean protein and packed with nutritious vitamins B12 and D, calcium and iron. The flavour is great and in my opinion tuna shouldn't be smothered with thick rich sauces, which is why I love this recipe: it's light, full of fresh flavour and the fish takes centre stage.

Bistecca di tonno con gremolata

serves 4

4 tuna steaks, each about 150g and 1cm thick
8 tablespoons extra virgin olive oil
50g crisp mixed salad leaves
100g rocket leaves
15 yellow cherry tomatoes, halved
3 tablespoons balsamic vinegar
Salt and black pepper, to taste

for the gremolata:
4 tablespoons flatleaf parsley
2 garlic cloves, peeled
Zest of 1 large unwaxed lemon

1   Preheat a griddle pan over a high heat.

2   To prepare the gremolata dressing, place the parsley and the garlic on a chopping board and finely chop together using a sharp knife. Place in a bowl and grate over the lemon zest. Mix together and set aside.

3   With your fingertips, rub the tuna steaks with 3 tablespoons of oil. Cook on the hot griddle pan for 2 minutes on each side.

4   Place the tuna steaks on a chopping board, season with salt and pepper and leave to rest for 1 minute.

5   Meanwhile, place all the salad leaves and the tomatoes in a large bowl, pour over the remaining oil and the balsamic vinegar. Season with salt and pepper and mix well using your fingertips. Arrange the salad on a serving plate.

6   Using a long sharp knife, cut the tuna on the diagonal into 1cm slices and lay alongside the salad leaves.

7   Sprinkle over the gremolata and serve with a bottle of chilled Italian white wine.

TUNA AND RED ONION SALAD

with

TOASTED GARLIC BREAD

This recipe reminds me of my time fishing with my father and grandfather. We always used to make this dish and take it in huge plastic containers on our little boat when we went out on a trip together: a great memory. This simple salad is brilliantly tasty and refreshing to eat in the heat of summer, yet it really fills you up for the day. We may not have always brought back any fish but we always returned with empty containers!

Insalata di tonno

serves 4

1 x 400g can cannellini beans,
drained and rinsed
1 x 400g can red kidney beans,
drained and rinsed
1 x 400g can butter beans,
drained and rinsed
1 large red onion, peeled and
finely sliced
Juice of ½ unwaxed lemon
6 tablespoons extra virgin
olive oil
3 tablespoons freshly chopped
flatleaf parsley
8 slices of ciabatta, 1cm thick
2 garlic cloves, peeled
3 x 200g cans tuna chunks in
oil, drained
Salt and white pepper, to taste

1 Put all the beans in a large bowl with the sliced onion.

2 Squeeze in the lemon juice and pour over the oil.

3 Add the parsley and season with salt and pepper. Mix together, cover the bowl with a tea towel and set aside for 10 minutes at room temperature. Stir every couple of minutes.

4 Meanwhile, toast the bread and once cool enough to handle, gently rub the garlic on both sides.

5 Gently fold the tuna into the bean salad and serve immediately with the toasted garlic bread.

COD FILLETS

in

A SPICY GARLIC AND TOMATO SAUCE

I love a good simple Arrabbiata sauce and often have it with pasta. This recipe came about when I had extra sauce left over. I decided to top some fish with the remaining sauce and to be honest I was a little bit worried that the chilli in the sauce might overpower the fish but it worked surprisingly well. You'll want some fresh crusty bread to mop up every bit of sauce on your plate.

Merluzzo Arrabbiata

serves 4

4 tablespoons extra virgin olive oil
3 garlic cloves, peeled and quartered
1 large red chilli, deseeded and finely chopped
2 x 400g cans cherry tomatoes
3 tablespoons freshly chopped flatleaf parsley
4 x 200g skinless cod fillets
Salt, to taste

1. Heat the oil in a medium frying pan and fry the garlic and chilli for 30 seconds. Add the cherry tomatoes with the parsley, stir together with a wooden spoon and bring to the boil.

2. Season with salt and gently simmer for 6 minutes, uncovered. Stir occasionally.

3. Carefully slip the cod fillets into the sauce, cover with a lid and cook for 4 minutes on each side. If the sauce is getting too thick, add a couple of tablespoons of hot water.

4. To serve, remove the cod from the pan and place on a large serving plate.

5. Spoon the sauce over the fish and serve hot with your favourite salad on the side.

COD FILLETS

with

SALAMI, CHERRY TOMATOES AND ROSEMARY

Cod is such an excellent fish – firm, meaty and delicious served simply with salt and olive oil or with a sauce; it really is a fish that can go with most things. I like this recipe as the ingredients remind me of my home in Naples. You can substitute the salami with chorizo or pancetta if you prefer.

Merluzzo alla Napoletana

serves 4

500g baby potatoes, skin on
30g salted butter
3 tablespoons olive oil
100g salame Napoli, skin removed, cut into 1cm cubes
4 cod fillets, each about 150g, skin on
100ml white wine
300g cherry tomatoes, halved
1 tablespoon fresh rosemary leaves, finely chopped
Salt and black pepper, to taste

1   Put the potatoes in a large saucepan, cover with boiling water from the kettle, add a teaspoon of salt and boil for 10 minutes. Drain, cut the potatoes in half and set aside.

2   Heat the butter and oil in a large frying pan over a medium heat and fry the salami for 2 minutes. Stir occasionally with a wooden spoon.

3   Add the cod to the frying pan, skin-side down first, and cook for 4 minutes. Gently turn the fillets and cook for a further minute. Lift the fish out of the pan and place onto a warm plate, cover with foil and set aside.

4   Add the wine, tomatoes and rosemary to the pan and let everything bubble away for 2 minutes. Add in the cooked potatoes and continue to cook for a further minute to heat through. Season with salt and pepper.

5   Spoon the potatoes and sauce into the centre of each serving plate and gently place the cod fillets on top. Serve immediately.

ROASTED SEA BREAM

with

LEMON COUSCOUS SALAD

If you like fresh fish that just melts in the mouth, this recipe is for you. It is so tasty with hardly any ingredients added to it. You could also use sea bass or monkfish if you prefer but sea bream definitely has a more delicate flavour, which is beautifully enhanced by the rosemary and garlic.

Orata al forno con couscous

serves 4

4 whole sea bream, about 400g each, scaled and gutted
20 sprigs of fresh rosemary
4 garlic cloves, peeled and halved
4 tablespoons extra virgin olive oil
Salt and black pepper, to taste

for the couscous:
250g couscous
650ml hot vegetable stock
50ml extra virgin olive oil
grated zest and juice of 3 unwaxed lemons
3 tablespoons capers in vinegar, drained
6 tablespoons fresh mint leaves, finely shredded
20 cherry tomatoes, halved

1 Preheat the oven to 200ºC/gas 6.

2 Put each fish on a chopping board and with the help of a sharp knife slash each side twice diagonally.

3 Insert 3 rosemary sprigs and 2 garlic halves into the belly cavity of each sea bream: place the remaining rosemary in the slashes. Allow the rosemary to hang out as this will burn, giving an extra flavour to the fish.

4 Put all the fish on a large roasting tray, drizzle with the oil and sprinkle with salt and pepper.

5 Roast in the middle of the oven for 18 minutes until the flesh is white and the skin crispy.

6 Meanwhile, put the couscous into a large bowl and pour over the vegetable stock. Cover tightly with clingfilm and leave it to rest for 5 minutes. Use a fork to fluff up the couscous and separate the grains.

7 Gently fold the remaining ingredients into the cooked couscous and set aside for 5 minutes allowing all the flavours to combine.

8 Serve the lemon couscous with the roasted sea bream.

BAKED RED MULLET

with

OREGANO, CHERRY TOMATOES AND WHITE WINE

Considering how simple this recipe is to prepare, the 'Ooohhs!' I get when I serve it up always amaze me. I don't know whether it's the smell of the fish and wine or the way you have to peel open your own foil parcel to reveal your meal, but whatever it is, everyone seems to love it. You can serve this with a crisp salad or with couscous, rice or potatoes.

Triglie al forno

serves 4

4 whole red mullet, each about 250g, scaled and gutted
1 small bunch of fresh oregano
4 garlic cloves, peeled and halved
100ml extra virgin olive oil, plus extra for brushing
100ml dry white wine
Juice of 3 lemons
16 cherry tomatoes, halved
Sea salt and black pepper, to taste

1 Preheat the oven to 220°C/gas 7.

2 Season the fish with salt and pepper inside and out. Put 3 sprigs of oregano and 2 pieces of garlic in the cavity of each one.

3 Prepare four 30cm squares of foil. Brush with a little oil on each square and lay a fish diagonally across the centre of each piece. Bring the sides of the foil up around the fish and crimp together tightly at each end, leaving the top part open.

4 Pour 2 tablespoons of wine into each parcel with 2 tablespoons of lemon juice and 2 tablespoons of extra virgin olive oil.

5 Scatter the cherry tomatoes equally over the top of the mullet.

6 Seal the parcels well and transfer to a baking tray. Bake in the middle of the oven for 10 minutes.

7 To serve, place the unopened parcels on 4 warm serving plates and take them to the table with a large bowl of crisp salad leaves.

8 Enjoy with a cold glass of dry white wine.

GRILLED FILLETS OF MACKEREL

with

OLIVES AND CHERRY TOMATOES

Sgombro con olive e pomodorini

Mackerel is an 'oily fish' and not really eaten as much as it used to be. Many of the older generation still love to use this fish but I think we are losing that tradition, which is a real shame. If you tend only to buy mackerel in its canned form, in oil or tomato sauce, this recipe using fresh fillets will make you think again – it's an absolute treat cooked Italian-style: marinated first, then cooked super-fast on a hot griddle. Historically in England, this fish was not preserved, but was consumed only in its fresh form but now with proper refrigeration we can enjoy this fish more often and so I have created this recipe for those of you who love fish and want to try something a little different.

serves 4

5 tablespoons extra virgin olive oil
Juice of 1 large lemon
½ teaspoon smoked paprika
4 whole fresh mackerel, each about 350g, filleted to give 8 pieces in total
60g rocket leaves
100g yellow cherry tomatoes, halved
100g red cherry tomatoes, halved
100g pitted green olives in brine, drained and halved
2 tablespoons balsamic vinegar
Salt, to taste

1 Pour the oil into a medium bowl with the lemon juice. Season with the paprika and ½ teaspoon of salt and mix together.

2 Brush some of the marinade on both sides of the mackerel fillets and leave to marinate on a flat plate for 10 minutes at room temperature.

3 Meanwhile, preheat a griddle pan to high and preheat a medium frying pan.

4 Arrange the rocket leaves in the middle of 4 serving plates.

5 Cook the fillets of mackerel on the hot griddle pan, skin-side down first, for 30 seconds. Turn the fillets and cook the other side for a further 30 seconds.

6 Arrange the mackerel, cherry tomatoes and olives on and around the rocket leaves, trying not flatten the leaves too much.

7 Pour the remaining marinade into the hot frying pan and cook for 30 seconds, stirring continuously with a wooden spoon.

8 Spoon the hot dressing all over the salad and fish and finally drizzle over the balsamic vinegar.

9 Serve hot with crusty bread on the side.

PASTA

La pasta

Pasta is often the dish that people turn to for a quick midweek meal when they're tired and hungry and the cupboards are almost bare. So here are a few ideas to pep up your usual pasta dinners using a range of pasta from fettuccine, spaghetti and linguine to farfalle, rigatoni and penne. If you want to speed up the recipes even more you can always substitute dried pasta with fresh egg pasta, which will roughly halve your cooking time.

FILLET OF SALMON

with

SUN-DRIED TOMATO PESTO

I often top fish such as cod and haddock with a green pesto sauce but I wanted to come up with a red pesto fish recipe. I love red pesto and the intense flavour of the sun-dried tomatoes and the kick of the chilli are really potent here. The salmon works so well with these flavours and the dish looks amazing with its pink/red bright colours against a serving of plain white rice. A good glass of Italian red completes the theme.

Salmone al pesto rosso

serves 4

4 salmon fillets, each about 200g, skin on or off

for the pesto:
1 x 400g can chopped tomatoes
1 garlic clove, peeled
8 basil leaves
50g capers in brine, drained
1 teaspoon dried chilli flakes
200g sun-dried tomatoes in oil, drained
1 tablespoon extra virgin olive oil
Salt, to taste

1   Preheat the oven to 190ºC/gas 5.

2   Put the tomatoes, garlic, basil, capers, chilli flakes and sun-dried tomatoes in a food processor, drizzle over the extra virgin olive oil and blitz until you have a smooth creamy paste. Season with a little salt.

3   Put the salmon fillets on a baking tray and spoon the spicy paste over each one. (Place them skin-side down if the salmon comes with the skin on.)

4   Cook in the hot oven for 15 minutes.

5   Remove the tray from the oven and leave the salmon to rest for 1 minute.

6   Serve hot with simple boiled rice to accompany the fish and a big glass of Italian red wine.

SALMON
and
SPINACH FISHCAKES

Many people buy ready-made fishcakes, perhaps because they feel it's going to be a long difficult process to make them. Well, it couldn't be easier: you put most of the ingredients in a food processor, coat the mixture in cracker crumbs and cook – done. I guarantee they will taste better, you will get much more fish than in any ready-made ones, and they probably cost less. Try this recipe – you will never go back!

Tortine di salmone

serves 4

150g frozen leaf spinach, defrosted
16 cream crackers
2 x 180g can salmon chunks in brine, drained
Zest of 1 unwaxed lemon
1 large egg, separated
2 tablespoons freshly chopped flatleaf parsley
4 tablespoons olive oil
3 tablespoons mayonnaise
2 tablespoons wholegrain mustard
Salt and black pepper, to taste

1. Squeeze any excess water from the spinach, roughly chop and set aside.

2. Place 6 crackers in a food processor and blitz to make fine crumbs then tip on to a flat plate and set aside for coating the fishcakes later.

3. Put the remaining crackers in the food processor and blitz until fine. Add in the salmon, spinach, lemon zest, egg yolk, parsley and season with salt and pepper. Blitz until fully combined. Set aside.

4. Put the egg white in a bowl and whisk with a fork.

5. Shape the salmon mixture into 4 patties, dip each one into the egg white and then coat in the reserved cracker crumbs.

6. Heat the oil in a medium frying pan over a medium heat and cook the fishcakes for 5 minutes on each side, until beautiful and golden all over.

7. Meanwhile, put the mayonnaise and mustard in a small bowl and stir.

8. Serve the salmon fishcakes hot with the mustard and mayonnaise dip.

SHELL PASTA

with

PEPPERS, SUN-DRIED TOMATOES AND PINE NUTS

This has to be the ultimate vegetarian pasta recipe. There is so much goodness in this dish and it's also really filling and extremely tasty. Some might think that the peppers could make it slightly bitter but together with the pine nuts and basil, it screams freshness and will be enjoyed by herbivores and carnivores alike.

Conchiglie vegetariane

serves 4

1 orange pepper
1 red pepper
8 tablespoons olive oil
2 garlic cloves, peeled and finely sliced
8–10 sun-dried tomatoes, sliced
25g pine nuts
500g medium conchiglie shells
Basil leaves, to garnish
Salt and black pepper, to taste

1   In a large saucepan, bring 5 litres of water to the boil with 1½ tablespoons of fine salt.

2   On a chopping board, with the help of a sharp knife, cut the peppers in half, discard the seeds and chop into 1cm cubes.

3   Heat the olive oil in a large frying pan over a medium heat and fry the garlic and peppers for 5 minutes. Stir occasionally with a wooden spoon. Season with salt and pepper before adding in the sun-dried tomatoes and pine nuts. Cook for 2 minutes.

4   Meanwhile, cook the pasta in the boiling water until al dente. To get the al dente perfect bite, cook the pasta for 1 minute less then instructed on the packet and always leave the pan uncovered. A good-quality dried pasta will take 8–10 minutes to cook.

5   Once the pasta is cooked, drain and tip it back into the same saucepan that you cooked it in.

6   Pour over the prepared sauce, put the saucepan over a medium heat and mix all of the ingredients together for 30 seconds allowing all the flavours to combine beautifully. Scatter with basil leaves then divide the pasta between 4 serving plates and serve immediately.

FETTUCCINE

with

GOAT'S CHEESE, CHERRY TOMATOES AND FRESH BASIL

Goat's cheese is a favourite in our house but it can be quite heavy when melted, so using it in a pasta recipe can sometimes not work, unless it's a baked pasta dish. However, I came up with the perfect solution – don't melt it completely. My family love the strong yet fresh flavour of this recipe and actually getting protein, calcium, vitamins and carbs in one dish is not bad going. If you're a fan of goat's cheese you too will love this, but it also works well with feta if you prefer a slightly milder flavour.

Fettuccine velocissime

serves 4

8 tablespoons extra virgin olive oil
2 garlic cloves, peeled and finely sliced
300g cherry tomatoes, halved
500g fresh egg fettuccine
10 basil leaves, finely sliced, plus extra to garnish
150g firm goat's cheese
Salt and white pepper, to taste

1 Bring 5 litres of water to the boil in a large saucepan with 1½ tablespoons of fine salt.

2 In a medium frying pan, add the oil and gently fry the garlic and cherry tomatoes for 2 minutes, stirring with a wooden spoon. Season with salt and pepper then remove from the heat and set aside.

3 Meanwhile, cook the pasta in the boiling water until al dente. To get the al dente perfect bite, cook the pasta for 1 minute less than instructed on the packet and always keep the pan uncovered. A good-quality fresh egg pasta will take 4–6 minutes to cook.

4 Once the pasta is cooked, drain and tip back into the same saucepan in which you cooked it.

5 Pour over the cherry tomato mixture, add the basil and crumble in the goat's cheese. Gently fold together, away from the heat, for 30 seconds allowing all the flavours to combine.

6 Serve immediately, garnished with fresh basil leaved and accompanied with a glass of your favourite cold beer.

PASTA

with

CRISPY FOUR CHEESE SAUCE TOPPING

You will often find this recipe in Italian cookery books and I did think twice about putting it in this book but it would be so wrong to leave out such a wonderful classic. I always make this dish with the four wonderful Italian cheeses below but, to be honest, most cheeses will work. What's great about this particular dish is that if you don't have time to prepare it when your friends/family/guests arrive, you also have the option of preparing it in the morning and simply baking it when needed.

Penne ai quattro formaggi

serves 4

250ml full-fat milk
100g Gorgonzola, cut into cubes
100g Taleggio, cut into cubes
1 teaspoon smoked paprika
500g penne rigate
1 x 125g mozzarella ball, drained and cut into cubes
100g freshly grated Parmesan cheese
Salt, to taste

1 Bring 5 litres of water to the boil in a large saucepan with 1½ tablespoons of fine salt.

2 Pour the milk into a medium saucepan over a medium heat and add the Gorgonzola and Taleggio cheese. Gently melt the cheeses in the milk for 5 minutes, stirring with a wooden spoon.

3 Once the cheeses are melted, stir in the smoked paprika and season with a little salt. Set aside.

4 Preheat the grill to its highest setting (if you intend to serve the dish straight away).

5 Meanwhile, cook the pasta in the boiling water until al dente. To get the al dente perfect bite, cook the pasta for 1 minute less than instructed on the packet and always keep the pan uncovered. A good-quality driespasta will take 8–10 minutes to cook.

6 Once the pasta is cooked, drain and tip back into the same saucepan in which you cooked it.

7 Pour over the cheese sauce, add the cubes of mozzarella and half of the grated Parmesan and stir together for 10 seconds allowing the sauce to coat the pasta perfectly. Tip the pasta into an ovenproof dish and sprinkle over the remaining Parmesan cheese. Put under the hot grill for 3 minutes until golden and crispy.

FETTUCCINE

in

A CLASSIC BASIL AND TOMATO SAUCE

I know you might think this is quite a basic recipe but I am a true believer in 'less is more'. The small number of ingredients speak for themselves and I've never met anyone who doesn't like this dish, especially if you have a house full of kids. Do use fresh pasta for this recipe, although you could make it with the ribbon pasta tagliatelle if you prefer.

Fettuccine pomodoro e basilico

serves 4

1 medium white onion, peeled and finely chopped
6 tablespoons extra virgin olive oil
2 x 400g cans chopped tomatoes
10 basil leaves
500g fresh egg fettuccine
Salt and black pepper, to taste
Crusty bread, to serve

1 Bring 5 litres of water to the boil in a large saucepan with 1½ tablespoons of fine salt.

2 Place a medium saucepan over a low heat and fry the onion in the oil for 5 minutes until golden, stirring occasionally with a wooden spoon.

3 Pour in the chopped tomatoes, add the basil, and season with salt and pepper. Continue to cook for 10 minutes, uncovered, stirring the sauce every couple of minutes.

4 Cook the pasta in the boiling water until al dente. To get the al dente perfect bite, cook the pasta for 1 minute less than instructed on the packet and always keep the pan uncovered. A good-quality fresh egg pasta will take 4–6 minutes to cook.

5 Once the pasta is cooked, drain and tip back into the same saucepan in which you cooked it.

6 Pour over the tomato and basil sauce and stir together for 30 seconds allowing the sauce to coat the pasta perfectly.

7 Serve immediately with plenty of warm crusty bread on the side to mop up the delicious tomato sauce.

BOW PASTA

with

RICOTTA AND SUN-DRIED TOMATOES

If you enjoy creamy sauces but don't actually like cream (there are hundreds out there who have this problem), this recipe is for you. Ricotta cheese is an amazing substitute: light, creamy, but without the fat. The sun-dried tomatoes add the essential flavour to what could otherwise be a bland dish; it makes my mouth water just thinking about it.

Farfalle e ricotta

---

serves 4

4 tablespoons pine nuts
250g ricotta cheese
150g sun-dried tomatoes in oil, drained and cut into thin strips
5 tablespoons freshly chopped flatleaf parsley
½ teaspoon freshly ground black pepper
4 tablespoons extra virgin olive oil
500g farfalle
Salt, to taste

1 Bring 5 litres of water to the boil in a large saucepan with 1½ tablespoons of fine salt.

2 In a medium frying pan, toast the pine nuts for 2 minutes until golden brown all over. Watch carefully as they burn easily. Set aside.

3 Put the ricotta in a large bowl with the sun-dried tomatoes, parsley, pine nuts and black pepper. Pour over the oil, add 4 tablespoons hot water and season with salt. Mix together and leave to rest at room temperature.

4 Meanwhile, cook the pasta in the boiling water until al dente. To get the al dente perfect bite, cook the pasta for 1 minute less than instructed on the packet and always keep the pan uncovered. A good-quality driedpasta will take 8–10 minutes to cook.

5 Once the pasta is cooked, drain and tip back into the same saucepan in which you cooked it.

6 Pour over the ricotta mixture and gently fold together for 30 seconds allowing the sauce to coat the pasta perfectly.

7 Serve immediately.

POTATO DUMPLINGS

in

SPICY TOMATO SAUCE WITH MOZZARELLA

The ingredients in this sauce are similar to those you would find on a Margherita pizza, but with the addition of onion and chilli. This is pure comfort food – you feel completely satisfied, content and relaxed after a plate of *gnocchi piccanti alla Napoletana*. Gnocchi is a great substitute for pasta and kids love the little potato dumplings.

Gnocchi piccanti alla Napoletana

serves 4

4 tablespoons extra virgin olive oil
1 medium white onion, peeled and finely chopped
1 teaspoon dried chilli flakes
1 x 700ml bottle of passata
10 fresh basil leaves, plus extra to garnish
500g ready-made plain gnocchi (at least 70 per cent potatoes)
2 x 125g mozzarella balls, drained and cut into 1cm cubes
Salt, to taste

1   Bring 5 litres of water to the boil in a large saucepan with 1½ tablespoons of fine salt.

2   Heat the oil in a medium saucepan over a medium heat and fry the onion and chilli for 3 minutes until golden.

3   Pour in the passata and continue to cook for a further 10 minutes, uncovered. Stir occasionally with a wooden spoon.

4   Stir in the basil, season with salt and remove from the heat.

5   Cook the gnocchi in the boiling salted water until they start to float to the surface. (A good-quality gnocchi will take 3–5 minutes to cook). Drain well and add to the saucepan with the cooked tomato sauce.

6   Return the saucepan to a low heat and cook for 1 minute. Stir occasionally allowing the sauce to coat the potato dumplings.

7   Scatter over the mozzarella and continue to cook, stirring continuously, for a further 30 seconds allowing the mozzarella to melt slightly.

8   Serve immediately, garnished with fresh basil.

SPAGHETTI
with
GARLIC, OLIVE OIL, CHILLI AND CAPERS

If you are on a first date or are hoping to continue your evening maybe this isn't the recipe for you. You risk slurping your spaghetti, dribbling oil on your clothes and reeking of garlic but for any other occasion, this recipe is always a winner. I love the combination of simple yet strong flavours.

Spaghetti aglio, olio, peperoncino e capperi

serves 4

8 tablespoons extra virgin olive oil
4 garlic cloves, peeled and finely sliced
2 medium hot red chillies, deseeded and finely chopped
3 tablespoons salted capers, rinsed under cold water and drained
4 tablespoons freshly chopped flatleaf parsley
500g spaghetti or linguine
Salt, to taste

1 Bring 5 litres of water to the boil in a large saucepan with 1½ tablespoons of fine salt.

2 Heat the oil in a small frying pan over a low heat and fry the garlic for 1 minute until golden, stirring with a wooden spoon. Add the chillies, capers and parsley and fry for a further minute.

3 Pour over 6 tablespoons of the salted water from the saucepan in which you will cook the pasta. Mix and set aside.

4 Meanwhile, cook the pasta in the boiling water until al dente. To get the al dente perfect bite, cook the pasta for 1 minute less than instructed on the packet and always keep the pan uncovered. A good-quality dried pasta will take 8–10 minutes to cook.

5 Once the pasta is cooked, drain and tip back into the same saucepan in which you cooked it.

6 Pour over the chilli and garlic mixture and, over a medium heat, stir together for 15 seconds allowing the flavours to combine beautifully.

7 Serve immediately with a glass of cold Italian dry white wine.

RIGATONI

in

A CREAMY SAFFRON SAUCE

Most people love traditional creamy sauces but I wanted to create one with a bit of a difference, with a special flavour that we don't use very often: saffron. Saffron has a distinctive hay-like fragrance and has a really long medicinal history of healing, some people claim it is cancer-suppressing and even the petals can be helpful for depression. Iran now accounts for some 90 per cent of the world production of saffron; I personally love its unique flavour and extraordinary deep-yellow colour. It's a very expensive ingredient but happily a few threads are all that you need.

Rigatoni allo zafferano

serves 4

2 pinches of saffron threads
40g salted butter
150g Neapolitan salami, roughly chopped
250ml double cream
100g frozen peas, defrosted
500g rigatoni
3 egg yolks
60g freshly grated Pecorino cheese
Salt and black pepper, to taste

1 Bring 5 litres of water to the boil in a large saucepan with 1½ tablespoons of fine salt.

2 Put the saffron in a small bowl with 4 tablespoons of hot water. Set aside to infuse for 5 minutes.

3 Melt the butter in a medium saucepan and gently fry the salami for 2 minutes, stirring occasionally with a wooden spoon.

4 Pour over the cream and the saffron water. Add the peas and gently simmer for 5 minutes. Season with salt and pepper and set aside.

5 Meanwhile, cook the pasta in the boiling water until al dente. To get the al dente perfect bite, cook the pasta for 1 minute less than instructed on the packet and always keep the pan uncovered. A good-quality dried pasta will take 8–10 minutes to cook.

6 Once the pasta is cooked, drain and tip back into the same saucepan in which you cooked it. Pour over the saffron sauce.

7 Put the pan over a low heat and add the egg yolks, stirring continuously for 15 seconds.

8 Serve immediately with grated Pecorino on top.

RIGATONI

with

CHICKEN, RED CHILLIES, GARLIC AND TOMATOES

I once overheard a friend tell her family that she needed to cook chicken because it was almost past its use-by date that night and they were all disappointed as they fancied pasta… hello, Gino to the rescue… I even surprised myself with this one to be honest, as I pretty much threw the ingredients together, but it works. The dish is now on their weekly supper menu at home and it's called 'Gino's night' – I'm very honoured.

Rigatoni con pollo Arrabbiata

serves 4

8 tablespoons extra virgin olive oil
2 medium skinless, boneless chicken breasts, cut into 2cm pieces
2 garlic cloves, peeled and finely sliced
2 medium-hot red chillies, deseeded and finely chopped
2 x 400g cans chopped tomatoes
500g rigatoni
Salt, to taste
Parmesan shavings, to serve (optional)

1   Bring 5 litres of water to the boil in a large saucepan with 1½ tablespoons of fine salt.

2   Heat the oil in a large frying pan over a medium heat and fry the chicken, garlic and chilli for 2 minutes. Stir with a wooden spoon.

3   Pour in the chopped tomatoes, stir well and gently simmer for 10 minutes, uncovered, stirring every couple of minutes. Season with salt once the sauce is ready.

4   Meanwhile, cook the pasta in the boiling water until al dente. To get the al dente perfect bite, cook the pasta for 1 minute less than instructed on the packet and always keep the pan uncovered. A good-quality dried pasta will take 8–10 minutes to cook.

5   Once the pasta is cooked, drain and tip back into the same saucepan in which you cooked it.

6   Pour over the chicken sauce and stir together for 30 seconds allowing the flavours to combine properly.

7   Serve immediately with Parmesan shavings scattered over the top if you wish.

PENNE

with

PANCETTA, ONIONS AND CHOPPED TOMATOES

I cook this recipe at least once a week at home. It is so simple to make, so full of flavour and never fails to remind me of Italy. My late father Ciro loved this pasta dish. Whenever I made it he would ask whether I had used good-quality canned tomatoes, as he didn't like to have skin on them – you would think he wouldn't need to ask, considering he worked for me importing perfect canned tomatoes, but the question would always come and I would always reply, 'Of course, papa'. I think of him every time I make this dish and now miss him asking me.

Penne Amatriciana

serves 4

6 tablespoons olive oil
2 large white onions, peeled and finely sliced
½ teaspoon dried chilli flakes
250g diced pancetta
2 x 400g cans chopped tomatoes
500g penne rigate
4 tablespoons freshly chopped flatleaf parsley
Salt, to taste

1   Bring 5 litres of water to the boil in a large saucepan with 1½ tablespoons of fine salt.

2   Heat the oil in a medium saucepan over a medium heat and fry the onions for 3 minutes, stirring occasionally with a wooden spoon. Add the chilli and pancetta and continue to cook for a further 5 minutes.

3   Pour in the chopped tomatoes, stir well and gently simmer for 10 minutes, uncovered, stirring every couple of minutes. Season with salt once the sauce is cooked.

4   Meanwhile, cook the pasta in the boiling water until al dente. To get the al dente perfect bite, cook the pasta for 1 minute less than instructed on the packet and always keep the pan uncovered. A good-quality dried pasta will take 8–10 minutes to cook.

5   Once the pasta is cooked, drain and tip back into the same saucepan in which you cooked it.

6   Pour over the sauce, add the parsley and stir together for 30 seconds allowing the flavours to combine.

7   Serve immediately with a large glass of Italian red wine.

BOW PASTA

with

EGGS, CRISPY PANCETTA AND PECORINO

Before you go out and buy cream, bacon and mushrooms, please read the ingredients for this recipe. It is a real traditional Italian Carbonara and the ingredients may surprise you. In Italy we make this pasta dish with eggs not cream, and the flavour is far superior. If you prefer you can use Parmesan cheese instead of Pecorino and if making for your kids, omit the parsley.

Farfalle Carbonara

---

serves 4

3 tablespoons extra virgin olive oil
3 tablespoons salted butter
250g diced pancetta
4 large eggs
6 tablespoons freshly grated Pecorino Romano
4 tablespoons freshly chopped flatleaf parsley
½ teaspoon freshly ground black pepper
500g farfalle
Salt, to taste

1 Bring 5 litres of water to the boil in a large saucepan with 1½ tablespoons of fine salt.

2 Heat the oil and butter in a medium frying pan over a medium heat and fry the pancetta for 5 minutes until golden and crispy, stirring occasionally. Remove from the heat and set aside.

3 Whisk the eggs in a bowl with half the Pecorino cheese, the parsley and black pepper. Season with salt.

4 Meanwhile, cook the pasta in the boiling water until al dente. To get the al dente perfect bite, cook the pasta for 1 minute less than instructed on the packet and always keep the pan uncovered. A good-quality dried pasta will take 8–10 minutes to cook.

5 Once the pasta is cooked, drain and tip back into the same saucepan in which you cooked it.

6 Add the fried pancetta to the pasta and pour over the egg mixture. Mix together for 30 seconds with a wooden spoon. (The heat from the pasta cooks the egg sufficiently to create a creamy and moist texture.) Check if it needs a little more salt and serve immediately with the remaining cheese sprinkled on top.

BOW PASTA

with

TRADITIONAL CREAMY SAUCE, MUSHROOMS AND HAM

When I first came to England, I ordered a Carbonara and got spaghetti with ham, cream and mushrooms. I was surprised as this wasn't Carbonara that a native Italian would recognise but, at the same time, I did like the flavour. I felt it was missing something, though, and came up with this recipe, which I think is a fantastic mixture of the versions of Carbonara made in England and Italy. It makes the dish more interesting, in my opinion, and it's certainly a big success with customers at My Pasta Bar in London.

Farfalle Boscaiola

serves 4

6 tablespoons olive oil
1 large white onion, finely sliced
250g diced cooked ham
100g frozen peas, defrosted
200g chestnut mushrooms, sliced
2 x 400g cans chopped tomatoes
150g mascarpone cheese
500g farfalle
3 tablespoons freshly chopped basil
60g freshly grated Parmesan cheese
Salt and black pepper, to taste

1 Bring 5 litres of water to the boil in a large saucepan with 1½ tablespoons of fine salt.

2 Heat the oil in a large frying pan and fry the onion for 3 minutes over a medium heat, stirring occasionally with a wooden spoon. Add the ham, peas and mushrooms and continue to cook for a further 5 minutes.

3 Pour in the chopped tomatoes, stir well and gently simmer for 8 minutes, uncovered, stirring every couple of minutes. Add the mascarpone and season with salt and pepper. Mix together, remove from the heat and set aside.

4 Meanwhile, cook the pasta in the boiling water until al dente. To get the al dente perfect bite, cook the pasta for 1 minute less than instructed on the packet and always keep the pan uncovered. A good-quality dried pasta will take 8–10 minutes to cook.

5 Once the pasta is cooked, drain and tip back into the same saucepan in which you cooked it.

6 Pour over the sauce and add the basil; stir together for 30 seconds allowing the sauce to coat the pasta perfectly.

7 Serve immediately with the Parmesan cheese sprinkled on top.

BOW PASTA

with

BASIL PESTO AND PRAWNS

This recipe was created during an argument between my boys: Rocco wanted pasta with garlic, prawns and rocket leaves and Luci wanted pesto. Here we are – basil pesto with prawns. It really works; we all absolutely loved it and I got to please both boys without turning my kitchen into a restaurant! Please make sure you only buy fresh basil to make the pesto as the flavour is so much better.

Farfalle al pesto Genovese e gamberi

serves 4

60g basil leaves
50g pine nuts
1 garlic clove, peeled
130ml extra virgin olive oil
30g freshly grated Parmesan cheese
150g cooked peeled large prawns
500g farfalle
Salt and black pepper, to taste

1   Bring 5 litres of water to the boil in a large saucepan with 1½ tablespoons of fine salt.

2   Put the basil, pine nuts and garlic in a food processor. Drizzle in the oil and blitz until smooth.

3   Transfer the basil mixture to a large serving bowl and fold in the Parmesan. Season with salt and pepper and fold in the prawns. Set aside.

4   Meanwhile, cook the pasta in the boiling water until al dente. To get the al dente perfect bite, cook the pasta for 1 minute less than instructed on the packet and always keep the pan uncovered. A good-quality dried pasta will take 8–10 minutes to cook.

5   Just before the pasta is ready to be drained, remove 4 tablespoons of the boiling water from the pan and add to the bowl with the pesto mixture.

6   Once the pasta is cooked, drain and tip it into the bowl with the pesto mixture.

7   Fold together for 30 seconds allowing the pesto to coat the pasta.

8   Serve immediately.

FETTUCCINE

with

ANCHOVIES, TOMATOES, GARLIC AND CAPERS

Anchovies are like Marmite – you either love them or hate them. If you are a lover like me, you have to try this recipe. It is a really strong, rich-flavoured pasta dish. I love this sauce so much I've even used it to marinate cod and chicken fillets – it's great on nearly everything and the best part is dunking bread in any leftover sauce.

Fettuccine con acciughe

serves 4

8 tablespoons olive oil
2 garlic cloves, peeled and finely sliced
12 anchovy fillets in oil, drained and chopped
½ teaspoon dried chilli flakes
50g capers in salt, rinsed under cold water and drained
100g good-quality pitted green olives, halved
2 x 400g cans chopped tomatoes
500g fresh egg fettuccine
3 tablespoons freshly chopped flatleaf parsley
Salt, to taste
Crusty bread, to serve

1   Bring 5 litres of water to the boil in a large saucepan with 1½ tablespoons of fine salt.

2   Heat the oil in a large frying pan over a medium heat and fry the garlic and anchovies for about 2 minutes, stirring occasionally with a wooden spoon.

3   Add in the chilli, capers and olives and continue to cook for a further 2 minutes. Continue to stir.

4   Pour in the tomatoes, stir well and gently simmer for 10 minutes, uncovered, stirring every couple of minutes. Once ready, season with salt if necessary, remove from the heat and set aside.

5   Meanwhile, cook the pasta in the boiling water until al dente. To get the al dente perfect bite, cook the pasta for 1 minute less than instructed on the packet and always keep the pan uncovered. A good-quality fresh egg pasta will take 4–6 minutes to cook.

6   Once the pasta is cooked, drain and tip back into the same saucepan in which you cooked it.

7   Pour over the anchovy sauce, add the parsley and stir together for 30 seconds, allowing the flavours to combine properly.

8   Serve immediately with a cold Italian beer. Don't forget some bread for mopping up the sauce.

LINGUINE

in

A TUNA AND SMOKED SALMON SAUCE

This is a very tasty yet light pasta dish, which is incredibly easy to prepare. Seafood can be expensive, though, so I created a recipe that will give you your fish fix and yet won't make you feel as if you're being extravagant. As smoked salmon is expensive; I've increased the fish factor here by using a can of tuna as well. Please make sure you use tuna in oil and not brine – the flavour is so much better.

Linguine al tonno e salmone

serves 4

10 tablespoons extra virgin olive oil
2 garlic cloves, peeled and finely sliced
100g Kalamata pitted olives, drained and halved
150g smoked salmon, cut into strips
10 cherry tomatoes, quartered
½ teaspoon dried chilli flakes
1 x 200g can tuna chunks in oil, drained
2 tablespoons freshly chopped flatleaf parsley
500g linguine
Salt, to taste

1 Bring 5 litres of water to the boil in a large saucepan with 1½ tablespoons of fine salt.

2 Heat the oil in a large frying pan over a medium heat and fry the garlic, olives and smoked salmon for 1 minute. Stir with a wooden spoon.

3 Add in the tomatoes along with the chilli and continue to cook for a further 3 minutes. Stir occasionally.

4 Scatter over the tuna chunks and the parsley, season with a little salt and mix together for a further minute. Remove from the heat and set aside.

5 Meanwhile, cook the pasta in the boiling water until al dente. To get the al dente perfect bite, cook the pasta for 1 minute less than instructed on the packet and always keep the pan uncovered. A good-quality dried pasta will take 8–10 minutes to cook.

7 Once the pasta is cooked, drain and tip back into the same saucepan in which you cooked it.

8 Pour over the tuna and salmon sauce and, over a low heat, stir together for 30 seconds allowing the flavours to combine beautifully.

9 Serve immediately and please, please, DO NOT grate any kind of cheese on top.

SPAGHETTI

with

CRAB, CHERRY TOMATOES AND FRESH RED CHILLIES

If you are having guests over but don't have much time to prepare a meal, this is the recipe for you. Crab is a real treat and makes the dish seem really extravagant. The ingredients are simple and uncomplicated allowing the crabmeat to shine. You could also use lobster if you prefer – I guess it would depend on your budget and how much you like your guests!

Spaghetti con granchio e peperoncino

serves 4

500g spaghetti
8 tablespoons extra virgin olive oil
2 garlic cloves, peeled and finely sliced
1 medium hot red chilli, deseeded and finely sliced
200g cherry tomatoes, halved
100ml white wine
200g white crabmeat
3 tablespoons freshly chopped chives
Salt, to taste

1   In a large saucepan, bring 5 litres of water to the boil with 1½ tablespoons of fine salt.

2   Cook the pasta in the boiling water until al dente. To get the al dente perfect bite, cook the pasta for 1 minute less then instructed on the packet and always leave the pan uncovered. A good-quality dried pasta will take 8–10 minutes to cook.

3   Meanwhile, gently heat the oil in a large frying pan and fry the garlic and chilli together for 30 seconds.

4   Add the tomatoes and cook for 2 minutes before deglazing the pan with the wine. Bring to a simmer before stirring in the crab. Cook for 1 minute to warm the crab through.

5   Once the pasta is cooked, drain well before tipping into the pan with the crab sauce. Stir to combine, sprinkle over the chopped chives and serve immediately.

LINGUINE

with

CLAMS AND WHITE WINE

I absolutely love this recipe, so much so I would say it's my favourite in this chapter. I lived on freshly landed seafood when I was a young boy and miss it hugely. This was, and still is, number one for me. It's so easy and yet you really feel that you have been spoiled when someone makes it for you. Please be careful when making the sauce and ensure that you do not stir the clams too vigorously or you run the risk of breaking bits of the shell into the sauce.

Linguine vongole e vino bianco

serves 4

700g fresh clams in their shells
50ml dry white wine
8 tablespoons extra virgin olive oil
3 garlic cloves, peeled and sliced
½ teaspoon dried chilli flakes
15 cherry tomatoes, halved
4 tablespoons freshly chopped flatleaf parsley
500g linguine
Salt, to taste

1 Bring 5 litres of water to the boil in a large saucepan with 1½ tablespoons of fine salt.

2 Wash the clams under cold running water, discarding any broken ones and any that do not close when tapped firmly.

3 Put a large saucepan over a high heat, carefully add the clams and pour over the wine. Cover with a lid and cook for 3 minutes until they have opened. Discard any that remain closed. Tip into a colander placed over a large bowl and set aside, reserving the cooking liquor.

4 Pour the oil into the same saucepan in which you cooked the clams and gently fry the garlic for 1 minute until it begins to sizzle. Add the chilli, tomatoes and parsley and pour in the reserved liquor from the clams. Cook over a medium heat for 5 minutes. Season with salt.

5 Meanwhile, cook the pasta in the boiling water until al dente. To get the al dente perfect bite, cook the pasta for 1 minute less than instructed on the packet and always keep the pan uncovered. A good-quality dried pasta will take 8–10 minutes to cook.

6 Once the pasta is cooked, drain and tip back into the same saucepan in which you cooked it.

7 Pour over the sauce, add the clams and very gently stir together over a low heat for 30 seconds allowing the sauce to thicken and coat the pasta evenly. Serve immediately.

VEGETABLES

La verdura

Vegetables are the stars of the show in these recipes where the 20-minute cooking time maximises their freshness and flavour. I've even managed to include a vegetable tart using ready-made pastry for a handy shortcut and a quick vegetable risotto made with microwaveable rice, so you can still enjoy these dishes without wasting time with lots of stirring or baking. Ready-made polenta is also a great storecupboard staple and is a brilliant base for Italian-style vegetable dishes.

HONEY BEETROOT

with

BALSAMIC VINEGAR AND FETA

Fresh beetroot takes a long time to cook. However, in the chilled vegetable section of the supermarket you can find vacuum-packed cooked beetroot. It's a brilliant ingredient to use in quick recipes as the long, boring bit of the cooking has been done for you.

Barbabietola con miele e aceto balsamico

serves 4

3 x 250g packets of cooked beetroot
2 tablespoons extra virgin olive oil
2 tablespoons runny honey
A few sprigs of thyme
3 tablespoons balsamic vinegar
100g feta cheese
Salt and black pepper, to taste

1 Put a large frying pan over a high heat.

2 Remove the beetroot from the packet and quarter each one.

3 Add the oil to the pan and then the beetroot. Fry for 2 minutes before stirring in the honey and thyme. Cook for a further 2 minutes to allow the honey to caramelise.

4 Pour in the vinegar and deglaze the pan by stirring continuously with a wooden spoon.

5 Allow everything to bubble for 1 minute then spoon out into a serving bowl.

6 Crumble over the feta cheese, season to taste and serve.

GRIDDLED AUBERGINES

with

TOMATOES AND HERB YOGURT

Vegetarian food can often lack texture and interest, but this dish is the complete opposite: soft aubergines, spicy tomato sauce and cooling yogurt, perfectly balanced by the texture of crunchy chickpeas. It makes a delicious vegetarian main course, but also works well as a side dish with a steak.

Melanzane grigliate

serves 4

3 large aubergines, cut into
1cm-thick rounds
6 tablespoons olive oil
1 garlic clove, peeled and sliced
Pinch of dried chilli flakes
400g cherry tomatoes, halved
1 teaspoon vegetable stock
powder
1 x 400g can chickpeas, drained
and rinsed
A few basil leaves, to garnish
Crusty bread, to serve
Salt and black pepper, to taste

for the herb yogurt:
250g Greek yogurt
1 garlic clove, peeled
Pinch of sugar
Small bunch of mixed soft herbs
(basil, parsley and chives all
work well)

1 Preheat the grill to moderate.

2 Put the aubergine rounds on a large baking tray. Drizzle with half the olive oil and season with salt and pepper. Pop the tray under the grill until the aubergines turn golden brown – this will take 2–4 minutes on each side.

3 While the aubergines are cooking on the first side, heat the remaining olive oil in a medium frying pan and add the garlic. Fry for 30 seconds, then add the chilli flakes and halved tomatoes. Cook for 2 minutes until the tomatoes start to release their juices.

4 Check the aubergines and if they are cooked and golden brown turn off the grill and leave them in the oven to keep warm.

5 Add 150ml water and the vegetable stock powder to the frying pan with the tomatoes and stir. Add the chickpeas and continue to cook over a low heat while you make the yogurt dressing. Stir occasionally.

6 Put the yogurt in a bowl and finely grate in the garlic. Season with a pinch of sugar, salt and pepper. Finally, chop the herbs and stir them into the yogurt.

7 Remove the aubergines from the oven and place them on a large platter. Spoon over the tomato and chickpeas, drizzle with the yogurt and scatter with a few fresh basil leaves. Serve with crusty bread.

BLUE CHEESE

and

ARTICHOKE DIP

Dips are a brilliant starter as they can be served from one or two bowls set in the middle of the table so that everybody can tuck in, which creates a great atmosphere. This dip combines the strong flavours of blue cheese and bitter walnuts with earthy artichokes. Sweet pears and crunchy radishes make ideal scoops.

Crema rustica di carciofi e Gorgonzola

serves 4

1 x 250g jar of artichoke hearts
in oil, drained
100g mayonnaise
100g Gorgonzola cheese, cut into
cubes
25g freshly grated Parmesan
cheese
40g walnut halves, roughly
chopped
1 ciabatta
2 tablespoons olive oil
2 pears
12 small radishes
Black pepper, to taste

1 Preheat the oven to 200°C/gas 6 and put a griddle pan over a high heat.

2 Roughly chop the artichokes and put in a ceramic baking dish with the mayonnaise, Gorgonzola and Parmesan.

3 Scatter over the walnuts. Season with a little black pepper and transfer the dish to the oven for 10 minutes to warm through. Stir after 5 minutes.

4 Meanwhile, cut the ciabatta into thin slices and brush with the olive oil. Put the slices on the griddle pan and cook for 1 minute on each side until crisp.

5 Cut the pears into quarters, remove the core and cut into thin slices. Arrange on a serving plate with the washed radishes.

6 Remove the dip from the oven and serve with the toasted ciabatta, sliced pear and radishes.

CREAMY PEA

and

SPINACH BRUSCHETTA

Who needs canned beans on toast when you can just as quickly rustle up this recipe? Peas are always in my freezer as my kids love them and they are super quick to cook and so good for you. In this recipe they are the star of the show rather than a side dish.

Bruschetta calda con spinaci

---

serves 2

1 ciabatta
2 tablespoons olive oil
400g bag of washed baby spinach leaves
2 garlic cloves, peeled, one left whole, one halved
250g frozen peas
50ml vegetable stock
100g mascarpone cheese
Small bunch of chives
50g Parmesan cheese
Salt and black pepper, to taste

1 Put a griddle pan and a frying pan over a high heat.

2 Cut 4 thick slices of ciabatta and brush on both sides with 1 tablespoon of the olive oil. Toast on the griddle pan for 2 minutes on each side until crisp. Set aside.

3 Pour 1 tablespoon of olive oil into the frying pan and add the spinach. Once it starts to wilt, use a fine grater to grate in 1 garlic clove. Cook for 1 minute before stirring in the frozen peas.

4 Pour in the stock, bring to a simmer then stir in the mascarpone. Once it has melted and the sauce is hot, use scissors to chop in the chives and then grate in the Parmesan. Finally season with black pepper and a little salt if needed. Set aside.

5 Rub the toasted bread with the remaining garlic clove.

6 Place 2 slices of toasted garlic bread on each plate and spoon over the pea and spinach mixture. Enjoy.

CRISPY MOZZARELLA SANDWICH

with

CRANBERRY SAUCE

This is my take on the French classic, deep-fried Brie with cranberry sauce; it makes a great alternative to a boring cheese sandwich. It has all the right elements: warm gooey cheese, crispy toasted bread and cool crunchy lettuce.

Panini con mozzarella croccante

serves 2

2 x 125g balls of cow's milk mozzarella
150g ready-made fine dried breadcrumbs
50g flour
2 eggs, beaten in a small bowl
2 small baguettes
4 tablespoons olive oil
3 tablespoons cranberry sauce
2 handfuls of mixed lettuce leaves
Salt and black pepper, to taste

1 Preheat the grill to moderate.

2 Rip each mozzarella ball into about 8 pieces.

3 Put the breadcrumbs on a plate and the flour on another. Season the flour with salt and pepper.

4 Dip the pieces of mozzarella in the flour, then in the beaten egg and then in the breadcrumbs. Pop each piece back into the egg and once more into the breadcrumbs. Set aside.

5 Cut the baguettes in half lengthways then place them cut-side up under the grill. Grill until golden brown.

6 Heat the olive oil in a frying pan and fry the mozzarella pieces for 3 minutes, turning frequently, to get the pieces crispy and brown all over. Place on kitchen paper to absorb any excess oil and set aside.

7 Remove the bread from under the grill and spread the cut sides with cranberry sauce. Place the crispy mozzarella onto the baguette, top with some salad leaves and cover with the other half of the baguette. Enjoy your sandwich!

VEGETABLE COUSCOUS

with

PESTO DRESSING

Couscous, like pasta, needs a helping hand with flavours and should be well seasoned. Making it with stock powder – far quicker than using a stock cube – adds a great base flavour and the pesto dressing gives this side dish an all-Italian twist.

Couscous al pesto

serves 6-8

300g couscous
2 teaspoons vegetable stock powder
4 tablespoons olive oil
1 aubergine, trimmed and cut into 2cm cubes
2 courgettes, trimmed and cut into 1cm rounds
1 x 280g jar of red and yellow peppers, drained and roughly chopped
A handful of pitted black olives
100g semi-dried tomatoes in oil, drained

for the pesto dressing:
Large bunch of basil
1 small garlic clove, peeled
30g pine nuts
150ml olive oil
50g freshly grated Parmesan cheese
Salt and black pepper, to taste

1 Fill and boil the kettle and put a frying pan over a high heat. Have a small blender ready for later.

2 Place the couscous in a large heatproof bowl, sprinkle in the stock powder and mix together. Pour in 500ml of boiling water, stir well, cover with clingfilm and set aside.

3 Pour the oil into the hot pan and fry the aubergines and courgettes for 8 minutes until golden brown; remove from the heat.

4 While the courgettes and aubergines cook, make the dressing. Put the basil into the blender with the garlic and pine nuts. Pour in half the olive oil and blend until smooth. Add the Parmesan and blend once more, adding in the rest of the oil to create a dressing. Season with salt and black pepper.

5 Use a fork to loosen the couscous grains, then stir in the chopped peppers, olives, semi-dried tomatoes, aubergines and courgettes.

6 Stir the pesto dressing into the couscous and spoon onto a large serving plate.

STUFFED FOCACCIA

In Italy you often get a beautiful basket of bread before the start of the meal to nibble on. In the south of Italy it is often rubbed with tomatoes and it is absolutely delicious. I dedicate my Panuozzo to my brother-in-law Orlando, because every time he comes to see me in London he always asks me to make it for him.

Panuozzo

serves 4

1 large focaccia
200g cherry tomatoes
150g green pitted olives in brine, drained
200g Taleggio cheese, sliced
200g rocket leaves

1 Preheat the grill to moderate.

2 Cut the focaccia in half horizontally. Place it on a baking tray, cut-side up, and grill for 5 minutes until lightly golden brown.

3 Remove the bread from under the grill. Now it's time to get messy. Cut the tomatoes in half then squeeze them in your hands over the bottom half of the toasted bread so that all the juices are soaked up and the crushed tomatoes remain on top.

4 Roughly chop the olives and scatter them over the tomatoes, then top with the slices of Taleggio.

5 Finally add the rocket leaves and top with the other piece of bread.

6 Place the giant sandwich back under the grill, on a slightly lower rack this time, and grill for 5 minutes. You want it to slowly go crispy and golden brown on the top so that the centre has a chance to warm through.

7 Remove from the oven, cut into four and serve with a cold Italian beer.

BAKED MUSHROOMS
ON TOAST

This is my take on mushrooms on toast and it makes a perfect midweek supper. It is easily adapted for the meat eaters in the family with a little bit of pancetta placed on top before cooking. You can always add a touch of paprika or cayenne if you like a spice kick. Italian Taleggio is a great cheese for cooking as it melts most satisfyingly.

Funghi al forno

serves 4

8 large flat field mushrooms, stalks removed
250g Taleggio cheese, cut into small cubes
8 sun-dried tomatoes in oil, drained then cut into strips
3 tablespoons olive oil
4 thick slices of sourdough bread
Salt and black pepper, to taste

For the side salad:
¼ cucumber
1 tablespoon wholegrain mustard
Pinch of caster sugar
2 tablespoons balsamic vinegar
4 tablespoons extra virgin olive oil
100g peppery green salad

1 Preheat the oven to 190°C/gas 5.

2 Put the mushrooms on a large baking tray, gills facing up.

3 Scatter the Taleggio cubes on top of the mushrooms. Top the cheese with the strips of tomatoes. Drizzle with the olive oil and season with salt and pepper.

4 Bake for 10 minutes until the cheese has melted and the mushrooms are soft.

5 Meanwhile, cut the cucumber into matchsticks and put in a large bowl.

6 Toast the sourdough bread.

7 Whisk together the mustard, caster sugar and balsamic vinegar in a small bowl. Slowly whisk in the extra virgin olive oil with 1 tablespoon of cold water. Season with salt and pepper.

8 Dress the salad leaves and cucumber with the dressing.

9 Place the toasted bread in the middle of each serving plate and top each slice with 2 mushrooms. Serve with the green salad.

GRIDDLED POLENTA

with

WILD MUSHROOM RAGÙ

Mushrooms are a great base for a vegetarian meal even if you are a meat eater. They have a naturally meaty texture and are very filling, so even the most avid carnivore won't miss the steak! Italians love wild mushrooms and I'm no exception. Try this creamy ragù for a simple midweek supper.

Polenta alla griglia con ragù di funghi

serves 4

25g salted butter
3 tablespoons olive oil
450g chestnut mushrooms, sliced
150g button mushrooms, halved
**250g mixed wild mushrooms,
roughly chopped**
1 garlic clove, peeled
1 tablespoon plain flour
A good splash of white wine
300ml hot vegetable stock
300ml double cream
500g block of ready-made polenta
**1 tablespoon freshly chopped
tarragon**
Parmesan shavings, to serve
Salt and pepper, to taste

1   Preheat a griddle pan.

2   Heat the butter and 1 tablespoon of oil in a large frying pan and when melted add the mushrooms. Try not to move them around too much as this will allow them to take on some colour. Once lightly golden brown, grate in the garlic. Cook for 30 seconds before adding the flour. Stir well before pouring in the white wine. Bring to the boil, then pour in the stock and cream.

3   Stir everything together and allow to simmer for 5 minutes. Stir occasionally with a wooden spoon.

4   While the mushrooms cook, slice the polenta into 12 slices. Brush both sides with the remaining olive oil then place on the hot griddle for 1 minute on each side.

5   Stir the tarragon through the mushroom ragù and season well with salt and pepper.

6   Arrange the griddled polenta on 4 serving plates, spoon over the creamy mushroom ragù and top with some Parmesan shavings.

BAKED POLENTA

with

TOMATO AND RED PEPPER SAUCE

The ready-made blocks of polenta that you can now buy in the supermarket are great for a quick supper. Half the work is already done for you and there is no need to boil, whisk, cool and set it. I often have a packet in my kitchen for when I just don't feel like any other form of carbohydrate or for when I just feel like something a bit different.

Polenta al forno con peperoni rossi

serves 2

**3 tablespoons olive oil, plus
a little extra for brushing
1 x 290g jar of roasted red
peppers in brine or oil, drained
and sliced
2 medium courgettes, cut into
1cm cubes
1 garlic clove, peeled and sliced
Pinch of dried chilli flakes
1 x 400g can cherry tomatoes
100g pitted black olives in brine,
drained
500g block of ready-made polenta
1 x 125g ball of mozzarella,
drained
25g fresh breadcrumbs
10 basil leaves
Salt and white pepper, to taste**

1   Preheat the grill to moderate.

2   Heat the olive oil in a medium frying pan and fry the peppers and courgettes for 1 minute. Stir with a wooden spoon.

3   Add the garlic and chilli and continue to fry for a further minute.

4   Pour in the tomatoes, add the olives and simmer for 5 minutes, uncovered. Stir occasionally.

5   Put a second frying pan over a medium heat.

6   Slice the block of polenta into 1cm thick slices, brush both sides with a little olive oil and fry in the preheated frying pan for 1 minute on each side. Arrange the polenta in a small ovenproof dish so that the slices are just overlapping.

7   Tear the mozzarella into pieces and set aside.

8   Season the tomato and pepper sauce with salt and pepper. Spoon it over the polenta and scatter over the mozzarella.

9   Sprinkle the fresh breadcrumbs and basil leaves on top and drizzle with a little more olive oil. Season with salt and pepper. Put under the grill for 2 minutes or until the cheese has melted and the breadcrumbs are crispy. Serve hot.

NEW POTATO SALAD
with
RED ONIONS AND CAPERS

Adding just-boiled new potatoes into a dressing means they absorb all the flavours as they cool; it is as if they open up and suck in all the flavour. Italians use a lot of red onions, which are much milder than white or yellow ones – perfect for salads – and capers add a lemony tang. This recipe couldn't be easier, and is a great little trick to have up your sleeve.

Patate e cipolle rosse

serves 6

800g baby new potatoes, washed
1 medium red onion, peeled and sliced
2 tablespoons capers in brine, washed and drained
6 tablespoons extra virgin olive oil
Juice of 1 lemon
100g pitted green olives, drained and halved
3 tablespoons freshly chopped chives
Salt and black pepper, to taste

1 Fill a large saucepan with boiling water from the kettle and put over a high heat. Add a good pinch of salt and the potatoes. Boil for 10 minutes or until tender.

2 Meanwhile, put the onion in a large bowl with the capers, extra virgin olive oil and lemon juice. Mix everything together and set aside.

3 Add the olives to the bowl.

4 When the potatoes are tender, drain them and pop them straight into the bowl with the dressing. Add in the chives, season with salt and pepper and stir all together.

5 Serve warm to accompany any of your favourite dishes.

QUICK RISOTTO

with

LEMON, PEAS AND PARMESAN

Risotto is one of my favourite meals to eat, but sometimes I don't have the time to stand and stir for 20 minutes. This is my speedy version; its beautiful creaminess comes from the mascarpone and a good helping of Parmesan cheese.

Risotto veloce con limone e piselli

serves 4

4 tablespoons olive oil
4 spring onions, finely sliced
2 x 200g packets of microwaveable packet rice
1 tablespoon vegetable stock powder
100ml hot water
200g frozen peas, defrosted
Grated zest of 1 unwaxed lemon
4 tablespoons mascarpone cheese
60g freshly grated Parmesan cheese
Salt and white pepper, to taste

To serve:
3 tablespoons freshly chopped flatleaf parsley
150g pea shoots
Parmesan cheese
Extra virgin olive oil, to drizzle

1 Heat the olive oil in a medium saucepan.

2 Fry the spring onions in the hot oil for 2 minutes. Stir occasionally with a wooden spoon.

3 Stir in the packets of rice (no need to microwave them first) then add the stock powder and water. Stir well, breaking up the rice with the wooden spoon. Cook for 2 minutes.

4 Add the peas and cook for a further 2 minutes. Continue to stir with the wooden spoon.

5 Reduce the heat and add the lemon zest and mascarpone cheese. Sprinkle over the grated Parmesan and season with salt and pepper. Stir all together.

6 Spoon onto 4 warm serving plates, top with the fresh parsley and a handful of pea shoots then use a speed peeler to create shavings of Parmesan on top. Finish with a drizzle of extra virgin olive oil.

SUMMER VEGETABLE TART

This is a beautifully simple summer tart. The pastry is cooked blind while you make the filling so it is super quick to prepare. If you have a couple of courgettes in the fridge, or some fresh herbs, add them to the sautéed vegetables; you can make this dish up as you go along.

Tartina di asparagi

serves 4

1 sheet of ready-made rolled puff pastry
150g spring onions
1 tablespoon olive oil
150g fine asparagus spears, trimmed
100g frozen peas, defrosted
100ml crème fraîche
100g mascarpone cheese
50g freshly grated Parmesan cheese
50g rocket leaves
2 tablespoons extra virgin olive oil
Salt and black pepper, to taste

1   Preheat the oven to 200°C/gas 6.

2   Unroll the pastry and place on a non-stick baking tray. Use the point of a sharp knife to mark a border 2cm from the edge all the way round the sheet, taking care not to go all the way through. Use a fork to gently prick the pastry inside the border; this will stop it rising too much. Bake the pastry in the oven for 12 minutes.

3   Meanwhile, trim the spring onions to the same length as the asparagus spears. Heat the olive oil in a frying pan and fry the spring onions and asparagus for 1 minute.

4   Place the peas in a bowl and pour over 50ml boiling water from a kettle. Give them a quick stir and then set aside for 2 minutes, until the water has evaporated. Season with salt and pepper.

5   Mix together the crème fraîche, mascarpone and Parmesan in a large bowl. Season with a little salt and pepper.

6   Once the pastry is golden brown and risen, remove it from the oven and use a clean tea-towel to push down the puffed up central area of pastry so that you are left with a clear and defined border.

7   Spoon the cheese mixture over the central area of the pastry and spread out with a palette knife. Scatter over the cooked vegetables and top with the rocket leaves. Finish with a drizzle of extra virgin olive oil and a little salt and black pepper. Serve hot.

DESSERTS

I dolci

Pudding can often be an afterthought, particularly for everyday meals, so here are some ideas to quickly satisfy any after-dinner sweet cravings. From a simple fruit sorbet to a speedy chocolate pudding that you can whip up in the microwave, it's possible to make a range of dishes with only a little time. There's no need to wait for anything to cook or set so you can indulge in these delicious treats straight away.

FROZEN FRUITS SORBET

with

LIMONCELLO

This has to be the easiest and quickest recipe in the book. I have actually made this in less than 5 minutes and yet no one believed it. The taste is incredible and it can be counted towards your five a day – win, win!

Sorbetto tutti frutti

serves 4

500g mixed frozen fruits (blueberries, raspberries, strawberries, mangoes)
80g icing sugar
2 tablespoons limoncello liqueur, cold

1 Put the frozen fruits and the icing sugar in a food processor. Pour over the limoncello and blitz for about 2 minutes until smooth. It may need another blast to break up the frozen fruits.

2 Spoon the Sorbetto Tutti Frutti into dessert glasses and serve immediately. Alternatively, you can freeze the sorbet in a plastic sealed container for up to 2 months.

STRAWBERRIES AND ALMONDS

with

AMARETTO LIQUEUR AND GREEK YOGURT

Strawberries are on sale in supermarkets all year round but more often than not, the flavour isn't good unless they are in season. This recipe is perfect for those months when the berries are lacking their full taste and sweetness, as the Amaretto and honey add that extra something the fruit needs. This is a lovely refreshing dessert that will look really impressive if served in cocktail glasses.

Fragole, Amaretto e mandorle

serves 4

800g strawberries
3 tablespoons Amaretto liqueur
2 tablespoons runny honey
300g plain Greek yogurt
4 tablespoons flaked almonds
4 fresh mint leaves, to decorate

1 Wash the strawberries under cold water, drain and pat dry with kitchen paper.

2 Remove and discard the green stalks and cut the strawberries in half. Place in a large bowl.

3 Pour in the Amaretto liqueur and drizzle over the honey.

4 Mix well and leave to marinate for 10 minutes at room temperature. Stir occasionally.

5 Divide the yogurt between 4 dessert glasses and spoon over the marinated strawberries.

6 Drizzle with the remaining juices from the marinade and scatter over the flaked almonds. Top each glass with a fresh mint leaf.

SUMMER BERRIES

with

WHITE CHOCOLATE SAUCE

During the summer my fridge is always filled with a variety of berries for the kids to nibble on when they are hungry. This is the most simple of desserts with ingredients that are usually in the cupboard or fridge. It's a crowd-pleaser for adults and kids alike.

Frutta d'estate con cioccolata bianca

serves 6

200g good-quality white chocolate, broken into small pieces
50ml double cream
50g flaked almonds
3 tablespoons icing sugar
750g chilled summer berries (raspberries, strawberries or blueberries)
2 tablespoons crème fraîche

1. Put the chocolate pieces and the cream in a heatproof bowl. Set the bowl over a saucepan of just simmering water and allow to gently melt.

2. Meanwhile, heat a frying pan over a high heat and get a piece of baking paper out on the work surface.

3. Put the flaked almonds into the pan and dust with the icing sugar. Stir them constantly over a high heat for 1–2 minutes until they start to turn golden brown. Once lightly golden and caramelised, tip them out onto the baking paper to cool.

4. Divide the berries between 6 glasses or bowls.

5. Once the chocolate has melted, remove the bowl from the heat and stir in the crème fraîche. Spoon the sauce over the berries and scatter with the caramelised almonds.

6. Serve immediately while the sauce is still hot.

THIN PANCAKES

with

FRESHLY SQUEEZED LEMON JUICE

Say 'pancakes' in our house and everyone associates it with Saturday mornings when chocolate and banana pancakes are my speciality. I didn't really serve them as desserts after a meal until recently and now I can't understand why I didn't. If you are having fish or a light meal, this is a perfect dessert, now firmly on my top ten list. The flavours really round off your meal perfectly.

Crespelle al limone

serves 4

100g plain white flour
Pinch of salt
1 large egg
300ml full-fat milk
Zest of 1 unwaxed lemon
2 teaspoons sunflower oil
Juice of 2 lemons
1 tablespoon caster sugar
4 tablespoons Cointreau
300g strawberries, hulled and sliced

1   Sift the flour and salt into a large mixing bowl. Add the egg, milk and lemon zest and whisk together until smooth.

2   Heat a small, heavy-based frying pan over a medium heat. Add a few drops of oil and rub it over the base to allow it to heat. Pour in an eighth of the batter and tilt the pan so that the mixture spreads evenly over the base to make a thin pancake.

3   As soon as the pancake has set and bubbles appear on the surface, flip it over to cook the other side. Repeat the process to make 8 pancakes in total, transferring them to kitchen paper as you cook them. Once all the pancakes are cooked, fold them into triangles.

4   Wipe the frying pan clean with a piece of kitchen paper. Pour in the lemon juice and add the sugar. Heat gently to dissolve the sugar then pour in the Cointreau.

5   Return all the pancakes to the frying pan, overlapping them to fit. Cook gently for 30 seconds.

6   Serve 2 pancakes per person with slices of strawberries scattered over the top.

CAPPUCCINO MOUSSE

I love my coffee; it's the first thing I have in the morning and I keep my cup topped up during the day. So this dessert is for those of you who, like me, also enjoy a hit of coffee at the end of the day too.

Cappuccino mousse

Makes 4 large or 6 small

150g marshmallows
50g salted butter
50g caster sugar
250g dark chocolate (approx. 70 per cent cocoa solids), finely chopped
60ml espresso coffee
300ml double cream

for the topping:
8 tablespoons crème fraîche
1 tablespoon icing sugar
1 teaspoon vanilla bean paste
Chocolate-covered coffee beans, to decorate
Cocoa powder or finely grated chocolate, to dust

1   Place the marshmallows, butter, sugar, chocolate and espresso in a small saucepan and warm slowly until melted.

2   Meanwhile, whip the cream to medium/firm peaks.

3   Remove the melted chocolate and marshmallow mixture from the heat and pour into a large bowl. Stir gently until cooled to room temperature and then fold in the cream.

4   Spoon the mixture into 4 or 6 glasses.

5   Mix together the crème fraîche, icing sugar and vanilla then spoon on top of the coffee chocolate mousse.

6   Scatter with a few chocolate-covered coffee beans, dust lightly with cocoa powder or grated chocolate, and serve.

SUPERFAST CHOCOLATE PUDDING

You might not believe me if I told you you could cook a chocolate pudding in just sixty seconds, but it's true!

Tortino al cioccolato velocissimo

serves 4

Butter, for greasing
4 tablespoons Nutella
6 tablespoons full-fat milk
12 tablespoons self-raising flour
5 tablespoons caster sugar
1 tablespoon cocoa powder
2 medium eggs
2 tablespoons sunflower oil
3 tablespoons Amaretto liqueur
100g white chocolate, cut into small pieces
Vanilla ice cream, to serve

1 Grease 4 coffee mugs with butter.

2 Put the Nutella in a small bowl and pour over 4 tablespoons of the milk. Mix and divide between the 4 coffee mugs. Set aside.

3 Put the flour, sugar and cocoa powder in a large bowl. Crack in the eggs and pour over the oil, the remaining milk and the Amaretto liqueur. Mix well with a wooden spoon to create a smooth paste. Fold in the small pieces of white chocolate.

4 Divide the mixture equally and neatly between the coffee mugs.

5 Microwave each mug, one at a time, on full power (1000W) for 1 minute.

6 Turn out the chocolate puddings on to a plate and serve with a ball of ice cream on top.

HOT CHOCOLATE ORANGE FONDUE

This is a great one for the kids. It takes more time to eat it than it does to make and they will be kept busy creating their own combinations on skewers ready for dunking.

Fonduta di cioccolato

---

serves 8

400g dark chocolate (approx. 70 per cent cocoa solids), broken into small pieces
85g salted butter
300ml double cream
300ml full-fat milk
Zest of 2 oranges
2 tablespoons orange liqueur (omit if making for children)

for dunking:
Strawberries
Marshmallows
Amaretti biscuits
Shop-bought sponge cake (chocolate or Madeira), cut into 2cm dice
Brazil nuts
Ready-prepared pineapple chunks
Blueberries

Wooden or metal skewers

1   Heat the chocolate, butter, cream and milk in a saucepan over a low heat. Warm gently until the chocolate has melted.

2   Meanwhile, prepare the tasty treats for dunking on a board or large plate.

3   Stir the orange zest and liqueur (if using) into the melted chocolate – if the chocolate seizes (becomes stiff and unwieldy) at this stage, add 1 tablespoon of boiling water and stir until it is once again smooth and melted.

4   Pour the chocolate fondue into a fondue pot or place the saucepan on the board alongside the fruit and other bits.

5   Don't forget the skewers for dunking, otherwise it's going to get messy!

CHOCOLATE AND CHERRY TRIFLES

I am a firm believer of 'fresh is best' but when cherries are out of season or when you just don't have the time to remove their stones, canned ones sold in their natural juice are perfect. The juices are used in this recipe to moisten the sponge, adding yet more flavour.

Zuppetta Inglese

serves 4

190g dark chocolate (approx. 70 per cent cocoa solids)
150ml double cream
250ml ready-made custard
175g mascarpone
250g Madeira or chocolate sponge cake
1 x 425g can pitted cherries in natural juice, 4 reserved for decoration
4 tablespoons Amaretto liqueur

1   Break up 150g of the chocolate into small pieces and put in a heatproof bowl set over a saucepan of just simmering water. As soon as it has melted, remove the bowl from the heat and set aside.

2   Pour the cream into a separate bowl, whip to soft peaks and set aside.

3   Mix together the custard and mascarpone in a third bowl.

4   Cut the sponge into 1cm cubes and place a layer in the base of 4 straight-sided glasses. Spoon over some of the canned cherries, along with their juices, and add 1 tablespoon of Amaretto to each glass.

5   Stir the cooled melted chocolate through the custard.

6   Spoon half the custard mixture over the soaked sponge and cherries. Top with a little more sponge and some more cherries, then finish with the remaining custard mix.

7   Top with a spoonful of whipped cream and place a cherry on top.

8   Grate the remaining chocolate over the top and serve.

ZABAGLIONE

with

MARSALA WINE

What a fantastic, easy, classic Italian dessert. Who would think you could create something so delicious with three ingredients? It looks fantastic when served and always tastes amazing. Do be careful when warming the egg yolks over the pan of simmering water: the bowl must not touch the water and the water must be simmering not boiling. This recipe is not at all tricky but those rules are a must.

Zabaglione

---

serves 4

5 large eggs
250ml Marsala wine
80g caster sugar

1 Break the eggs into a small bowl and use your fingertips to lift up the egg yolks and place them in a large heatproof glass bowl. (Cover the egg whites with clingfilm and keep in the fridge for the next time you decide to make a meringue.)

2 Pour the Marsala wine into a medium saucepan and simmer gently until reduced by half. Leave to cool then stir in 20g of the sugar.

3 Put the remaining sugar in the bowl with the egg yolks and beat with an electric whisk for 5 minutes until thick and pale yellow.

4 Set the bowl over a saucepan of just simmering water (make sure the water is not in contact with the bowl) and continue to whisk for a further 10 minutes, gradually drizzling in the Marsala wine.

5 The egg mixture should almost triple in volume and have a light, foamy texture and be able to hold soft peaks when you lift the whisk. Make sure that the egg mixture doesn't become too hot or it will start to cook around the edges of the bowl – resulting in sweet scrambled egg!

6 Spoon the zabaglione into 4 tall glasses and serve immediately.

Index

fantastico!

GINO D'ACAMPO

fantastico!

Modern Italian Food

Photography by **Kate Whitaker**

KYLE BOOKS

To my grandfather who is no longer with us,
but his passion for food still lives in me!

Contents

Introduction

I grew up in the south of Italy, in Napoli, surrounded by a very large family, so it is no wonder that I became passionate about food. The food we ate was very traditional; simple recipes based on fresh and healthy fruit, vegetables, fish and meat. My grandfather always said that a good recipe doesn't need many ingredients, because if the ingredients are good quality and full of flavour, why do you have to cover up or change their taste? In the summer of 1987 when I was eleven, I walked into my grandfather's restaurant for the first time and that's when I decided that this was the career for me too.

That same summer I decided to go to catering college so that I could train to be a chef. Why? Simple. To me there is nothing more satisfying than seeing people enjoy a meal that you have created. That is the reason why I decided to write a book – so that everyone can enjoy the same experience. I wanted to write a book that would finally answer all the questions that people ask me about Italian cuisine – because, believe it or not, some of you are still making the same mistakes over and over again.

Enough… let me tell you what I think: there is no such thing as 'I can't cook'. There is a chef in each and everyone of us, but the problem is that you don't know it yet. Let me explain why. Cooking comes from the heart. If you feel down or upset, it will show in the taste of your dishes and, no matter how hard you try to follow my recipes, I guarantee you that it will be a disaster. My grandfather used to say to me that practice makes perfect; he was right, but I also say that practising for the wrong reasons will never be a success. My first rule of cooking therefore is: if you are not in a good mood, don't attempt to cook. Get a takeaway!

My second rule is cook alone. Don't try to cook with someone else, or in a group. Cooking is a personal experience, as I've just explained, and your personality will show in the food you prepare, so communal cooking will only confuse the dish. Cooking should be a selfish and relaxing experience; selfish because it is probably the only time that you should think about what YOU like and how to satisfy yourself, and relaxing because it is definitely the only time you shouldn't think about anything else, especially your problems – otherwise refer back to rule number 1.

Rule number 3 is don't try to make a 'healthier' version of a recipe; get your arse down the gym. This is self-explanatory.

The fourth rule: never cook onions and garlic together. I remember very clearly my first day at catering school. I was 14 years old and on my first attempt at making a simple tomato sauce, as I was frying my onions and garlic together, the headteacher came to me and said, 'remember Gino, the secret of a good dish is respecting the ingredients that you use'. Soon afterwards he taught me to understand the unique flavours that onions and garlic have and explained that these two great ingredients should never be mixed together. Today, none of my recipes have onions and garlic cooked together and I choose my flavours very carefully.

Rule number 5: put all your energy and concentration into the flavour of a dish and worry less about what a dish looks like. If you get the recipe right, it will look so appetising that you won't need to worry about its presentation.

Finally, and I can't say this often enough, spend less time on cooking a dish and more time on buying the right ingredients. How many times have you had to cook something for a long time with so many herbs and spices just to give an extra kick to the dish? Take a curry, for example. Some people say 'hoooo!, it's an explosion of flavours'. I say, tell me, what am I supposed to taste in a curry? The experience and the enjoyment of eating a good dish is by tasting, recognising and appreciating every single ingredient that you have put together. Next time you pick up a carrot, close your eyes, smell it, and then you will know what I mean.

I hope this book will prove to you that you don't need to spend a lot of time in the kitchen to enjoy a good Italian meal. It will also give you a good idea of the food you will find in Italy now. I have chosen some traditional recipes, exactly as my grandfather would have cooked them, some modern dishes, sometimes with a twist of my own, and a few that have been influenced by food that I love from other countries. None of the recipes are complicated or fussy – just get the ingredients right, buy a sharp knife and fantastico!

My book will tell you everything you need to know about Italian cooking – all my rules, tips and secrets – so by the time you have tried the recipes, you will understand my motto:

Minimum effort, maximum satisfaction!

First Aid for Food

1. If you want to make a good tomato salad but the tomatoes aren't as good as they could be, make sure that, after you have sliced them, you season them with salt and pepper, a good drizzle of extra virgin olive oil and a few fresh basil leaves. This will bring out their maximum flavour.

2. When you buy Mozzarella in a tub or bag filled with water from a supermarket, it is usually the commercially produced sort with not a lot of flavour. To get the best out of it, drain the Mozzarella, slice it on a serving plate, sprinkle over some salt and drizzle with good extra virgin olive oil.

3. If you have to use strawberries out of season, to get the best flavour, marinate them in Amaretto liqueur, or alternatively, add some caster sugar and freshly squeezed lemon juice. Leave to marinate for at least 20 minutes.

4. If your fruit is unripe but you still want to make a tasty fresh fruit salad, place your chopped or sliced fruit in a large bowl and dress it with Limoncello liqueur and icing sugar. Leave to marinate for at least 30 minutes.

5. If you have salad leaves that are reaching their sell-by date and are starting to wilt, remember you can always use them for cooking as you would use rocket leaves.

6. If your apples are too ripe, use them to make a fantastic apple sauce like the one used for the Maiale al Pepe e Sciroppo on page 101.

7. If your recipe only requires egg yolks, please do not throw away the whites. You can use them to make a great meringue like the one on page 149 (Cesto di Frutta).

8. If your avocados are too ripe or have gone dark in the middle, blitz them with some balsamic vinegar, salt and olive oil until smooth, to make an exquisite dipping sauce for your favourite crisps or pitta bread.

9. If you have bought too many lemons and they are past their best, squeeze the juice into an ice-cube tray. Once they have hardened, pop them out, place them in a plastic food bag and keep in the freezer. Great to add to a soft drink or plain water instead of an ice cube.

10. If your bread is becoming stale, do not throw it away. Cut into chunks, place on a baking tray and cook in a preheated oven set to 180°C/350°F/gas mark 4 for about 20 minutes. Once golden and brown, remove from the oven and allow to cool. Blitz in a food processor to make toasted breadcrumbs. Store in a plastic food bag in your cupboard for up to three months. Excellent for making escalope or fried fish.

In Italy brunch doesn't exist. We start the morning with a croissant and a cappuccino and we starve ourselves until lunchtime, but let me tell you, an Italian lunch is not a regular lunch; it is a two-hour feast with a four-course meal followed by a siesta. Since I've been living here (nearly 13 years), my way of life has changed and the hours in my day are filled differently. I never get the chance to have a long meal followed by a siesta anymore.

So mid-morning is probably my worst dilemma. It's 11am and I'm hungry. It's definitely too early for a big lunch, so I'm going to choose something lighter and probably skip lunch – what do I choose?

Cooking tips – only one…

1. Make sure you have some kind of small snack lying around for about 4pm – you will be hungry again before your dinner!

Date and Raisin Pancakes with Caramel Sauce

PANCAKES ALLA FRUTTA

Serves 4

100g pitted dates, chopped

90g raisins

1 teaspoon bicarbonate of soda

250g self-raising flour

90g soft brown sugar

250g sour cream

3 medium eggs, separated

Melted butter, for greasing

Pineapple, mango, papaya, banana, or a seasonal selection of fresh fruit of your choice

FOR THE SAUCE

250ml single cream

180g soft brown sugar

200g salted butter

This is my little sister Marcella's favourite recipe. Obviously, it's not very Italian, but it's still good enough to be in my book. I absolutely love the texture and the fruits that I have chosen. Make sure that when you prepare the pancakes, you stack them one on top of each other, creating a tower effect, and completely cover them with the warm caramel sauce. Also great for dessert.

Put the dates and raisins in a small saucepan with 250ml of water and bring to the boil. Remove from the heat, stir in the bicarbonate of soda and set aside to cool. Place in a food-processor and blitz until smooth.

Sift the flour into a large bowl and use a wooden spoon to mix in the sugar and the raisin mixture.

Beat together the sour cream and egg yolks in a separate bowl and pour into the flour mixture. Stir until you have a smooth batter and set aside for 20 minutes.

Whisk the egg whites in a large, spotlessly clean bowl until soft peaks form and fold into the batter.

Heat a medium frying pan over a medium heat and lightly brush with melted butter.

Pour about 1 ladleful of batter into the pan and cook for 3 minutes until bubbles form on the surface. Turn over and cook the other side for 2 minutes. Transfer to a warm plate and cover with a tea-towel while you make up the rest of the pancakes.

To prepare the caramel sauce, place all the ingredients in a medium saucepan over a medium heat and allow to dissolve. Gently simmer for 4–5 minutes, stirring occasionally.

Serve the sauce over the warm pancakes with some fresh fruit.

Eggs with Mediterranean Vegetables in Tomato Sauce

UOVA IN CAMICIA

Serves 4

3 tablespoons olive oil

1 medium onion, sliced

3 medium courgettes, roughly chopped

1 large yellow pepper, roughly chopped

400g tinned chopped tomatoes

5 fresh basil leaves

50g pitted Kalamata olives

4 medium eggs

70g freshly grated Cheddar cheese

Salt and pepper

This is a fantastic way to cook your eggs. The combination of the ingredients is just unbelievable. You can prepare the sauce well ahead and when you are ready, reheat it and break in the eggs as the recipe explains. Ensure you serve plenty of bread with this dish to soak up the delicious sauce.

Heat the olive oil in a large frying pan and fry the onion, courgettes and pepper until soft and browned, stirring occasionally. Season with salt and pepper, add in the tomatoes, basil and olives. Cook, uncovered, over a medium heat for about 10 minutes or until the water from the tomatoes is well reduced.

Meanwhile, preheat the grill. Make four slight hollows in the tomato mixture and very gently break one egg into each. Sprinkle over the cheese and cook under the grill for about 10 minutes or until the eggs are set as you like them.

Serve immediately with warm crusty bread.

The Ultimate Egg-fried Bread
with Melted Mozzarella

MOZZARELLA IN CARROZZA

Serves 2

3 medium eggs

3 tablespoons freshly grated Parmesan cheese

2 cow's milk Mozzarella balls, drained and sliced

4 slices of country-style nut bread, about 2cm thick

2 tablespoons pesto sauce

4 slices of cooked ham

10 tablespoons olive oil

Salt and pepper

Every time my father visits, he always ensures that I have all these ingredients. Since I can remember, this has always been his favourite dish. Make sure you use a cow's Mozzarella not buffalo Mozzarella, because the latter contains too much milk.

Beat the eggs and Parmesan together in a large bowl and season.

Divide the Mozzarella slices between two slices of bread, spread with pesto and top with two slices of ham, then place the remaining bread on top.

Heat the oil in a large frying pan. Dip the sandwiches into the egg mixture, then lower them into the hot oil and cook over a medium heat for about 2 minutes on each side to allow the Mozzarella to melt and the outside to become crisp. When cooked, transfer to kitchen paper to allow any excess oil to drain and rest for 2 minutes. Cut the sandwiches in half and serve with some of your favourite crisps.

Scrambled Eggs with Pancetta, Peas and Asparagus

UOVA STRAPAZZATE

Serves 2

150g asparagus spears, trimmed

2 tablespoons olive oil

150g pancetta, finely chopped

100g frozen peas, thawed

5 medium eggs

50ml full-fat milk

50g salted butter

1 small ciabatta loaf, sliced

Salt and pepper

Cook the asparagus in a small pan of boiling salted water for no longer than 4 minutes. Drain and rinse gently under cold water to prevent the asparagus from discolouring. Pat dry on kitchen paper, then roughly chop the stalks and reserve the tips.

Heat the olive oil in a small pan and fry the pancetta and peas for about 10 minutes or until the pancetta is golden and crisp.

Whisk the eggs with the milk in a large bowl and season.

Melt the butter in a medium frying pan, add the egg mixture and stir with a wooden spoon over a medium heat until it starts to set. Tip in the pancetta, peas and the asparagus stalks and stir until the eggs are lightly set.

Serve the eggs immediately topped with the asparagus tips and accompanied with toasted ciabatta bread.

The Ultimate Toasted Ciabatta with Italian Hummus and Grilled Sausages

Serves 2

4 Italian sausages

1 large ciabatta loaf

A few salad leaves of your choice

FOR THE HUMMUS

400g tinned chickpeas, drained and rinsed

Juice of 1 lemon

1 garlic clove

50ml light tahini paste

2 tablespoons extra virgin olive oil, plus extra for drizzling

50g pitted Kalamata olives

Salt and pepper

Since I left catering college, I've been everywhere in the Mediterranean to experience different cuisines, and after Italian food (of course), I think that Greek is probably my favourite. During the weekend, I often find myself in need of a hearty snack and this panino is always top of my list. The combination of crusty ciabatta bread, Italian sausages and hummus is absolutely divine.

With a sharp knife, cut the sausages lengthways, but without completely splitting into two halves, and cook on a hot griddle pan over a medium heat.

In the meantime, make the hummus. Put the chickpeas in a food-processor with the lemon juice, garlic, tahini paste, extra virgin olive oil and olives, blitz to a smooth paste. Once ready, season with salt and pepper.

With a serrated knife, slice the ciabatta lengthways, drizzle with some olive oil and grill with the sausages until it is crisp on both sides.

Once the sausages and the bread are ready, spread some of the Italian hummus on each side of the toasted bread, add the sausages, place some salad on top and enjoy immediately.

Neapolitan-style Pizza Topped with Anchovies

PIZZA ALLA NAPOLETANA

Makes 2 pizzas

Pinch of salt

1 teaspoon dried yeast

140ml warm water

180g strong plain flour, plus extra for dusting

1 tablespoon extra virgin olive oil, plus extra for greasing

FOR THE TOPPING

400g tinned chopped tomatoes

1 teaspoon dried oregano

10 anchovy fillets in oil

2 garlic cloves, finely sliced

4 tablespoons extra virgin olive oil

Salt and pepper

Napoli is a city well known for three things: 1. Vesuvius, 2. Gino D'Acampo and 3. Pizza. I could have written a whole book about pizzas, but I thought that I would show you the oldest pizza recipe known, which is actually the base for all other pizzas. I could eat pizza every day and I hope that everybody will try this recipe and enjoy making it. This is a great recipe to get children involved in cooking and there are no limits (except for pineapple!) for topping choices. Please make sure that the oven is preheated before you cook the pizza and that you place the topping on the pizza dough just before the pizza is ready to go in the oven.

To prepare the dough, mix the salt and yeast together in a jug with the water. Sift the flour into a large bowl, make a well in the centre and add the water mixture, along with the olive oil. Use a wooden spoon to mix everything well to create a wet dough.

Turn out the dough onto a clean well-floured surface and work it with your hands for about 5 minutes or until smooth and elastic. Place in a bowl and cover with a tea-towel. Leave in a warm place to rest for at least 45 minutes until the dough nearly doubles in size.

Meanwhile, preheat the oven to 220°C/425°F/gas mark 7.

Once rested, turn out the dough onto a floured surface, and divide it into two. Use your hands to push each out from the centre, creating two round discs about 25cm in diameter. Place the pizza bases on two oiled baking trays.

Spread the tomatoes on top of the pizza dough using a tablespoon and season with salt and pepper. Add a couple of pinches of oregano, the anchovies and garlic and drizzle with extra virgin olive oil. Cook in the middle of the oven for about 20 minutes or until golden and brown. Serve immediately.

Italian-style Cornish Pasty

CALZONE DI CARNE

Serves 4

250g plain flour

Pinch of salt

70g salted butter, cut into small dice

70g lard, cut into small dice

1 medium egg, beaten

FOR THE FILLING

250g beef steak, cut into small dice

1 medium swede, peeled and diced

1 onion, finely chopped

3 large potatoes, peeled and diced

150g smoked pancetta, diced

1 teaspoon finely chopped rosemary

Salt and pepper

To tell you the truth, I am such a big fan of the Cornish pasty that I had to create an Italian version of this dish. I can eat it hot, warm or cold and would always be satisfied by the flavours. Make sure you rest the dough for at least half an hour before you roll it out so that it relaxes, making it easier to work with.

Sift the flour into a large bowl with the salt. Use your fingers to rub in the butter and the lard and knead the dough to a firm consistency. Leave to rest for 30 minutes.

Preheat the oven to 200°C/400°F/gas mark 6.

Mix together the filling ingredients in a large bowl and season with salt and pepper. Divide the pastry into four balls and roll out into discs about 5mm thick. Share out the filling equally and pile in the middle of the discs. Dampen the edges of the pastry with water. Bring together the edges to enclose the filling. Pinch to seal and turn over the edges to make a rope-like effect.

Use the tip of a sharp knife to make a small slit on top of each calzone to let the steam out. Brush the top with beaten egg and place the calzone on an oiled baking tray.

Bake in the oven for 25 minutes, then reduce the heat to 180°C/350°F/gas mark 4 and cook for a further 25 minutes.

Serve immediately with your favourite salad.

Spicy Spaghetti Cake

FRITTATA DI SPAGHETTI

Serves 4

400g spaghetti

7 tablespoons olive oil

1 medium onion, finely chopped

1 teaspoon dry chilli flakes

2 medium courgettes, finely chopped

100g salame, finely sliced and chopped

5 medium eggs

200g freshly grated Pecorino cheese

4 tablespoons finely chopped parsley

Salt

If you like spaghetti, eggs and salame, you must try this recipe! The flavours are unbelievable and if you leave out the chilli, it is also a very child-friendly recipe. I've been eating this pasta dish since I can remember and I have to cook it for myself at least once a month to remind me of my home in Napoli. If you don't have spaghetti you can use tagliatelle or linguine and any hard cheese will do. Great to prepare the night before as it can be eaten cold for lunch the next day.

Cook the spaghetti in a large saucepan of boiling salted water until al dente. Drain and rinse under cold water to stop the pasta cooking. Drain again.

Heat 4 tablespoons of the olive oil in a large frying pan and fry the onion, chillies, courgettes and salame on a medium heat for 10 minutes until golden and soft. Season with salt and allow to cool.

Beat together the eggs, Pecorino and parsley in a large bowl. Add in the cooked onion mixture and the spaghetti. Mix well.

Heat the remaining olive oil in the same pan used to cook the onions. Add the spaghetti mixture and cook on a medium heat for 8 minutes on each side. You can finish off cooking the top side by placing the frying pan under a hot grill. Make sure that the spaghetti cake is a fantastic golden brown colour all over with a crispy texture.

Spinach and Gorgonzola Puffs

FAGOTTINI DI SPINACI

Serves 4

30g salted butter

½ onion, finely chopped

130g spinach leaves, washed

Whole nutmeg, for grating

100g Gorgonzola cheese

Ready-to-roll puff pastry
(2 x 25cm squares)

40g pistachio nuts, finely
chopped

1 medium egg, beaten

Olive oil, for greasing

FOR THE SALAD

250g rocket leaves

4 tablespoons extra virgin olive oil

2 tablespoons good-quality
balsamic vinegar

Salt and pepper

Often when I have friends coming round to my house and I want to prepare a lot of nibbles for them, I choose this recipe because it is so simple and I can prepare it before they arrive. My tip would be not to bother making puff pastry because the ready-made versions are perfectly fine. You can be very adventurous with this recipe; add Neopolitan salame, salame Milano or spicy chorizo, replace spinach with rocket leaves, or leave out any ingredients that you particularly don't like. For best results, serve them hot with a cold beer.

Melt the butter in a medium saucepan and gently fry the onion for 3 minutes or until softened. Add the spinach with plenty of grated nutmeg and cook for 5 minutes, stirring occasionally until the spinach is soft and the excess juice has evaporated. Season with salt and pepper, remove from the heat and leave to cool.

Preheat the oven to 200°C/400°F/gas mark 6. Cut each pastry square in half diagonally. Divide the spinach into four portions and place on one half of each pastry triangle. Top with Gorgonzola and sprinkle with pistachio nuts. Dampen the edges of the pastry with a little water, then fold over the pastry and press the edges to seal well. Brush with beaten egg to glaze.

Place the parcels on an oiled baking tray and cook in the oven for about 15 minutes or until golden brown and puffy.

Meanwhile, place the rocket leaves in a large bowl and dress with the olive oil and balsamic vinegar. Season with salt and pepper, mix well and serve with the puffs.

I love antipasti – this is the part of the meal that wakes up your taste buds. You will never go to an Italian house for dinner and not have some kind of antipasti, whether hot or cold or even both. Italians feel that this is probably the most important part of the meal. If you are serving aperitivi (drinks), offer them about 20 minutes before the antipasti, and make sure that they are good quality, so that you raise your guests' expectations of dinner.

You can have many different choices or just stick to one in particular, but the most important thing is to match it correctly to first your main dish and then your dessert.

Cooking tips

1. Try not to make anything too heavy – remember it's just a taste before your main meal arrives
2. Don't choose any fishy antipasti if your main meal is meat, otherwise you will ruin your palate
3. Don't serve too much antipasti which will fill up your guests too soon
4. If you have many people dining, choose easy antipasti, but impress them with good aperitivi
5. Make sure the aperitivi are always served cold
6. If you don't fancy making a main course, you can always make a meal based on antipasti
7. Never serve bread with olive oil – nobody does this in Italy

ADAMO

Any great dinner party should start with great aperitivi and this is definitely one of them. Make sure it is always served cold and prepare it at least five minutes before serving.

Serves 4

120ml freshly squeezed lemon juice

40ml sugar syrup (add 1½ tablespoons caster sugar to a pan with 100ml water and reduce to make 40ml)

240ml white rum

200g crushed ice cubes

Place the ingredients in a cocktail shaker. Shake for about 1 minute and serve immediately in tall glasses.

LUCIANO

I wanted to dedicate these two drinks to my two boys and the reasons are very simple: they are both sweet and beautiful, but at the same time they can be feisty and hazardous.

Serves 4

280g green apple nectar (available in supermarkets, but choose the thick nectar, not the juice)

40ml sugar syrup (add 1½ tablespoons caster sugar to a pan with 100ml water and reduce to make 40ml)

480ml Champagne

Mix the apple nectar and sugar syrup together and divide between four tall narrow glasses. Top up with cold Champagne and serve immediately.

EVA

I think the title says it all – untrustworthy if you abuse it but delicious if you respect it. You can substitute the Prosecco for a good-quality Champagne and make sure that you serve Eva in a martini glass.

Serves 4

320ml freshly squeezed mandarin juice

480ml cold Prosecco

Divide the mandarin juice between four glasses. Top up with cold Prosecco and serve immediately in Martini glasses.

ROCCO

Serves 4

120ml good-quality gin

120ml Cointreau

30ml freshly squeezed lime juice

160g fresh pineapple, cut into small cubes

80g small strawberries (ideally wild)

200g crushed ice cubes

Place all the ingredients in a cocktail shaker. Shake for about 30 seconds, and pour immediately in Martini glasses.

Mushrooms Stuffed with Gorgonzola and Honey

Serves 4

16 large button mushrooms

100g runny honey

400g Gorgonzola cheese (it must be at room temperature)

6 tablespoons extra virgin olive oil

1 ciabatta loaf, sliced

2 garlic cloves, cut in half

Salt and pepper

The combination of the strong cheese and the sweetness of the honey has always appealed to me. Try not to have fish after this recipe as I feel that its flavour is too powerful for fish.

Preheat the oven to 180°C/350°F/gas mark 4. Carefully remove the stalk from each mushroom to create a cavity ready to be stuffed. Discard the stalks. Rub a little honey on the inside of the mushrooms with the tip of your finger, then stuff each one with 1–2 teaspoons of Gorgonzola.

Place the mushrooms on a baking tray, season and drizzle with extra virgin olive oil. Cook in the oven for about 10 minutes.

Meanwhile, toast the bread on a hot griddle pan for about 3 minutes on each side or until dark brown and crusty, then rub the cut side of the garlic over the slices. Arrange the stuffed mushrooms on a large serving plate surrounded by the garlic bread and serve with cold beer.

Toasted Ciabatta Topped with Tomatoes and Basil

BRUSCHETTA CLASSICA

Serves 4

1 ciabatta loaf

4 tablespoons olive oil

400g small plum tomatoes

10 fresh basil leaves, sliced

6 tablespoons extra virgin olive oil, plus extra to serve

2 garlic cloves

This reminds me of my childhood when I went camping with my parents. My mother often served bruschetta for lunch. The secret is to add the topping at the last minute.

Cut the loaf into 8 slices, each 2cm thick, brush both sides with olive oil and toast on a hot griddle pan for about 3 minutes on each side or until dark brown and crusty. Leave to cool slightly.

Meanwhile, quarter the tomatoes and place in a bowl. Add the basil, extra virgin olive oil and season. Mix well and set aside, covered and at room temperature, for 5 minutes.

Lightly rub the garlic over the bread. Place 2–3 tablespoons of the tomato mixture on top of each slice and arrange the bruschette on a large serving plate. Drizzle with extra virgin olive oil, and enjoy.

Baked Aubergine with Mozzarella and Tomato Sauce

MELANZANE ALLA PARMIGIANA

Serves 4

6 large aubergines

Sea salt

10 tablespoons olive oil

200g plain flour

4 medium eggs, beaten and seasoned

3 Mozzarella balls, drained and sliced

300g freshly grated Parmesan cheese

20 fresh basil leaves

Sea salt and pepper

FOR THE TOMATO SAUCE

5 tablespoons olive oil

1 medium onion, finely chopped

2 sticks celery, finely chopped

1 large carrot, finely chopped

4 x 400g tinned chopped tomatoes

Salt and pepper

Sicily is a region in Italy that is famous for: 1. The Godfather, 2. The Mafia and 3. Melanzane alla Parmigiana. I remember when I was at catering college that one of the dishes I was really excited about learning to make was this one. Believe you me when I say that this is the ultimate Italian recipe. This dish is great eaten hot, warm or even cold.

To prepare the sauce, heat the olive oil in a large saucepan and gently fry the onion, celery and carrot until soft. Add the chopped tomatoes, season with salt and pepper and cook, uncovered, over a medium heat for about 10 minutes. Remove from the heat and leave to cool.

Meanwhile, cut the aubergines lengthways into slices about ½cm thick. Place in a sieve, sprinkle with sea salt and leave over the sink for about 1 hour to allow the excess water to drain from the aubergine. Place the slices on kitchen paper and pat dry.

Heat the oil in a large frying pan. Dust the aubergine slices first in flour, then dip in the eggs, and fry them in the hot oil until golden on both sides (you may need to work in batches). Transfer the slices to kitchen paper to drain off any excess oil.

Preheat the oven to 180°C/350°F/gas mark 4. Place a layer of aubergines in the base of a large ovenproof dish (about 40 x 20cm and 7cm deep). Spread about a fifth of the tomato sauce, then place some Mozzarella slices over the sauce. Sprinkle over a handful of Parmesan and some of the basil leaves. Repeat the process three times. Finally, spread the remaining tomato sauce on top and sprinkle with the remaining Parmesan. Cover with kitchen foil and bake in the oven for 20 minutes. Remove the foil and continue to bake for a further 30 minutes.

Remove from the oven and leave to rest for about 10 minutes before serving generous portions.

Deep-fried Taleggio with Strawberry Sauce

Serves 4

4 thick slices of Taleggio cheese
(each weighing about 100g)

100g plain flour

2 medium eggs, beaten

200g toasted breadcrumbs

1 litre vegetable oil, for frying

FOR THE STRAWBERRY SAUCE

4 tablespoons water

3 tablespoons balsamic vinegar

300g fresh strawberries, finely
chopped

Salt and pepper

Like most people, I am a big fan of all deep-fried food, but one of my favourites has to be deep-fried cheese. There is nothing better than the combination of crisp coating with melting cheese oozing inside, especially when it's served with a cool fruity sauce. You can substitute Taleggio for Brie, and if strawberries are out of season, you can use any other berries of your choice.

To prepare the sauce, reduce the water and balsamic vinegar in a saucepan by half, add the strawberries and gently cook for 3 minutes. Remove from the heat and leave to cool.

Meanwhile, dust each slice of Taleggio first in the flour, then dip in the eggs, and finally coat in breadcrumbs. Place the prepared cheese on a plate and leave to rest in the fridge for about 2 hours before cooking.

When you are ready to cook, heat the oil in a large, high-sided pan. Coat the Taleggio once again in the breadcrumbs. Carefully lower the slices into the hot oil and cook for about 3 minutes until they turn a golden colour. Transfer to a plate covered with kitchen paper to drain off any excess oil.

To serve, place 2–3 tablespoons of strawberry sauce in the centre of four plates and place a slice of Taleggio on top. Serve immediately to ensure that the cheese oozes out as soon as you break into the golden crust.

Courgettes with Truffle and Mint Dressing

ZUCCHINE E TARTUFO

Serves 4

4 medium courgettes

16 thin slices of white or black truffle

FOR THE DRESSING

6 tablespoons extra virgin olive oil

3 tablespoons good-quality balsamic vinegar

1 garlic clove, finely sliced

3 tablespoons finely sliced fresh mint leaves

Salt and pepper

This recipe sums up what this book is all about – minimum effort, maximum satisfaction! If you cannot find fresh truffles you can always use truffles preserved in jars or even truffle-flavoured olive oil.

To make the dressing, whisk together the olive oil, vinegar, garlic and mint in a large bowl and season with salt and pepper.

Thinly slice the courgettes lengthways using a swivel-blade potato peeler. Place the slices in the bowl with the dressing, season with more salt and pepper, mix well and leave to marinate for about 10 minutes.

To serve, pile the courgettes in the centre of four plates and top each serving with four slices of truffle. Serve with some warm crusty bread to mop up the dressing.

Figs and Soft Cheese Rolled in Parma Ham

Serves 4

6 large plum tomatoes

Extra virgin olive oil

6 large very ripe figs

200g soft cheese

5 tablespoons finely chopped fresh chives

12 slices Parma ham

4 tablespoons runny honey

Salt and pepper

This is a gorgeous antipasto that needs very little effort to prepare, yet looks and tastes fantastic. It was one of the first recipes I wrote as a chef, because I thought that the saltiness of the ham would go beautifully with the sweetness of the figs. The key to this dish is to prepare it just before you want to serve, otherwise the ham will go soggy. If you can't find fresh figs, use dark plums or mangoes instead. A typical Italian antipasto, these figs will go well with Bruschetta Classica or the Mushrooms Stuffed with Gorgonzola and Honey (both on page 29) – a contrast of hot and cold.

Preheat the grill. Cut the tomatoes in half and place on a baking tray, skin-side down. Season with salt and pepper, drizzle with extra virgin olive oil and grill for about 10 minutes until softened. Leave to cool.

Meanwhile, cut the figs in half, discarding the skin.

Mix the soft cheese with the chives and 1 tablespoon of extra virgin olive oil. Season with salt and pepper.

Lay a slice of ham lengthways on a chopping board. Place a fig half on one end. Drop a teaspoon of the soft cheese mixture on top of the fig, then place a tomato half on top of the cheese. Carefully roll up the ham to enclose the fig, cheese and tomato. Repeat with the remaining ingredients to make 12 parcels.

To serve, allow three parcels per portion. Drizzle with extra virgin olive oil and honey and enjoy with some toasted bread soldiers.

Deep-fried Polenta Sandwiches Stuffed with Salame Milano and Cheddar

BIGNÈ DI POLENTA ALLA MILANESE

Serves 4

400g polenta (use quick-cook polenta)

5 tablespoons finely chopped flat-leaf parsley

2 tablespoons plain flour, plus extra for dusting

16 slices Cheddar cheese

8 slices salame Milano

2 medium eggs

About ½ glass full-fat milk

1 litre vegetable oil, for frying

4 handfuls mixed salad leaves

4 tablespoons extra virgin olive oil

Juice of 1 lemon

Salt and pepper

If you travel anywhere in Italy north of Roma, you will find recipes using polenta. This recipe comes from Milano, but I've added an English twist. If you have not yet tried polenta, this is the best recipe to taste, because it's just full of flavour. My suggestion would be to always eat it hot or warm, because when cold, polenta tends to harden and become heavier in texture and taste. You can prepare large batches and warm them up before your guests arrive (great for parties). Make a batch without the salame for veggies.

Cook the polenta in boiling salted water according to the instructions on the packet until it thickens. Season with salt and pepper, add the parsley and stir well. Pour into a 15 x 11cm tray and level the top, ensuring that the polenta is about 1cm thick. Leave to cool until firm.

Once the polenta is cold and firm, use a drinking glass to cut out 16 discs about 7cm in diameter. Transfer them to a well-floured chopping board.

Place a slice of cheese on 8 discs, then a slice of salame and top with another slice of cheese. Cover with the remaining polenta discs to create small round sandwiches.

Beat the eggs in a large bowl with the flour, a couple of pinches of salt and pepper, then add enough milk to make a smooth batter.

Heat the oil in a large saucepan. Dip the polenta sandwiches into the batter and fry until golden and brown – work in batches, no more than four sandwiches at time. Once cooked, transfer the sandwiches to kitchen paper to allow the excess oil to drain. Serve immediately on a bed of fresh salad leaves dressed with extra virgin olive oil and freshly squeezed lemon juice.

Avocado with Saffron Crab

AVOCADO CON GRANCHIO

Serves 4

2 tablespoons olive oil

1 small onion, finely chopped

2 pinches of saffron stems

4 tablespoons ready-made mayonnaise

2 tablespoons tomato paste

Zest and juice of ½ unwaxed lemon

2 tablespoons finely chopped fresh chives

250g white crab meat, flaked

2 ripe avocados

Paprika, to garnish

Salt and pepper

Before I came to this country, I didn't have a clue what an avocado was — unfortunately in the south of Italy it is not part of our diet. Well, let me tell you, I am now converted and therefore I had to create a recipe using this fantastico fruit. Ensure that you buy ripe avocados and that they always come with a little stalk attached, because if not you might find that they are rotten on the inside.

Heat the olive oil in a small frying pan and gently fry the onion with the saffron for about 5 minutes or until soft. Remove from the heat and leave to cool.

Mix the mayonnaise with the tomato paste and the lemon zest and juice. Add in the chives and season with salt and pepper. Fold in the crabmeat with the onion and mix well.

Halve the avocados lengthways and gently remove the stones. Spoon the crab filling into the centres, sprinkle with paprika and serve.

Sardines Coated in Black Pepper with Italian Salsa

SARDINE AL PEPE NERO

Serves 4

300ml olive oil

2 garlic cloves, finely sliced

6 large plum tomatoes, chopped, seeds and skin included

100g pitted black olives, sliced

5 tablespoons chopped fresh basil

10 tablespoons toasted fine breadcrumbs

7 tablespoons black peppercorns, crushed

16 fresh sardines, gutted, heads and spines removed

200g plain flour

3 medium eggs, beaten and seasoned

100ml extra virgin olive oil

Salt and pepper

In Napoli, we eat a lot of sardines, especially cooked on the barbecue. The reason why I created this recipe is because sardines can be a very 'fishy' fish, but the black pepper coating balances this flavour perfectly. Always use fresh sardines and once cooked, do not reheat them. Absolutely fantastico eaten cold the next day for breakfast.

Heat 5 tablespoons of the olive oil in a large frying pan and fry the garlic until golden. Add the tomatoes and olives, season with salt and pepper and leave to cook over a medium heat for about 5 minutes. Add the chopped basil, then remove the salsa from the heat and leave to cool.

Meanwhile, mix the breadcrumbs and black pepper together on a plate.

Wash the sardines under cold running water and dry with kitchen paper. Dust each sardine first in the flour, dip into the eggs, then coat in the breadcrumbs and pepper.

Heat the remaining oil in a large frying pan and fry the sardines for about 2 minutes on each side – work in batches, no more than six sardines at a time. Once they look brown and crunchy, transfer to kitchen paper to allow any excess oil to drain.

Arrange four sardines on the plates with 2–3 tablespoons of the salsa. Drizzle with extra virgin olive oil and serve immediately.

Tuna and Sun-dried Tomato Fishcakes

POLPETTE DI TONNO E POMODORI SECCHI

Serves 4

250g potatoes, peeled

2 slices white bread, soaked in water and squeezed

2 medium eggs

2 x 200g tinned tuna chunks in oil, drained

100g sun-dried tomatoes in oil, drained and chopped

1 garlic clove, finely chopped

4 tablespoons chopped fresh flat-leaf parsley

Zest of 1 lemon, preferably unwaxed, and juice of half

150g toasted fine breadcrumbs

300g French green beans

50g sesame seeds

1 tablespoon extra virgin olive oil

Salt and ground black pepper

If there is one tinned food that I absolutely love, it would have to be tuna. This recipe is a mixture of flavours and colours that will never bore you. Great for picnic food or to pack in your children's lunchbox. Fantastico when it's hot and still fantastic when it's cold. My only tip would be to use good-quality tinned tuna (stored in olive oil not brine).

Boil the potatoes in a large pan of salted water until soft. Drain, mash and tip into a large bowl and leave to cool. Add the bread, eggs, tuna, sun-dried tomatoes, garlic, parsley, salt and pepper, and mix well together. Add the lemon zest and a little juice and keep stirring until evenly combined.

Preheat the oven to 180°C/350°F/gas mark 4. Use your hands to make balls the size of snooker balls, flatten gently and coat in the breadcrumbs. Place the fishcakes on a tray lined with baking paper and bake in the oven for about 15 minutes or until golden brown.

Meanwhile, cook the green beans in boiling salted water until al dente. Drain and place in a large bowl with the sesame seeds. Dress with extra virgin olive oil, a squeeze of lemon and season with salt.

Once the fishcakes are cooked, serve them with the crunchy green beans and enjoy with your friends.

This is probably the most versatile chapter in this book. Here you will find recipes from exciting salads to barbecue dishes. Being brought up in the south of Italy gave me the chance to understand the importance of choosing healthy and tasty ingredients and I strongly believe that the secret of a healthy dish is in the simplicity of the cooking. Rely on good-quality ingredients, tasty dressings and fantastic flavours.

Cooking tips

1. Choose a recipe with seasonal ingredients – it will be much healthier, colourful and usually cheaper

2. Do not overcook – let the natural freshness of the flavours come through

3. If you choose a salad dish, do not dress it until the last minute otherwise the leaves will cook and go soggy

4. Salads are great as light meals or as accompaniments to meat and fish dishes, but never serve with a pasta, soup or risotto dish – the cold crunch of a salad will ruin the warm comfort of the hot dish

5. See my recipe for Schiacciata Toscana (page 137) for a great Tuscan-style bread to serve with your barbecue or salad

6. Barbecues are a simple cooking method. My only tip: don't place the grill too close to the coals

French Beans with Sun-dried Tomatoes, Feta and Mozzarella

INSALATA DI FAGIOLINI

Serves 4

400g fine French beans

70g sun-dried tomatoes in oil, drained and sliced

50g shelled walnuts

5 tablespoons extra virgin olive oil

1 tablespoon freshly squeezed lemon juice

130g feta cheese

2 buffalo Mozzarella balls, drained and cut into chunks

Salt and pepper

This recipe (like most of my recipes) happened by accident. I was hosting a barbecue party and a friend of mine challenged me to make something that resembled the colours of the Italian flag. I went to the fridge, got hold of everything green, white and red and came up with this masterpiece. Today, it has become one of my signature dishes among my friends and we still enjoy it at every barbecue party. Make sure that the French beans are not overcooked and use a good-quality buffalo Mozzarella.

Trim ½cm from both ends of the beans, then cook in a large pan of boiling salted water for about 5 minutes until al dente. Drain well and place in a large bowl.

Lightly toss the hot beans with the sun-dried tomatoes, walnuts, extra virgin olive oil and lemon juice. Season with salt and pepper and leave to cool.

Once the beans have cooled, crumble in the feta and gently mix in the Mozzarella. Serve immediately.

Spinach and Watercress Salad with Bacon and Pears

INSALATA DI SPINACI

Serves 4

150g smoked streaky bacon rashers

2 ripe pears

130g young spinach leaves, trimmed

100g watercress, trimmed

FOR THE DRESSING

3 tablespoons extra virgin olive oil

2 teaspoons hazelnut oil

1 teaspoon wholegrain mustard

2 teaspoons white wine vinegar

2 tablespoons sesame seeds

Salt and pepper

Once again I find myself in a very lucky position, because I can use the best of Italy and the best of Britain to create something unique. The combination of spinach, bacon and pears is just exceptional. If you don't have pears, you can always use your favourite apples or even papayas.

Grill the bacon until crispy, then transfer to kitchen paper to drain any excess oil and roughly chop.

Halve the pears, remove the cores and thinly slice.

Whisk together the dressing ingredients in a medium bowl.

Place the spinach and watercress in a large salad bowl with the bacon and pears. Pour over the dressing and toss lightly. Serve with warm crusty bread.

Tuna and Mixed Bean Salad

Serves 4

150g dried cannellini beans

150g dried borlotti beans

10 tablespoons extra virgin olive oil

5 tablespoons freshly squeezed lemon juice

400g tinned tuna in oil

2 medium red onions, sliced

2 garlic cloves, finely sliced

3 tablespoons roughly chopped flat-leaf parsley

Salt and pepper

Even today I have no idea which region in Italy this recipe comes from and, to be honest with you, it doesn't make any difference, because I would love it anyway. I often use beans in my salads, but this recipe is definitely my favourite one. If you don't want to soak dried beans, you can always use tinned ones, but just ensure that you drain the juice and rinse the beans under cold water. For best results, use good-quality tuna — one that has been tinned in olive or sunflower oil, never brine.

Put the beans in a large bowl, cover with cold water and leave to soak overnight.

The following day, drain the beans, place in a saucepan and cover with fresh water. Bring to the boil, then reduce the heat and cook, covered, for about 45 minutes until tender. Drain.

Whisk the extra virgin olive oil and the lemon juice together in a large bowl, season with salt and pepper and gently fold in the warm beans. Set aside to cool.

Drain the tuna and very gently flake the fish into the cooled beans. Lightly stir in the onions, garlic and parsley, adjust the seasoning and serve with your favourite bread.

Northern Italian Salad
with Roasted Red Peppers

PANZANELLA

Serves 4

3 red peppers

2 tablespoons olive oil

1 small country-style loaf, cut into chunks

100g frisée lettuce

100g radicchio

1 small cucumber, cut into 1cm cubes

1 large red onion, finely sliced

3 ripe tomatoes, roughly chopped

2 tablespoons capers in vinegar

10 fresh basil leaves, roughly sliced

8 anchovy fillets in oil, drained and chopped

FOR THE DRESSING

3 tablespoons red wine vinegar

5 tablespoons extra virgin olive oil

1 teaspoon sugar

Salt and pepper

An authentic northern Italian salad full of flavour, crunchiness and colour. For perfection, try to use bread which is at least 2–3 days old. The beautiful thing about this salad is that you can add or take away any ingredient that you don't like, but believe you me when I tell you that I'm sure you will love it just the way it is. Remember to always dress the salad just before you serve it.

Preheat the oven to 180º/350°F/gas mark 4. Place the whole peppers in a large roasting tin with the olive oil and roast for about 20 minutes until the skins are blackened all over. Remove from the oven, place in a large bowl and cover with clingfilm.

Meanwhile, scatter the bread in a large roasting tin and toast in the oven for about 10 minutes or until golden and crisp.

Mix together the salad leaves, cucumber, onion, tomatoes, capers, basil and anchovies in a large bowl. Mix together the dressing ingredients, and add to the bowl, stirring to coat.

Remove the skin, stalk and seeds from the roasted peppers and cut the flesh into strips. Add to the salad bowl, along with the warm bread. Stir well and serve immediately.

Parma Ham with Minted Citrus Salad and Limoncello

Serves 4

2 papayas

1 small cantaloupe melon

1 grapefruit

1 ugli fruit (if you can't find ugli fruit, use pink grapefruit instead)

3 tablespoons finely sliced fresh mint leaves

2 tablespoons Limoncello liqueur

12 slices Parma ham

Fresh mint sprigs, to garnish

A wonderful, stylish recipe with refreshing flavours and fantastic colours. I guarantee that you will impress your friends with the Limoncello and fresh mint dressing. A great dish to prepare if you have a lot of guests coming for dinner. If you don't like Limoncello, you can always use Cointreau.

Peel the papayas, halve and remove the seeds. Slice the flesh and place in a large bowl.

Halve the melon and scoop out the seeds. Use a melon baller to scoop out the flesh and add to the bowl, along with the juice.

Use a sharp serrated knife to peel and segment the grapefruit and ugli fruit, discarding all the white pith – hold the fruit over the bowl to catch the juices.

Add the mint and Limoncello and lightly toss together.

Cover and chill for 30 minutes to allow the flavours to blend.

To serve, form a loose nest with three slices of Parma ham in the centre of each serving plate and fill the nest with the citrus salad in the middle. Garnish with the mint sprigs.

The Ultimate Warm Salad

Serves 4

200g new potatoes, unpeeled

8 quail's eggs

8 slices Parma ham

70g frisée lettuce

70g radicchio

50g white cabbage, shredded

150g pitted Kalamata olives

100g shelled walnuts

300g tuna chunks in oil, drained

70g Pecorino cheese, freshly shaved

FOR THE DRESSING

3 tablespoons apple cider vinegar or white wine vinegar

6 tablespoons extra virgin olive oil

1 tablespoon sherry liqueur

Salt and pepper

I often really fancy a good, tasty salad, but sometimes they can be quite boring. I like this one because of the contrast of flavours and especially the contrast between cold and warm ingredients. The saltiness of the Parma ham against the sweetness of the eggs works beautifully.

Cook the potatoes in a large saucepan of boiling salted water until al dente. Drain, cut in half and set aside.

Boil the eggs for 5 minutes. Peel and halve the eggs while still warm and set aside. Preheat the grill.

Place the Parma ham on a baking tray and grill for about 2 minutes on each side until crispy.

Put the salad leaves and cabbage into a large bowl. Add the olives, walnuts, tuna, the warm potatoes, crisp Parma ham and warm eggs. Season with salt and pepper.

Mix together the dressing ingredients in a small bowl. Season with salt and pepper, then pour over the salad and toss lightly.

Pile the salad onto a large serving plate, sprinkle the Pecorino shavings on top and serve immediately with warm crusty bread.

Griddled Lamb with Rosemary, Garlic and Courgettes

Serves 4

15 large garlic cloves, unpeeled

8 lamb loin chops (about 130g each)

8 long rosemary sprigs

6 medium courgettes, halved lengthways

Olive oil, for brushing

Salt and pepper

If you like lamb and Italian food, it is impossible not to like this recipe, as it sums up what Italian food is all about.

Drop the garlic into boiling salted water and cook for 5 minutes. Drain and set aside to cool.

Use a skewer to make a hole lengthways through each chop. Remove the skewer and thread with rosemary sprigs. Brush the meat and courgettes with olive oil.

Heat a griddle pan and start cooking the chops on one side for 5 minutes. Turn the chops and add the garlic and courgettes to the pan too. Griddle for a further 8 minutes, turning the vegetables every 2 minutes. Season, then transfer everything to a large flat tray to rest for 30 seconds.

Arrange three slices of courgette in the centre of each serving plate, scatter the charred garlic around it and arrange two chops on top of the courgettes. Serve immediately.

Barbecued Citrus and Honey Chicken Drumsticks

COSCETTE DI POLLO AL MIELE

Serves 4

16 chicken drumsticks (skin on) or pork ribs, if you prefer

FOR THE MARINADE

5 tablespoons runny honey

5 tablespoons dark soy sauce

Zest and juice of 2 unwaxed lemons

Zest and juice of 2 oranges

1 teaspoon paprika

Every time I have a barbecue, my two boys Luciano and Rocco ask me to prepare this. They not only love to eat this dish, but they love to help me prepare it because they can get their hands dirty, coating the drumsticks in the marinade.

Mix together the ingredients for the marinade in a large bowl.

With a sharp knife score the drumsticks and place in the bowl with the marinade. Cover and leave to marinate in the fridge for 2 hours, turning the chicken occasionally.

Meanwhile, preheat the barbecue and bring the chicken to room temperature. Cook the drumsticks for about 20 minutes, turning frequently and brushing with the marinade. Serve hot with a salad.

Poussin with Peperonata and Mozzarella

POLLETTO CON PEPERONATA

Serves 4

4 poussin

FOR THE MARINADE

4 teaspoons English mustard

4 tablespoons olive oil

1 glass red wine

5 tablespoons fresh rosemary, stripped from stalks

½ onion, sliced

Salt and pepper

FOR THE PEPERONATA

5 tablespoons olive oil

1 garlic clove, finely sliced

800g tinned or jarred roasted peppers, drained and sliced

1 tablespoon capers in salt, rinsed

100g pitted Kalamata olives

1 tablespoon chopped flat-leaf parsley

2 Mozzarella balls, drained and sliced

8 wooden skewers, presoaked in water

This recipe definitely shows the carnivorous side of me. I don't think that there is anything better in this world than to cook a whole poussin on the barbecue. I love using my fingers and eating the meat off the bones, experiencing all the flavours and textures and, of course, served with roasted peppers and melted Mozzarella, it becomes the ultimate meal. You can always substitute poussin for quails or pigeon. Perfect with a glass of dry Italian red wine.

Clean the poussin and use a sharp knife to cut along the backbone. Spatchcock the birds by flattening them down on a chopping board and inserting two crossed skewers through the centre of each bird to keep them flat. Transfer to a deep-sided baking tray.

Mix together the marinade ingredients in a large bowl. Pour over the poussin, cover with clingfilm and place in the fridge to marinate for about 20 minutes.

Meanwhile, preheat the barbecue or griddle pan and bring the poussin to room temperature. Transfer the poussin to the barbecue or griddle and cook for about 7 minutes on each side.

Heat 3 tablespoons of the olive oil in a medium saucepan and gently fry the garlic until golden, then add the peppers, capers and olives. Season with salt and pepper, stir well and simmer over a medium heat for about 5 minutes. Stir in the parsley and cook for a further 5 minutes.

Place the pepper mixture in a dish measuring 20 x 10cm and cover with the sliced Mozzarella. Drizzle with the remaining olive oil, grind over some black pepper and grill for about 5 minutes or until golden and melted. Serve the poussin with the peperonata.

Marinated Seafood Skewers

Serves 4

130g shelled scampi (langoustines)

400g shelled scallops (with corals)

150g salmon steak, cut into pieces the size of the scallops

150g tuna steak, cut into pieces the size of the scallops

2 lemons, cut into wedges, to serve

FOR THE MARINADE

6 tablespoons olive oil

Zest and juice of 1 unwaxed lemon

1 tablespoon chopped fresh oregano

1 teaspoon fennel seeds

Salt and pepper

This recipe was created by my mother and I remember she always used to prepare these marinated seafood skewers in the summer. I guess one of the reasons she did this was because they were very easy to prepare and very quick to cook. Of course, if you don't want to cook them on a barbecue, you can always cook them under a hot grill for the same amount of time.

First make the marinade. Whisk the olive oil with the lemon zest and juice in a large bowl. Add the oregano and fennel seeds and season with salt and pepper.

Skewer the seafood and fish alternately onto four metal skewers and place in a shallow dish measuring 35 x 20cm. Pour over the marinade, cover and chill in the fridge for 2 hours, turning frequently.

Preheat the barbecue or grill and bring the fish skewers back to room temperature. Remove the skewers from the marinade and cook on the hot barbecue or under the grill for about 6 minutes, turning and basting frequently with the remaining marinade.

Serve immediately on a bed of crisp salad leaves with the lemon wedges.

Pasta This is a subject I can talk about forever. I have been eating pasta since I can remember and a plate of pasta is to me the ultimate comfort food. Have a look at Veg Out (page 110) for some fantastic veggie pasta dishes.

Cooking tips on pasta. OK, where do I start...
1. To cook the perfect pasta, you should always ensure that you have enough water in the pan (500g dried pasta to 2.5 litres of water)
2. Make sure that the water is always fast boiling before you start cooking
3. The water should always be salted
4. Never cook pasta with the lid on
5. Keep tasting as you cook, ensuring the pasta remains al dente (firm to the bite)
6. ALWAYS put the pasta into the sauce NEVER the sauce on top of the pasta!
7. THE MOST IMPORTANT RULE OF ALL: never add cheese to seafood or fish pasta!

Soups I must admit I appreciate soups much more now than I have ever done before. When I lived in Napoli, we never ate soup, as it is hot there for most of the year. The closest we came to it was bean soup, but now living in London, there is nothing better than a tasty soup with some warm crusty bread.

The secret to a good soup? Only one tip.
1. Endless combinations of ingredients that you like — anything goes

Risotto In my opinion, making a risotto is the only way of doing justice to a simple grain of rice. The most popular rice used in Italy is Arborio, which you will recognise by its short grain essential for an authentic risotto. The thing I like most about a risotto is that it is a meal in itself and can be as versatile as you want. I still can't believe how many people are afraid of preparing risotto and have difficulty in getting the consistency right.

Like everything else in life there are rules to follow...

1. If you can't find risotto rice (Arborio and Carnaroli are the most common), DON'T use anything else. It won't work

2. Always cook the risotto in a large saucepan

3. Never cook the risotto with the lid on

4. Toast the rice in the saucepan before adding any stock

5. Always stir the risotto with a wooden spoon

6. When adding stock, always ensure that it is well absorbed before adding any more

7. Never leave the pan alone while cooking the risotto (keep stirring)

8. If you want to add cheese, it should always be added at the end, but do not ever add cheese to a seafood or fish risotto

9. If you want a creamy finish, stir in a couple of knobs of butter with the cheese

Seafood and Asparagus Risotto

Serves 4

150g thin asparagus stalks

150g fresh mussels

5 tablespoons olive oil

1 onion, finely chopped

350g Arborio rice

Pinch of saffron powder or strands

100ml dry white wine

1.2 litres warm fish stock (made from 2 fish stock cubes)

150g fresh raw prawns, peeled, heads and tails removed

100g large scallops with the coral, cut in half

Zest of 1 small unwaxed lemon

80g salted butter

Salt and pepper

For anyone who likes seafood, this is the recipe to try because the combination of saffron, asparagus, rice and seafood works perfectly. I wish my grandfather was still here to try it, because he loved risotto with seafood. Please make sure you use fresh mussels and if they are not in season, leave out the asparagus.

Cut off the tips of the asparagus and peel the stalks. Cut into 4cm lengths and set aside.

Place the mussels in the sink, and under cold running water, scrape off any grit. With your fingers, pull away the hairy beards that protrude from the shells. Using the back of a knife, tap any mussels that remain open, and if they refuse to close, throw them away. Rinse again in cold water until there is no trace of sand. Set aside.

Heat the olive oil in a large saucepan and fry the onion on a medium heat for about 2 minutes or until softened. Add in the asparagus stalks and continue to cook for a further 3 minutes, stirring continuously.

Add the rice and, using a wooden spoon, keep stirring for 3 minutes, allowing the rice to toast in the oil and begin to absorb all the flavours.

Add in the saffron and the wine and continue to cook for a further 3 minutes to allow the alcohol to evaporate.

Start to add the warm stock a little at a time, season and cook gently, stirring until the stock is absorbed. Continue adding the stock as each addition is absorbed. If you need to, add more warm water to the stock.

Just before most of the stock has been absorbed (about 15 minutes), add in the prawns, scallops, mussels, lemon zest and asparagus tips, and continue to cook for a further 5 minutes.

When the risotto is ready, take the saucepan off the heat and add the butter. It is very important that you stir the butter into the rice for at least 1 minute so you can create a fantastic creamy texture. Serve immediately.

Three-mushroom Risotto with Peas

RISOTTO FUNGHI E PISELLI

Serves 4

5 tablespoons olive oil

1 medium onion, finely chopped

100g portobello mushrooms, sliced

80g chestnut mushrooms, sliced

20g sliced dried Porcini mushrooms, soaked in cold water for 30 minutes to soften

150g frozen peas, thawed

400g Arborio or Carnaroli rice

100ml dry white wine

1 tablespoon fresh thyme leaves

1.2 litres warm vegetable stock, made with 2 stock cubes

50g salted butter

100g freshly grated Parmesan cheese

Salt and pepper

Once when I was cooking for my wife and her girlfriends, they all described this dish as warm and comforting, like a cuddle. Of course, I thought that this was my lucky night, but once the risotto was finished, I was ditched. When in season, substitute the dry Porcini for fresh ones (150g) and use good-quality rice for perfect results. Don't be afraid to make this dish; remember it's a one-pot dish and if you follow my instructions, you will actually find it quite easy.

Heat the olive oil in a large saucepan and fry the onion over a medium heat for about 2 minutes or until softened. Add in all the mushrooms and the peas and continue to cook for a further 3 minutes. Add the rice and stir continuously using a wooden spoon for 5 minutes to allow the rice to toast in the olive oil and begin to absorb all the mushroom flavours. Add the wine and continue to cook for a further 3 minutes to allow the alcohol to evaporate.

Add the thyme and the warm stock a little at a time, stirring occasionally, allowing the rice to absorb the stock before adding more. Season well and cook gently (if you need extra liquid, use warm water).

After about 20 minutes, when most of the stock has been absorbed, remove the pan from the heat and stir the butter into the risotto. It is very important that you stir the butter very fast into the rice for at least 1 minute – this creates a fantastic creamy texture.

Add the Parmesan and serve immediately.

Deep-fried Risotto Balls Served with Spicy Tomato Sauce

Serves 6

5 tablespoons olive oil

1 onion, finely chopped

500g Arborio or Carnaroli rice

1 litre warm vegetable stock

100ml passata (sieved tomatoes)

100g frozen peas, thawed

150g freshly grated Parmesan cheese

3 medium eggs, separated

200g toasted fine breadcrumbs

200g Mozzarella cheese, drained and cubed

1 litre vegetable oil, for deep-frying

Salt and pepper

FOR THE SAUCE

5 tablespoons olive oil

1 garlic clove, finely sliced

1 large hot chilli, deseeded and sliced

300g fresh plum tomatoes, chopped, skin and seeds included

Salt

Every Sunday my father used to take me around the town of Torre del Greco where I was born. We used to do our weekly shop in the markets and we would eat this in the middle of the road or sitting on the step of a church. Forget about burgers or hotdogs, this is the ultimate Neapolitan street food. The preparation will take at least one hour but once cooked, the rice balls are great to serve at parties.

Heat the olive oil in a large saucepan, and gently fry the onion until golden. Add the rice and continue to fry for about 3 minutes, stirring constantly with a wooden spoon.

Add the vegetable stock a little at a time, allowing the rice to absorb the stock before adding more (if you need extra, use warm water) and cook for about 20 minutes, stirring constantly. Season with salt and pepper, add the passata, the peas, the Parmesan and the egg yolks. Mix well then spread out the risotto on a tray and leave to cool.

Lightly beat the egg whites (you only want to break up the yolks) and spread the breadcrumbs on a plate. Once the risotto is cooled, place about 3 large tablespoons of rice in the centre of your hand (wet your hands in cold water so the rice doesn't stick to them) and roll the rice into a ball about the size of a snooker ball. Press some Mozzarella in the centre and form the rice into a ball again. Dip in the egg whites and cover with breadcrumbs. Repeat with the remaining risotto and Mozzarella. Put the rice balls on a tray and leave in the fridge for about 1 hour.

While the rice balls are resting, prepare the sauce. Heat the olive oil in a saucepan and fry the garlic and chilli until golden. Add the tomatoes, season with salt and cook over a medium heat for about 10 minutes.

Heat enough vegetable oil in a heavy-based saucepan to ensure that the rice balls can be completely submerged. Roll the rice balls in the breadcrumbs for a second time.

Deep-fry the balls for about 2 minutes or until golden (work in batches, if necessary), then transfer to kitchen paper to allow any excess oil to drain.

To serve, pour all the sauce in the centre of a large serving plate and place the rice balls on top, ready to be shared with your friends.

Pasta with Prawns and Rocket

LINGUINE AI GAMBERI E RUCOLA

Serves 4

5 tablespoons olive oil

2 garlic cloves, finely sliced

50g pine nuts

1 medium-hot red chilli, finely sliced and deseeded

300g large fresh raw prawns, peeled, heads and tails removed

½ glass dry white wine

3 tablespoons finely sliced fresh basil

500g linguine

100g rocket leaves

Salt

This is one of my signature dishes, created in the summer of 2003 on the island of Sardinia where my family and I were enjoying our holiday in our house on the beach. Make sure that you serve this dish as soon as you combine the pasta and the sauce. You can substitute the prawns for scallops.

Heat the olive oil in a large frying pan and shallow-fry the garlic, pine nuts and chilli for about 20 seconds, then add the prawns and cook for about 1 minute. Add the wine and basil, season with salt and simmer over a high heat for about 2 minutes. Remove the pan from the heat.

Meanwhile, cook the pasta in a large pan of boiling salted water until al dente. Drain and add to the frying pan. Return the frying pan to a high heat and immediately add in the rocket leaves, mix well for about 1 minute to allow the rocket to soften slightly and the pasta to absorb the flavour. Serve immediately.

Pasta Bows with Smoked Salmon and Peas

FARFALLE SALMONE E PISELLI

Serves 4

70g salted butter

1 tablespoon olive oil

3 shallots, finely chopped

150g frozen peas, thawed

100g smoked salmon, chopped

100ml single cream

500g farfalle

Salt and pepper

When I was a child, smoked salmon was always a treat for us, because at the time it was quite expensive and my mother would only make this dish once a month. To this day, I still love it.

Melt the butter and oil in a large frying pan and gently shallow-fry the shallots until golden. Add the peas and cook for about 3 minutes. Add the salmon, check the seasoning (be careful as smoked salmon is quite salty), and cook over a medium heat for a further 3 minutes. Add in the cream and cook for 2–3 minutes or until it starts to thicken slightly.

Meanwhile, cook the pasta in a large pan of boiling salted water until al dente. Drain and immediately add to the sauce. Mix well over a medium heat, stirring constantly to ensure the sauce coats the pasta beautifully. Serve immediately with freshly ground pepper on top.

Baked Pasta with Four-cheese Sauce and Salame

Serves 4

500g penne rigate

80g salted butter

200g cream cheese

100g Gorgonzola cheese, cubed

100g grated Cheddar cheese

½ glass full-fat milk at room temperature

150g salame Milano, in small dice

3 tablespoons roughly chopped flat-leaf parsley

70g freshly grated Parmesan cheese

Whenever I think about this recipe, I think comfort food. It is impossible not to like this dish (unless you don't like cheese). You can substitute some of the cheeses for your favourite ones and, without the salame, it will make a great vegetarian dish.

Cook the pasta in a large pan of boiling salted water until al dente, bearing in mind it will also cook in the oven. Drain and return to the saucepan. Add the butter and the cheeses except the Parmesan. Mix well using a wooden spoon and slowly add in the milk. Stir constantly over a medium heat until the cheeses are melted and you have a creamy texture. Add in the salame, season and stir in the parsley.

Preheat the oven to 180°C/350°F/gas mark 4. Spoon the pasta mixture into a large baking tray (35 x 20 x 7cm), sprinkle over the Parmesan and bake in the centre of the oven for 15 minutes or until the top is golden and crisp. Serve immediately.

Pasta with Ham and Mushrooms in Cream

TAGLIATELLE PANNA E PROSCIUTTO

Serves 4

100g salted butter

200g button mushrooms, sliced

200g cooked ham, thickly sliced then cut into small squares

300ml single cream

Pinch of grated nutmeg

500g fresh tagliatelle

100g freshly grated Parmesan cheese

Salt and pepper

If you aren't watching your weight and you want to cook a very quick, easy and extremely tasty pasta dish, this is the recipe to choose. The combination of ingredients is classic and you really can't go wrong.

Melt the butter in a large frying pan and fry the mushrooms and ham over a medium heat for 10 minutes or until golden. Add the cream, season with salt, pepper and a pinch of nutmeg and cook, uncovered, for about 2 minutes.

Meanwhile, cook the pasta in a large pan of boiling salted water until al dente. Drain and immediately add to the sauce. Stir constantly, allowing the sauce to thicken slightly. Serve at once with plenty of Parmesan on top.

Spaghetti Rolled in Aubergines
with Melted Cheese

INVOLTINI DI MELANZANE E SPAGHETTI

Serves 4

2 whole aubergines

5 tablespoons olive oil

1 garlic cloves, chopped

500g tinned chopped tomatoes

10 fresh basil leaves

350g spaghetti

Butter, for greasing

2 Mozzarella balls, drained and sliced

100g freshly grated Pecorino cheese

Extra virgin olive oil

Salt and pepper

This is definitely a wow plate of pasta. Simple flavours, a bit fiddly to put together, but believe me you will enjoy every minute of it. A dish that you can prepare at least half an hour before your guests arrive and no need to accompany anything with it. You can serve it as a starter or main course and, if you don't want to use spaghetti, you can always use linguine. My tip would be not to overcook the pasta and make sure that the aubergines are cooked enough, otherwise they can get very leathery.

Slice the aubergines in lengths about 1cm thick. Place in a large sieve, sprinkle with salt and leave for about 30 minutes to allow the excess water to drain. Carefully dry each slice on kitchen paper.

Heat a griddle pan and cook the aubergines for about 3 minutes on each side, then set aside and leave to cool.

Heat the olive oil in a medium saucepan, gently fry the garlic until golden, then add the chopped tomatoes. Season and leave to simmer, uncovered, for 15 minutes, stirring occasionally. Remove from the heat, mix in the basil and leave the sauce to become tepid.

Meanwhile, bring a large pan of salted water to the boil and cook the spaghetti until al dente according to the packet instructions. Drain and mix into the tomato sauce to allow the pasta to absorb the flavours.

Preheat the oven to 200°C/400°F/gas mark 6. Place a slice of grilled aubergine on a greased baking tray measuring about 30 x 20cm and spoon some of the pasta in the middle. Add a slice of Mozzarella, roll up the aubergine and secure with a toothpick. Repeat the process until all the ingredients are used up.

Sprinkle the rolls with Pecorino and bake in the centre of the oven for 10 minutes.

Once the cheese has melted, drizzle with extra virgin olive oil, remove the toothpicks and serve immediately.

Pasta Shells with Spicy Sprouting Broccoli and Purple Basil

ORECCHIETTE CON BROCCOLETTI

Serves 4

6 tablespoons olive oil

200g sprouting broccoli

2 garlic cloves, finely sliced

1 medium red chilli, deseeded and finely sliced

100ml dry white wine

500g orecchiette pasta

100g freshly grated Pecorino cheese

5 tablespoons toasted pine nuts

10 purple basil leaves

Salt

This is an authentic traditional dish that comes from the region of Puglia in southern Italy. To be precise, it comes from a town called Bari where they are absolutely mad about orecchiette pasta. The translation of the shape of the pasta in English is little pretty ears, which of course doesn't sound very appetising, but trust me the flavour of the garlic, with the spiciness of the chilli and the crunchiness of the broccoli will send you straight to heaven (aren't I a poet!) Try not to but if you have to, you can substitute Pecorino cheese for Parmesan and if you can't find the orecchiette, use any shell-shaped pasta.

Heat the olive oil in a large wok and stir-fry the broccoli with the garlic and the chilli over a high heat for 3 minutes. Season with salt, add the white wine and continue to cook over a medium heat for a further 8 minutes. Make sure that the broccoli stays al dente.

Meanwhile, cook the pasta in boiling salted water until al dente. Drain and add to the wok. Increase the heat to high and add the Pecorino, pine nuts and basil. Toss well for 1 minute allowing all the flavours to combine with the pasta. Serve immediately.

Pasta with Meat Sauce and Parmesan Cheese

Serves 4

4 tablespoons olive oil

1 onion, finely chopped

450g minced beef

100ml red wine

600g passata (sieved tomatoes)

2 tablespoons sun-dried tomato paste or red pesto

100g frozen peas, thawed

4 tablespoons full-fat milk

400g fresh tagliatelle

100g freshly grated Parmesan cheese

Salt and pepper

I wanted to write a traditional bolognese recipe but to make such a recipe, you need more than 25 ingredients and 18 hours of cooking time. So I decided to create a meat sauce that is quicker to make but still with fabulous flavours. Every time my friends come round to watch football, I make this dish and it always goes down well, especially with a cold beer. You can substitute the minced beef for minced lamb, and you can use penne pasta instead of tagliatelle.

Heat the oil in a large saucepan and fry the onion over a medium heat until soft.

Add in the minced beef and fry for about 8 minutes, stirring constantly.

Add in the wine, stir well and continue to cook for a further 5 minutes, to allow the alcohol to evaporate.

Pour in the passata together with the sun-dried tomato paste and the peas and stir well. Half cover with the lid and cook over a low heat for 30 minutes, stirring occasionally.

Stir in the milk, season and allow to rest for 5 minutes.

In the meantime, cook the pasta in a large saucepan with plenty of boiling salted water until al dente.

Drain the pasta and add immediately to the sauce. Stir for 1 minute so that the pasta absorbs the flavours. Serve straightaway, with plenty of Parmesan cheese on top.

Leek, Potato and Rocket Soup

ZUPPA DI PORRI E RUCOLA

Serves 6

60g salted butter

1 onion, chopped

2 medium King Edward potatoes, diced

3 large leeks, chopped

900ml warm chicken stock

150g rocket leaves, roughly chopped

1 ciabatta loaf, halved lengthways

2 garlic cloves

150ml double cream

Salt and white pepper

One of my favourite British recipes has to be leek and potato soup. Such a simple recipe but with a unique balance of flavours. I decided to add rocket leaves to this fantastic soup, which adds a peppery flavour to the dish. Do serve this soup with my home-made garlic croûtons, you are going to love it! Make sure that the consistency of the soup is not too runny and use fresh leeks for best results.

Melt the butter in a large saucepan, add the onion, potatoes and leeks and stir to coat the vegetables in butter. Continue to fry over a medium heat for about 10 minutes until the vegetables start to soften. Pour in the stock and bring to the boil, then reduce the heat and cook, covered, for 20 minutes.

Pass the soup through a food mill and return to the rinsed-out pan. (Do not blitz the soup in a food-processor, as this gives the soup a gluey texture.) Add the rocket to the pan and cook, uncovered, over a medium heat for a further 6 minutes, stirring occasionally.

Meanwhile, toast the ciabatta halves under a grill until crisp and brown. Leave to cool slightly, then rub all over with the garlic cloves and cut into 2cm cubes.

Stir the cream into the soup, season with salt and pepper and ladle into warmed soup bowls. Serve immediately with a few garlic ciabatta croûtons on top.

Minestrone

Serves 6

5 tablespoons olive oil

2 onions, diced

2 carrots, peeled and diced

2 celery sticks, washed and diced

200g tinned cannellini beans, drained

300g King Edward potatoes, peeled and diced

200g dark green cabbage, roughly chopped

400g tinned chopped tomatoes

200g French beans, diced

2 litres vegetable stock, made with 4 stock cubes

120g conchigliette (baby shells)

4 tablespoons roughly chopped flat-leaf parsley

80g freshly grated Parmesan cheese

Salt and pepper

Every Italian cookery book has to have a minestrone recipe in it and this is the way I cook it – very light and the ingredients I have chosen don't need to be cooked for a long time. My children absolutely love this soup – if you have children, don't be scared to let them try this, it's a great way to get vegetables inside them without an argument. A great starter and accompanied with some fresh crusty bread, it also makes a fantastic and filling main course. My tip would be not to overcook it, otherwise the bright colours and the crunchiness of the vegetables will disappear.

Heat the olive oil in a large saucepan over a medium heat and fry the onions, carrots and celery for about 10 minutes or until golden.

Add the cannellini beans, potatoes, cabbage, chopped tomatoes, French beans and stock and bring to the boil. Season to taste. Reduce the heat, half cover the pan with the lid and cook for 30 minutes.

Remove the lid, add the pasta with the parsley and continue to cook over a medium heat for a further 25 minutes, stirring occasionally.

Check that all the vegetables are tender and the pasta is cooked, and serve immediately sprinkled with plenty of Parmesan.

Spicy Bean Soup with Pancetta and Sausages

Serves 6

5 tablespoons olive oil

3 garlic cloves, crushed

3 tablespoons fresh rosemary, stripped from stalks

200g pancetta, finely chopped

2 carrots, peeled and diced

1 celery stick, washed and diced

3 teaspoons dry chilli flakes

4 pork sausages, sliced into 2cm chunks

400g tinned cannellini beans, drained

400g tinned borlotti beans, drained

400g tinned chickpeas, drained

400g tinned green lentils, drained

500ml vegetable stock

80g freshly shaved Pecorino cheese

Salt and pepper

In May 2005, I was lucky enough to travel around Mexico filming a cookery series and this recipe was influenced by my time there. An earthy and rustic dish with a chilli kick, it will warm you in an instant. It's also a beautiful dish to make when you have loads of guests coming round and will save you washing up. Try to get good-quality sausages for a better result and my tip would be to let the casserole rest before serving, allowing all the flavours to develop.

Heat the olive oil in a large saucepan and fry the garlic, rosemary, pancetta, carrots, celery, chilli and sausage over a high heat for about 10 minutes or until golden brown.

Add all the beans and lentils with the stock. Bring to the boil. Season to taste, then reduce the heat, half cover the pan with the lid and cook for 30 minutes, stirring occasionally.

Remove from the heat and leave to rest for 10 minutes. Serve with freshly shaved Pecorino and your favourite crusty bread.

SOMETHING FISHY

Every day I hear people telling me that they are absolutely scared of cooking fish. Of course, it's very difficult for me to understand this, because I was born on the Napoli coast and so was brought up predominantly on a fish diet. I find cooking fish much easier than cooking meat or vegetables – if you buy a fresh piece of fish, there really is not much cooking involved.

If this is your first attempt at cooking fish, I would recommend Involtini di Pesce alle Olive (page 88), because it's easy to prepare and full of flavour.

Cooking tips

1. Do not overcook the fish – it should be flaky and not dry
2. The fish is ready when the bones can be pulled out easily
3. Never never never use a strong cheese as it will overpower the fish
4. When you buy fish, always smell it – if it's too fishy, it's not fresh
5. Fresh fish from your fishmonger will definitely taste better than supermarket produce and the fishmonger will usually prepare it for you, too
6. If you are having a dinner party, impress them with Spigola in Barchetta (page 93)
7. A fish dish should always be served as soon as it's been cooked
8. Please make sure that your fish comes from sustainable sources and is caught using environmentally responsible fishing methods

Crispy Fillet of Salmon with Cherry Tomato and Anchovy Sauce

Serves 2

2 medium eggs

2 tablespoons chopped flat-leaf parsley

100g toasted fine breadcrumbs

2 teaspoons coarse sea salt

50g plain flour

2 medium salmon or plaice fillets (about 120g each)

FOR THE SAUCE

200ml olive oil

½ red onion, finely sliced

4 anchovy fillets in oil, drained

400g tinned cherry tomatoes

3 tablespoons finely chopped flat-leaf parsley

Salt and pepper

This is the kind of fish dish that I love to eat when I want something light, colourful and very very tasty. My grandfather used to make this recipe in his restaurant in Sardinia and it was probably his best-selling dish, but he used plaice instead of salmon. If you can't find tinned cherry tomatoes, you can use tinned chopped tomatoes. Make sure you use anchovies in oil and not the ones marinated in vinegar, otherwise they will be too sharp for the sauce. To prepare the breadcrumbs, cut some stale bread into chunks, roast in the oven until brown and crisp, and once cooled, blitz them very finely (see page 8).

Beat the eggs in a large bowl with the parsley and a pinch of salt. Mix the breadcrumbs, sea salt and flour together on a large plate. Dip the fish fillets into the egg mixture and coat in the breadcrumb mixture.

Heat 4 tablespoons of the olive oil in a medium saucepan and fry the onion until golden. Add the anchovies, cherry tomatoes and parsley, season with salt and pepper and cook, uncovered, over a medium heat for 10 minutes.

Meanwhile, heat the remaining oil in a large frying pan and gently fry the breaded fish for about 3 minutes on each side until golden and crisp. Transfer to kitchen paper to allow any excess oil to drain.

To serve, spread the cherry tomato sauce in the middle of two serving plates and place the crispy fish on top. Perfect with a glass of cold white wine.

Monkfish Roasted with Parma Ham and New Potatoes

CODA DI ROSPO AL PARMA

Serves 6

80g salted butter

2 medium onions, sliced

800g new potatoes, quartered

5 sprigs fresh thyme

2 garlic cloves

8 anchovy fillets in oil, drained

5 tablespoons finely chopped
flat-leaf parsley

60g fresh white breadcrumbs

4 tablespoons olive oil

1kg monkfish tail, cut into 4 fillets
(if you can't find monkfish, use
cod instead)

16 slices Parma ham

Salt and pepper

This is a wonderful dish if you're looking for plenty of flavour, lots of food and very little washing up. As you can see from the recipe, it only needs a large baking tray and so is perfect for those busy people who still enjoy cooking. The Parma ham and anchovies will bring loads of flavour to the monkfish and, served with my roast potatoes, it makes a complete meal. If you have to, substitute the monkfish for fresh cod and you can definitely use rosemary instead of thyme. My tip would be to ensure you cook this dish in the middle of the oven for a better overall temperature.

Preheat the oven to 200°C/400°F/gas mark 6.

Grease a large roasting tray with half the butter and tip in the onions and potatoes. Season well with salt and pepper, sprinkle over half the thyme and dot with the remaining butter.

Roast in the middle of the oven for about 55 minutes or until golden and crisp (shake the tray every 10 minutes).

Meanwhile, place the garlic, anchovies, parsley and breadcrumbs in the bowl of a food-processor. Add 2 tablespoons of the olive oil, season with salt and pepper and process until well mixed. (If it looks dry, add extra olive oil.)

Lay two monkfish fillets flat-side up on a chopping board and sprinkle with the mixture. Place the remaining fillets on top to create two parcels. Wrap the Parma ham around each parcel and tie with fine string at 2cm intervals.

After 35 minutes, remove the tray from the oven, place the monkfish parcels on top of the potatoes and roast for a further 20 minutes.

To serve, transfer the potatoes and the fish onto a large serving plate, garnish with the rest of the thyme and enjoy immediately.

Fish Stew

Serves 6

6 tablespoons olive oil

1 large onion, finely chopped

5 anchovy fillets in oil, drained

1 red pepper, roasted, skinned, deseeded and sliced

200ml dry white wine

250ml fish stock

600g tinned chopped tomatoes

3 tablespoons finely chopped flat- leaf parsley

1 sachet of saffron powder (0.012g)

300g haddock, skinned and cut into large chunks

300g cod, skinned and cut into large chunks

300g red mullet, skinned and cut into large chunks

20 large raw prawns (shell on)

20 mussels, cleaned

Salt and pepper

No matter if it's winter or summer, spring or autumn, no dish will ever beat a good fish stew. After a long day or when you feel particularly tired, it will really give you the energy you need. An explosion of flavour with colour and texture that won't disappoint. It's also a great recipe to prepare in the afternoon ready to be served in the evening and it's often used in Italy as a starter with good warm crunchy bread. If you fancy it, you can substitute the red mullet for salmon and if you don't like mussels, you can always use fresh clams.

Heat the olive oil in a large saucepan and gently fry the onion, anchovies and pepper for about 5 minutes. Add the wine and cook for a further 2 minutes, allowing the alcohol to evaporate.

Stir in the fish stock with the tomatoes, parsley and saffron and season with salt and pepper. Bring to the boil, then reduce to a medium heat and cook, uncovered, for about 20 minutes.

Add in the fish, stir well and continue to cook for about 5 minutes. Add in the prawns and the mussels, cover and cook for a further 5 minutes over a medium heat or until the mussel shells have opened. (Discard any unopened ones.)

Transfer the stew to a large serving bowl and serve immediately.

Mixed Fried Fish

FRITTO MISTO

Serves 6

5 small red mullet, cleaned and filleted

200g sole, cleaned and filleted

150g haddock, cleaned and filleted

300g whitebait

600g squid, cleaned

100g plain flour, seasoned

15 large raw prawns, peeled

2 courgettes, sliced and cut into matchsticks

1 litre vegetable oil, for frying

2 lemons, cut into wedges

Salt and pepper

For anybody who isn't a big fan of fish, this is probably the safest way to introduce them to it. Let me give you an example. My best friend Marco says he absolutely hates fish and yet every time we go to Italy together, the only thing he seems to eat is Fritto Misto – because the fish has been fried in small chunks, he doesn't taste the stronger fishy flavours you get from cooking it any other way. Serve the fish with the courgettes because the balance works well. Ideal for dinner parties where you serve everything on one big platter – either as a main or a starter, but remember to salt the fish.

Cut the mullet, sole and haddock fillets into chunks. Slice the body of the squid into rings about ½cm thick. (If you have the tentacles of the squid, cut into 1cm pieces).

Place the flour on a large plate and toss all the fish, the prawns and the courgettes until well coated.

Heat the oil in a large wok and fry the fish, prawns and courgettes until crisp and golden brown, working in batches. Drain on kitchen paper and keep each batch warm while frying the remainder.

Place the fritto misto on a large serving plate and garnish with lemon wedges.

Fresh Sardines Stuffed with Ricotta and Herbs

SARDINE RIPIENE CON RICOTTA ED ERBE

Serves 4

12 fresh sardines, cleaned, gutted, heads and spines removed

6 large tomatoes, sliced

5 tablespoons olive oil

4 tablespoons extra virgin olive oil

Salt and pepper

FOR THE STUFFING

300g ricotta cheese

50g breadcrumbs

2 medium eggs

3 tablespoons finely chopped flat-leaf parsley

2 tablespoons finely chopped fresh chives

2 tablespoons capers in salt, rinsed and finely chopped

1 garlic clove, finely chopped

This is a traditional Sicilian dish usually made with sardines or anchovies. A perfect combination of soft cheese blended with fresh herbs complements the beautiful fish. I usually serve it as a main course, but it can also be a starter. If you don't want to use sardines, you can use fresh mackerel and you can substitute parsley for basil. As I suggest in the recipe, ensure you serve it on a bed of tomato salad to freshen your palate.

Wash the sardines in cold water and dry on kitchen paper. Open out and lay flat on a chopping board with the skin side down. Preheat the oven to 180°C/350°F/Gas Mark 4.

To prepare the stuffing, mix the ricotta, breadcrumbs, eggs, parsley, chives, capers and garlic in a large bowl to create a smooth paste. Season with salt and pepper.

Divide the mixture between half of the flattened sardines, spread and cover with another sardine, sandwich-fashion. Once they are ready, place on an oiled baking tray, drizzle with the remaining olive oil and cook in the oven for about 20 minutes.

Serve the sardines immediately on a bed of sliced tomatoes dressed with extra virgin olive oil, salt and pepper.

Devilled Oysters with Spicy Tomato Sauce

Serves 4

24 very fresh oysters

FOR THE SAUCE

10 tablespoons olive oil

2 garlic cloves, finely sliced

2 teaspoons dry chilli flakes

500g plum tomatoes, chopped, with seeds and skin

2 medium eggs

6 tablespoons finely chopped flat-leaf parsley

100g plain flour

150g toasted very fine breadcrumbs (see page 8)

Salt

I'm sure you've heard about food that acts as an aphrodisiac. Well, this is one of them! A dish that will definitely not disappoint your partner, in every sense of the word. My only advice would be not to eat this dish by yourself... You can use fresh chilli instead of the dry chilli flakes and, if you really don't like oysters, try it with fresh scallops.

To open the oysters, cover your hand with a tea-towel, hold the shell and insert the tip of a sharp knife into the muscle between the two halves. Remove the oyster and place on kitchen paper to dry.

To prepare the sauce, heat 3 tablespoons of the olive oil in a large frying pan and fry the garlic and chilli together until golden, then add the chopped tomatoes. Season with salt and cook over a low heat for about 10 minutes.

Mix the eggs with half the parsley in a large bowl and season with salt and pepper. Dust each oyster with flour, dip in the egg mixture, then coat in breadcrumbs.

Heat the remaining oil in a frying pan and gently fry the oysters for about 1 minute on each side.

To serve, put 4–5 tablespoons of the tomato sauce in the middle of each serving plate and arrange six oysters on top. Garnish with the remaining parsley and serve immediately with grissini (breadsticks) and a glass of chilled Italian Spumante.

Rolled Fillets of Plaice with Black Olive and Caper Dressing

INVOLTINI DI PESCE ALLE OLIVE

Serves 4

8 plaice fillets (about 80g each), skinned (or sea bass or Dover sole)

100g black olive paste or tapenade

160ml dry white wine

2 large plum tomatoes, deseeded and diced

50g pitted Kalamata olives, finely sliced

FOR THE DRESSING

Zest and juice of 1 unwaxed lemon

2 tablespoons capers in salt, rinsed

5 tablespoons extra virgin olive oil

10 fresh basil leaves

Salt and pepper

This is a perfect example of a dish from the region of Calabria, in southern Italy. Like the Neapolitans, they believe in fresh produce with a few tasty and simple ingredients. You could also try this dish with sea bass or Dover sole. If you don't like black olive paste, substitute it for green olive paste or sun-dried tomato paste. Please ensure you buy good-quality black olives — remember, the colour of a good black olive should never be black but the colour of an aubergine.

Lay the fillets of plaice on a chopping board skinned-side up and spread with the black olive paste. Roll them up and secure with cocktail sticks.

Place the rolled fish in a deep-sided frying pan and pour over the wine. Gently bring to the boil. Reduce the heat, cover and simmer for about 10 minutes. Do not season, because the black olive paste is salty.

Put 4 tablespoons of the cooking liquor from the fish in a large bowl with the tomatoes and olives. Make the dressing by adding in the lemon zest and juice, the capers, olive oil, then season with salt and pepper. Mix the dressing with a spoon, stirring to coat the tomatoes and olives.

Transfer the fish to a warmed serving dish using a slotted spoon and pour over the dressing. Garnish with fresh basil leaves.

Grilled Turbot with Basil and Tomato Cream Sauce

Serves 4

8 turbot steaks (about 80g each)

FOR THE SAUCE

300ml full-fat milk

4 shallots, sliced

10 black peppercorns

2 large tomatoes

40g salted butter

15g plain flour

1 teaspoon tomato paste

5 tablespoons finely sliced fresh basil

1 tablespoon freshly squeezed lemon juice

Salt and pepper

Unfortunately in Italy, turbot is not a fish that we eat often, but I had to include a recipe with it, because I think it's a fantastic fish. I created this beautiful cream of tomato to go with this dish, because the balance is just perfect and it brings the best out of the fish. Make sure you use freshly squeezed lemon juice for the sauce. You can substitute basil for parsley or 2 tablespoons of pesto. Perfect with Spicy Spinach with Garlic and Chillies (page 133).

For the sauce, put the milk in a small saucepan with the shallots and the peppercorns. Bring to the boil. Remove from the heat and leave to infuse for 15 minutes. Strain through a fine sieve.

In a second saucepan, dip the tomatoes into boiling water for 15 seconds, remove and peel off the skin. Cut in half, discard the seeds, slice into strips and set aside.

Melt 15g of the butter in a small saucepan, mix in the flour and, stirring with a wooden spoon, cook for about 1 minute. Remove from the heat and gradually stir in the infused milk. Season with salt. Bring the sauce to the boil, stirring constantly, then gently simmer for 2 minutes. Whisk in the tomato paste and basil and keep warm.

Preheat the grill. Melt the remaining butter and brush over both sides of the turbot. Grill for 5 minutes on each side.

Meanwhile, add the tomato strips to the sauce, along with the lemon juice. Stir and reheat gently.

To serve, place two turbot steaks on each plate and pour over the sauce.

Seared Tuna Steak with Courgettes and Capers

TONNO SCUE' SCUE'

Serves 4

100ml olive oil

4 tuna steaks (about 300g each)

3 garlic cloves, roughly sliced

5 tablespoons pine nuts

2 large courgettes, roughly sliced

200g cherry tomatoes, halved

5 tablespoons capers in salt, rinsed

1 tablespoon fresh thyme leaves, chopped

80g pitted green olives, halved

Salt and pepper

If you ever have the chance to visit the town where I was born, Torre del Greco, you will soon realise that every restaurant in town serves this dish. Southern Italian people, me included, are absolutely crazy about tuna. If you try to translate 'tonno scue' scue' into English, it would be 'tuna made with no effort'. The reason it is called this is because the few ingredients used are put together quite randomly with not much thought and yet the dish is still perfect with amazing flavours. Cooked in less than 15 minutes, it is something that I would definitely suggest after a long day.

Heat 5 tablespoons of the olive oil in a large frying pan and cook the tuna over a medium heat for 2 minutes on each side. Remove from the heat.

Heat the remaining oil in a second frying pan and fry the garlic, pine nuts and courgettes for 3–4 minutes over a high heat. Add in the cherry tomatoes, capers, thyme and olives and season with salt and pepper. Cook for a further minute.

Spoon the courgette mixture over the tuna and return the pan to a medium heat. Cook for a further 5 minutes, uncovered, to allow the fish to absorb the flavours.

To serve, place the tuna steaks in the centre of a serving plate and pour some of the courgette mixture over each portion.

Whole Baked Sea Bass Stuffed with Italian Salsa

Serves 4

4 whole sea bass (about 300g each)

6 unwaxed lemons

4 tablespoons finely chopped flat-leaf parsley

8 tablespoons extra virgin olive oil

4 tablespoons dry white wine

8 anchovy fillets in oil, drained and chopped

Salt and pepper

FOR THE SALSA

20 cherry tomatoes, quartered

1 red onion, finely chopped

200g roasted peppers from a jar, drained and chopped

100g pitted black olives, halved

10 tablespoons extra virgin olive oil

3 tablespoons white wine vinegar

This dish is definitely one of my top five signature dishes. I think I can comfortably say that I've shown how to make this dish in every cookery show I've appeared on. I strongly believe that this recipe is the best way to cook a whole fish. The only fiddly bit is boning the fish, but don't panic, have a look at the pictures and if you really feel worried, you can always ask your fishmonger to do it for you. (Please take my book with you, otherwise you may find it difficult to explain what you want). You can make this recipe by using a whole salmon, sea bream or a large trout.

To bone the fish (unless you can get your fishmonger to do it for you), place the whole fish on a chopping board, on its belly. Using a small sharp knife, cut down either side of the dorsal fin and along the backbone to free the two fillets from the central skeleton. Do not pierce the fish's belly. Work the backbone and ribs away from the flesh, from the head to within 2.5cm of its tail. Use kitchen scissors to sever the backbone at the head and tail. Gently pull out the backbone. Check for and remove any stray bones with your fingers.

Preheat the oven to 190°C/375°F/gas mark 5. Peel the lemons and chop up the skin. Mix the lemon skin in a large bowl with the parsley, olive oil, wine and anchovies. Season with salt and pepper. Mix well and spoon the mixture around the fish.

Slice the peeled lemons and spread to cover the bottom of a baking tray – this will prevent the fish from sticking to the tray and also infuse the fish with flavour. Place the prepared fish on top. Cook in the centre of the oven for about 20 minutes or until completely cooked.

Meanwhile, mix all the salsa ingredients together in a bowl and season.

Once the fish is cooked, use a tablespoon to gently remove the lemon mixture and discard.

Place the fish onto a serving plate and stuff with the Italian salsa. Serve immediately with a glass of dry Italian white wine.

I have to admit that I absolutely love meat. For me, it's the ultimate energy food. Whenever I feel down there is nothing that makes me happier than to have a really meaty dish; so much so that every time I do my tax return, my wife makes me a Polpettone alla Napoletana (page 104) that night.

I could easily write a thousand recipes about meat, but I have decided to go for my favourite regional dishes – with a Gino twist. The one I would choose for a dinner party is Rotolo di Maiale (page 103), because you can prepare it in advance, it's really easy to put together and it will look so good that your friends will think you are a genius.

Cooking tips

1. Do not overcook pork – it is safe to eat pork slightly more than medium
2. Ensure that chicken is always well cooked
3. To get the best flavour from beef, cook it medium or medium-rare
4. Do not season raw meat with salt as it will draw out the moisture from the meat
5. Good-quality meat from your butcher will make your dish taste ten times better
6. If you grill your meat, always make sure that the meat is at room temperature
7. If you are using a griddle pan, oil the meat not the pan, otherwise you will smoke out your kitchen. For beef and lamb, preheat the griddle pan until it is very hot, for pork it needs to be warm going on hot, so that the pork cooks through and is not pink
8. Never never never serve meat immediately after it's been cooked; always let it rest for at least one minute

Italian Shepherd's Pie

TORTA DEL PASTORE

Serves 6

5 tablespoons olive oil

1 large onion, finely chopped

3 carrots, chopped

70g button mushrooms, halved

500g minced beef

1 glass dry red wine

500g tinned chopped tomatoes

6 fresh basil leaves

700g sweet potatoes, chopped

30g salted butter

50ml full-fat milk

150g freshly grated Parmesan cheese

Salt and pepper

One of my favourite British dishes has to be shepherd's pie. You can't beat the combination of a perfectly textured mashed potato with a tasty meat sauce. Of course, like every great thing in life, you always try to improve it and I think with this dish, I've succeeded. My tip would be to use tinned chopped tomatoes, as their juice is thicker than the fresh ones, and plenty of fresh basil leaves – never use dry basil as it's horrible. You can bake this in a 2-litre pie dish or in smaller individual dishes.

Heat the olive oil in a large saucepan and fry the onion, carrots and mushrooms for 10 minutes until softened. Add the minced beef, season with salt and pepper and stir frequently with a wooden spoon for 5 minutes, separating any clumps of meat.

Add in the wine and simmer for about 10 minutes, stirring occasionally, until the alcohol has evaporated. Add the tomatoes and basil, taste for seasoning and cook, uncovered, over a medium heat for 30 minutes. Stir occasionally.

Meanwhile, preheat the oven to 200°C/400°F/gas mark 6. Cook the sweet potatoes in boiling salted water until soft. Drain and mash well, adding in the butter, milk and 100g of the Parmesan. Season with salt and pepper, then stir vigorously with a wooden spoon over a low heat for 2 minutes to give a creamy texture.

Pour the meat sauce into your pie dish(es) and carefully spread over the mashed potato, ensuring that the meat is completely covered. Use a fork to create small peaks and then sprinkle the remaining Parmesan on top. Bake in the centre of the oven for about 20 minutes or until the topping is crisp and golden. Serve immediately and enjoy with your friends.

Sirloin Steak in Pepper Crust with Peas

BISTECCA AL PEPE CON PISELLI

Serves 4

10 tablespoons olive oil

½ onion, finely chopped

2 celery sticks, finely chopped

1 medium carrot, finely chopped

400g frozen peas, thawed

200g tinned chopped tomatoes

100g toasted fine breadcrumbs (see page 8)

70g black peppercorns, crushed

4 sirloin steaks

2 medium egg whites, lightly beaten

Salt and pepper

I first read this recipe about ten years ago in an old Italian cookery book and once I saw the crusty steak served with the sweet peas, I couldn't resist trying it. I don't think I've altered the original recipe much and it definitely has to be one of my top 10 recipes that I've learned. If you fancy, you can always make it with a breast of chicken.

Heat 3 tablespoons of the olive oil in a frying pan and fry the onion until golden and soft. Add the celery and carrot and cook over a medium heat for 5 minutes until the vegetables soften. Add in the peas, stir well, and finally add in the chopped tomatoes. Season with salt and pepper and cook over a medium heat for about 10 minutes, stirring occasionally.

Meanwhile, mix together the breadcrumbs and crushed pepper in a bowl with a couple of pinches of salt. Dip the steaks into the egg white, then coat in the breadcrumb mixture..

Heat the remaining oil in a large frying pan and gently fry the steaks for about 2 minutes on each side until the coating is crisp and golden. Transfer to kitchen paper to allow any excess oil to drain.

To serve, place 3–4 tablespoons of the peas in the centre of each plate. Cut the steaks into thirds and place the pieces on top of the peas. Enjoy with a glass of dry Italian red wine.

Italian Sausage with Mushrooms and Cheesy Polenta

SALSICCE E POLENTA

Serves 4

6 tablespoons olive oil

1 large onion, finely sliced

6 Italian sausages with fennel, chopped into 2cm slices

100g chestnut mushrooms, sliced

100g oyster mushrooms, sliced

100g Porcini mushrooms, sliced

100g pitted Kalamata olives

200ml beef stock

Knob of butter

30g plain flour

400g quick-cook polenta

1 litre vegetable stock (or as much as your polenta packet recommends)

200g freshly grated Pecorino cheese

Salt and pepper

It is very traditional especially in northern Italy to serve sausages with polenta. A great dish to serve when you have loads of friends coming round, because you can serve it in the middle of the table and everybody can help themselves. If you can't find fresh Porcini mushrooms, use 15g of dried Porcini that has been soaked in 100ml of warm water together with 150g of flat mushrooms. Traditionally, this dish is always served on a wooden chopping board.

Heat the olive oil in a large saucepan and fry the onion, sausages and mushrooms over a medium heat for 8 minutes until golden, stirring occasionally. Add the olives, season with salt and pepper, add the beef stock and allow to simmer for about 10 minutes over a medium heat.

Dip the knob of butter into the plain flour, add to the sauce and stir, allowing the sauce to thicken very slowly.

Meanwhile, put the polenta and the vegetable stock into a medium saucepan and cook, stirring constantly with a wooden spoon, until it thickens. Add in the Pecorino, season with salt and pepper and stir well (the polenta should not be too hard; add some hot water, if necessary). Turn out onto a wooden board.

Spoon the sausages and sauce over the polenta and serve immediately on the board with a glass of dry Italian red wine.

Italian Lamb Casserole with Warm Salad

AGNELLO ALLA MENTA CON INSALATA CALDA

Serves 4

400g lamb steaks, cut into
2cm cubes

4 tablespoons finely chopped
fresh rosemary

5 tablespoons finely chopped
fresh mint

3 tablespoons white wine vinegar

3 tablespoons runny honey

5 tablespoons olive oil

2 large onions, finely chopped

100g button mushrooms

3 celery sticks, finely chopped

2 large potatoes, finely chopped

1 glass dry red wine

1 glass water

Salt and pepper

FOR THE WARM SALAD

5 tablespoons olive oil

3 courgettes, very finely sliced
like matchsticks

2 carrots, very finely sliced like
matchsticks

2 leeks, very finely sliced like
matchsticks

6 tablespoons toasted pine nuts

Salt and pepper

After five years of cookery school and over ten years of experience, I have to admit that I never stop learning. I always think I know the best ways of cooking lamb and yet I am still finding better ways. This recipe came to me about five years ago when I started to appreciate the combination of mint with lamb after spending many years cooking lamb with rosemary. I can now say that I am absolutely addicted to this dish and recommend it to anyone who loves lamb casseroles. You can use neck of lamb instead of lamb steaks and my tip would be to rest the casserole for at least ten minutes before serving with the warm salad.

Put the lamb with the rosemary, mint, vinegar, honey, salt and pepper in a bowl. Cover with clingfilm and place in the fridge for about 4 hours to marinate.

Heat the olive oil in a large cast-iron casserole and fry the onions, mushrooms, celery and potatoes for about 5 minutes, stirring continuously with a wooden spoon. Add the lamb steaks along with the marinade, mix well and cook, uncovered, for a further 5 minutes, stirring.

Add the wine and cook for about 2 minutes to allow the alcohol to evaporate. Add the water, season with salt and pepper, cover the casserole with a lid and cook over a low heat for about 1½ hours, stirring occasionally.

Once the casserole is ready, prepare the salad. Heat the olive oil in a large frying pan and fry the sliced vegetables over a high heat for about 4 minutes, tossing continuously. Add the pine nuts and season with salt and pepper.

To serve, place some warm salad in the centre of each plate to form a nest and pour some of the lamb casserole in the middle.

Roast Pork Chops with Maple Syrup and Green Peppercorns

Serves 4

2 tablespoons whole green peppercorns

8 tablespoons maple syrup

4 tablespoons olive oil

1 tablespoon paprika

4 pork chops (about 250g each)

3 apples, peeled, cored and diced

2 tablespoons wholegrain mustard

300g spinach leaves

2 tablespoons extra virgin olive oil

2 tablespoons freshly squeezed lemon juice

Salt and pepper

I have to admit that I'm not a big fan of sweet and sour flavours, but since I've designed my own version, I am now converted of course. The combination of maple syrup with paprika is just perfect and with my fresh apple sauce added to the dish, it is beautiful. You can try this dish with chicken thighs — it would work just as well. My tip is to use firm apples and good-quality pork chops.

Mix together the peppercorns, maple syrup, half the olive oil and paprika in a large bowl. Place the chops in the bowl and leave to marinate in the fridge for at least 2 hours and for as long as possible.

Preheat the oven to 180°C/350°F/gas mark 4. Heat the remaining oil in an ovenproof frying pan and seal the pork for about 1 minute on each side. Use tongs to hold the chops and seal the fat on the side for about 1 minute. Pour the marinade over the chops and place the pan in the oven. Cook for about 15 minutes.

Meanwhile, put the apples in a small saucepan with 3 tablespoons of water and cook over a medium heat, stirring until they make a soft pulp. Remove from the heat and leave to cool slightly, then add the mustard and season with salt and pepper.

Cook the spinach in boiling salted water, drain thoroughly and place in a bowl. Dress with extra virgin olive oil and lemon juice, season with salt and mix well.

Place a pork chop in the centre of each plate, drizzle over the hot marinade, and serve with spinach and apple sauce on the side.

Baked Pork Tenderloin with Rosemary-flavoured Yorkshire Pudding

ROTOLO DI MAIALE

Serves 4

500g pork tenderloin

3 tablespoons finely chopped fresh rosemary

150g Parma ham, sliced

150g black olive paste or tapenade

1 medium egg, beaten in a bowl

Salt and pepper

FOR THE YORKSHIRE PUDDING

130g plain flour

2 tablespoons very finely chopped fresh rosemary

1 medium egg

200ml full-fat milk

100ml sparkling mineral water

10 tablespoons vegetable oil

FOR THE PASTRY

220g plain flour, plus extra for dusting

100g salted butter, chopped

This is one of my grandmother's special Sunday dishes — without the Yorkshire pudding of course. My sister Marcella and I were always very excited when we knew that Nonna Assunta was cooking this dish. The saltiness of the olive paste works absolutely fantastically with the sweetness of the pork and, of course, the crusty pastry around it makes it perfect. I created a rosemary-flavoured Yorkshire pudding to go with.

To make the pastry, mix the flour with a pinch of salt in a large bowl. Rub in the butter to create a breadcrumb texture. Add about 2 tablespoons of cold water to bind the pastry. Mix to a firm dough, wrap in clingfilm and leave to rest in the fridge for about 30 minutes.

Meanwhile, preheat the oven to 200°C/400°F/gas mark 6. Generously season the pork with salt, pepper and the rosemary. Wrap it in the Parma ham, ensuring the meat is completely covered.

Roll out the pastry on a well-floured surface until it makes a rectangle large enough to cover the meat. Gently spread over the black olive paste. Place the meat in the centre and wrap the pastry around it. Press the edges together to seal. Brush the top with the beaten egg, place on a baking tray and cook in the centre of the oven for about 40 minutes until golden.

Meanwhile, prepare the Yorkshire pudding. Mix together the flour, rosemary and egg with a pinch of salt in a large bowl. Add about half the milk and use a wooden spoon to gradually work it into the flour. Beat until the mixture is smooth, then add the remaining milk and the sparkling water. Continue to beat until well mixed and the surface is covered with little bubbles. Leave to rest for 20 minutes.

Pour the vegetable oil into a baking tray (or a 12-hole Yorkshire pudding tray) and place in the oven for 10 minutes until the oil is very hot. Pour the batter into the tray and cook for about 40 minutes until risen and golden brown.

When the pork is cooked, leave to rest for about 5 minutes. Slice and serve immediately with the rosemary Yorkshire pudding.

Neapolitan-style Meat Loaf

POLPETTONE ALLA NAPOLETANA

Serves 4

400g minced beef

400g minced pork

1 carrot, finely chopped

2 celery sticks, finely chopped

3 tablespoons chopped flat-leaf parsley

2 medium eggs

150g freshly grated Parmesan cheese

1 tablespoon extra virgin olive oil

50g bread, crusts removed and broken into small pieces

1 glass full-fat milk

4 boiled eggs, peeled

4 slices ham

1 glass dry white wine

Salt and pepper

If you go anywhere in Napoli, you will be served this traditional recipe. Great if you have a large family, it also can be eaten cold the day after you've made it. If you don't want to use pork, you can use minced lamb instead. Please make sure the meat loaf rests for at least five minutes before cutting it, so that you get the perfect slice.

Put the beef and pork mince, the carrot, celery, parsley, raw eggs, Parmesan and extra virgin olive oil in a large bowl. Season with salt and pepper and using your hands, mix well to combine all the ingredients.

Briefly soak the bread in the milk, drain and mix well with the meat mixture.

Cover the base of a baking tray with baking paper, place half of the meat mixture on the tray and flatten with your hands. Place the 4 hard-boiled eggs evenly down the centre of the mixture, then cover with the remaining meat. Use your hands to mould the meat loaf into an oval shape, cover with clingfilm and leave to rest in the fridge for 30 minutes before cooking. Meanwhile, preheat the oven to 160°C/325°F/gas mark 3.

Remove the loaf from the fridge, bring to room temperature and remove the clingfilm. Cook in the oven for about 1½ hours.

Twenty minutes before the end of the cooking, remove the loaf from the oven. Place the slices of ham over the loaf, pour the glass of white wine on top and return to the oven.

Leave the meat loaf to cool slightly before you slice it. Serve with a fresh salad of your choice.

Italian Chicken Curry

Serves 4

3 tablespoons olive oil

1 large onion, finely sliced

4 curry leaves

1.2kg skinless, boneless chicken breasts, cut into 3cm cubes

50ml double cream

100g sliced salame Milano, cut into strips

180ml coconut milk

Fresh coriander leaves, to garnish

Salt

FOR THE CURRY PASTE

3 green chillies, deseeded and chopped

½ teaspoon ground coriander

½ teaspoon turmeric

3 garlic cloves

1 teaspoon grated fresh ginger root

½ teaspoon ground cinnamon

2 tablespoons olive oil

My best friend Marco once told me that it is impossible for an Italian to create a curry. Of course, I had to prove him wrong, but in doing, I broke my cardinal rule and used onion and garlic together! I'm going to dedicate this recipe to all my Asian fans and to all curry lovers. Please let me know if you like it. You can substitute the salame Milano for cubed pancetta.

To make the paste, put the chillies, coriander, turmeric, garlic, ginger and cinnamon in a blender with the olive oil, 2 tablespoons of cold water and a couple of pinches of salt. Blitz to make a coarse paste.

Heat the olive oil in a large wok and fry the onion with the curry leaves over a medium heat for about 3 minutes until the onions have softened. Add the paste and cook for a further minute.

Add the chicken to the wok, mix well to coat with the sauce and cook for 5 minutes, stirring occasionally.

Add the cream, salame and coconut milk and cook, uncovered, over a medium heat for a further 8 minutes until the sauce starts to thicken.

Serve immediately, sprinkled with fresh coriander and your favourite fluffy rice.

Chicken Breasts in Lemon and Sage Sauce

POLLO AL LIMONE E SALVIA

Serves 4

2 tablespoons plain flour

Zest and juice of 1 unwaxed lemon

2 garlic cloves, crushed

4 skinless and boneless chicken breasts

3 tablespoons olive oil

1 teaspoon fennel seeds

300ml chicken stock

3 tablespoons freshly chopped sage

2 medium egg yolks

Sprigs of sage and slices of lemon

Salt and pepper

Every time my wife cooks for her girlfriends, she always makes this dish. I guess it's the freshness of the flavours and the simplicity of the cooking that works for her. Make sure once the dish is cooked, it's eaten straightaway, because as it cools down the chicken will dry. If you don't like fennel seeds, you can leave them out. Make sure the lemons are fresh and juicy.

In a small bowl, mix together the flour, lemon zest and garlic to create a paste. Lightly coat the chicken breasts with the lemon paste.

Preheat the oven to 180°C/350°F/gas mark 4. Remove the chicken from the paste, reserving the paste.

Heat the olive oil in a flameproof casserole and gently fry the chicken with the fennel seeds until lightly browned, turning once or twice.

With a wooden spoon, stir in any remaining lemon paste.

Add in the stock and sage and season with salt and pepper. Mix well and bring to the boil. Once it comes to the to boil, cover and bake in the oven for about 30 minutes.

In a bowl, mix together the egg yolks with 2 tablespoons of lemon juice.

Take the casserole dish out of the oven, stir the egg mixture into the casserole and put the dish back on the stove over a medium heat until the sauce thickens, stirring frequently. (Do not allow to boil.)

Once ready, adjust the seasoning and serve garnished with sage sprigs and lemon slices. Serve with your favourite rice.

Crispy Chicken Breasts Topped with Taleggio and Serrano Ham

Serves 4

100g toasted fine breadcrumbs
(see page 8)

100g toasted mixed nuts, crushed

50g plain flour

2 medium eggs

1 tablespoon finely chopped
flat-leaf parsley

4 skinless, boneless chicken
breasts

10 tablespoons olive oil

300g Taleggio cheese

8 slices Serrano ham

Salt and pepper

FOR THE SAUCE

5 tablespoons olive oil

1 large red onion, finely sliced

8 anchovy fillets in oil, drained

800g tinned cherry tomatoes

2 tablespoons finely chopped
flat-leaf parsley

The worse thing you can do to a chicken breast is of course to overcook it and dry it out. The idea for this recipe came from a northern Italian dish called Vitello alla Milanese (Veal Milanese) and my twist is mixing the breadcrumbs with crushed nuts. This dish combines the crunchiness of the coating, the ooziness of the cheese and the saltiness of the ham – it would be impossible not to like it. Served with a cherry tomato sauce, it is colourful and full of flavour. You can adapt my recipe with any melting cheese and substitute the Serrano ham for any cured ham.

To prepare the sauce, heat the olive oil in a medium saucepan and fry the onion and anchovies for 6 minutes until golden. Add in the cherry tomatoes and parsley, season with salt and pepper and cook, uncovered, over a medium heat for about 10 minutes, stirring occasionally with a wooden spoon.

Meanwhile, preheat the grill. Mix together the breadcrumbs, nuts and flour on a large plate. Gently beat the eggs with the parsley and a pinch of seasoning in a large bowl.

With a meat mallet, beat the chicken breasts between two sheets of clingfilm on a board until the breasts are 1cm thin. Dip into the eggs, then coat in the breadcrumb mixture.

Heat the olive oil in a large frying pan and gently fry the chicken for about 4 minutes on each side until crisp and golden. Transfer to kitchen paper to allow any excess oil to drain.

Put the chicken on a baking tray and top each one with two slices of Taleggio. Place under a hot grill until the cheese has melted.

To serve, spread 4–5 tablespoons of the sauce in the centre of each plate and place a chicken breast on top. Gently arrange two slices of Serrano ham in folds over the melted cheese and serve immediately, accompanied by a glass of dry Italian white wine.

VEG OUT

I thought I would find this chapter very hard to write, simply because I love meat and fish and I often eat vegetarian dishes as a side dish. Luckily, a lot of Italian recipes are vegetarian so when I started writing, it proved to be easier than I had anticipated. Take pasta for example, I strongly believe that it's probably the most versatile vegetarian dish that you will ever find.

Most of the recipes that I have chosen are from southern Italy and are made with easy, accessible ingredients.

Cooking tips

1. Make sure you choose vegetables that are in season and if the ones I've used in my recipes aren't in season, experiment with alternatives
2. Veggie dishes are the ultimate quick meals, as they don't need much cooking
3. I can't stress enough how important it is not to overcook veg – not only will you lose their vibrant colour, but you will also lose their nutrients
4. If you fancy the Italian Shepherd's Pie (page 96), you can easily replace the minced beef with minced quorn
5. Try the Melanzane alla Parmigiana (page 30) – it will also make a fantastic main course

Italian-style Spring Rolls

BOMBE DI VERDURE

Serves 4

4 tablespoons olive oil

1 red pepper, deseeded and finely sliced

1 courgette, finely sliced like matchsticks

1 carrot, finely sliced like matchsticks

1 leek, finely sliced like matchsticks

150g button mushrooms, sliced

2 garlic cloves, finely chopped

½ teaspoon crushed dry chillies

16 sheets filo pastry (15 x 15cm)

100g melted butter

Salt and pepper

One of my favourite oriental dishes has to be vegetable spring rolls and I make it so often at home that I had to include it in my book. It's a fantastic dish to prepare when you have parties, because you can fry them in the afternoon and then reheat them in the oven ready for your guests. Ensure the vegetables are not too wet when putting them into the filo pastry, otherwise your spring rolls will go soggy. If you don't have one of the vegetables, don't panic – you can always do without. Please don't try to make fresh filo pastry, the ready-made type is perfectly fine.

Heat the olive oil in a wok or large frying pan and fry all the vegetables, the garlic and the chilli over a high heat, uncovered, for 15 minutes. Stir continuously and season with salt. Once all the vegetables are golden and soft, remove using a slotted spoon and leave to cool.

Preheat the oven to 180°C/350°F/gas mark 4. Brush all the filo pastry sheets with the melted butter and stick them together in twos to make eight strong ones. Brush these eight sheets with more melted butter and share out the cooled vegetables between them, placing them diagonally across each sheet. Start to roll one corner of the filo towards the middle. When you reach the centre, tuck in the sides to encase the filling, then continue to roll up, creating a large roll.

Place the prepared rolls on a greased baking tray and brush them with the remaining melted butter. Sprinkle with black pepper.

Bake in the oven for about 15 minutes or until browned and crispy. Serve immediately with sweet chilli sauce.

Spinach, Ricotta and Goat's Cheese Terrine

SFORMATO DI SPINACI

Serves 4

2 tablespoons olive oil, plus extra for greasing

3 spring onions, finely chopped

230g spinach leaves, chopped

200g ricotta cheese

150g goat's cheese

3 medium eggs

280ml double cream

100g shelled, toasted walnuts, to garnish

Salt and pepper

This recipe is probably one of my favourite ways to use goat's cheese. The balance of flavours between spinach, goat's cheese and toasted walnuts works beautifully. It is a great dish that can be served as a starter or main course. You can use rocket leaves instead of spinach if you prefer, and make sure that you serve my terrine with plenty of warm crusty bread – see page 137 for my bread recipe.

Lightly oil a 1.4-litre ovenproof terrine dish and line the base and sides with non-stick baking paper. Lightly brush with oil again.

Heat the olive oil in a large frying pan and gently fry the spring onions for 2 minutes. Add in the spinach, season with salt and pepper and cook over a medium heat until the spinach has wilted and all excess liquid has evaporated. Remove the pan from the heat and leave to cool.

Preheat the oven to 180°C/350°F/gas mark 4. Transfer the spinach mixture to a food-processor with the cheeses, eggs and double cream. Season with salt and pepper and blend until smooth.

Pour the mixture into the terrine and cover with a piece of oiled foil. Place the terrine in a deep-sided baking tray and pour in enough hot water to come halfway up the sides of the terrine.

Cook in the oven for about 2 hours or until a skewer inserted into the centre of the terrine comes out clean. Remove from the oven and leave to cool. When completely cold, pour off any excess liquid from the terrine and chill in the fridge for 2 hours.

Turn out the terrine onto a serving plate and cut into thick slices. Garnish with the walnuts and serve with toasted bread.

Asparagus and Gorgonzola Soufflé

Serves 2

350g trimmed asparagus spears

50g salted butter, plus extra for greasing

3 tablespoons plain flour

200ml full-fat milk

4 medium eggs, separated

120g Gorgonzola cheese

Salt and pepper

Many people think that you need to be a chef to make a soufflé, but I completely disagree. My friends have tried this recipe many times and every time they have come back to me saying that it is one of the easiest soufflés that they have ever made. Of course, the combination of the Gorgonzola cheese with the asparagus is amazing, but if you want to make it when asparagus is not in season, you can always use courgettes. This recipe will make everybody believe that you are a professional, because not only does it taste fantastic, but it also looks elegant and beautiful. Whenever you make a soufflé, make sure that you bake it in the middle of the oven to avoid burning the top.

Cook the asparagus in boiling salted water until soft. Drain, allow to cool and finely chop.

Preheat the oven to 180°C/350°F/gas mark 4. Grease a soufflé dish (about 1.3 litres).

Melt the butter in a medium saucepan, add in the asparagus and cook for about 2 minutes, allowing any excess moisture to evaporate. Mix in the flour and cook very gently for a further minute. Stir in the milk, season with salt and pepper and bring to the boil slowly. Reduce the heat and keep stirring with a wooden spoon until it thickens.

Cool slightly, then beat in the egg yolks a little at a time and half the Gorgonzola.

Whisk the egg whites in a large clean bowl until stiff and fold into the mixture.

Transfer the mixture to the soufflé dish and sprinkle with the remaining Gorgonzola. Bake in the centre of the oven for about 30 minutes until well risen. Serve immediately with your favourite salad.

Italian Fondue

Serves 4

1 garlic clove

3 tablespoons Kirsch

2 teaspoons cornflour

200g Emmental cheese, grated

100g Taleggio cheese, cut into small cubes

50g Gorgonzola cheese, cut into small cubes

100g Gruyère cheese, grated

220ml dry white wine

1 focaccia loaf, sliced

Paprika

Salt and pepper

This is what I call a fun dish, the kind of dish I like to do when I want something tasty, quick and with hardly any effort. The combination of the bread dipped in melted cheese is the ultimate taste experience. I remember very clearly that this used to be one of my grandmother's favourite dishes – she loved any kind of fondue. You can substitute the chunks of bread for chunks of celery, carrots or yellow peppers. If you find the Gorgonzola cheese too strong, use Dolcelatte.

Rub the garlic around the inside of a heavy-based saucepan or a fondue pan.

Whisk the Kirsch with the cornflour in a small bowl to make a smooth paste.

Put the four cheeses in the pan with the wine and the cornflour paste and gently bring to the boil, uncovered, stirring frequently with a wooden spoon. As soon as it starts to boil, reduce the heat and simmer for 3 minutes, stirring frequently. Season with salt and pepper (go easy with the salt, because the cheeses are salty).

Meanwhile, toast the focaccia slices and cut into bite-sized chunks. Once ready, set the pan over a fondue burner, sprinkle with paprika and bring to the table to share with your friends.

(If you don't have a fondue set, transfer the fondue to a warmed serving dish and keep warm over a heated serving tray.)

Cannelloni with Courgettes, Rocket and Mascarpone

CANNELLONI AL FORNO

Serves 4

4 tablespoons olive oil, plus extra for greasing

2 large courgettes, cut into small cubes

400g rocket leaves, roughly chopped

450g mascarpone cheese

1 teaspoon grated nutmeg

200g freshly grated Parmesan cheese

1kg tinned chopped tomatoes

5 tablespoons extra virgin olive oil

10 fresh basil leaves

16 sheets fresh lasagne or ready-rolled dried cannelloni tubes

100ml double cream

Salt and pepper

Cannelloni is what I call a traditional Italian recipe, and it is usually filled with ricotta and spinach. My twist on this Italian classic is to use rocket leaves and mascarpone cheese. Believe me, if you make them my way, they will be lighter and yet still full of flavour. Make sure that you rest this pasta dish for at least five minutes before serving, allowing all the flavours to marry together.

Heat the olive oil in a large frying pan and fry the courgettes and rocket leaves over a medium heat for 8 minutes or until soft. Season with salt and pepper and set aside to cool.

Preheat the oven to 200°C/400°F/gas mark 6. Mix the mascarpone with the courgettes and rocket in a large bowl. Add in the nutmeg and half the Parmesan. Season with salt and pepper and mix well.

Tip the chopped tomatoes into another large bowl, season with salt and pepper, and stir in the extra virgin olive oil and basil.

Lay the lasagne sheets on the work surface and divide the mascarpone mixture between them. Roll up the sheets to secure the filling. Place the prepared cannelloni, seam-side down, in a single layer in a greased baking dish measuring 25 x 30cm. Pour over the tomatoes and drizzle the double cream on top.

Bake in the centre of the oven for 15 minutes, then sprinkle with the remaining Parmesan and return to the oven for a further 15 minutes.

Remove from the oven, leave to rest for 5 minutes, then serve.

Potato Dumplings with Tomato and Basil Sauce

Serves 4

1kg floury potatoes (King Edward or Maris Piper), unpeeled

2 medium eggs, beaten

300g plain flour, plus extra for dusting

FOR THE SAUCE

4 tablespoons olive oil

1 medium onion, finely chopped

700g passata (sieved tomatoes)

10 fresh basil leaves

100g freshly grated Parmesan cheese

Salt and white pepper

If I had to choose one recipe that gives me the greatest pleasure to cook with my children, it would have to be this one! It's probably the only time that I don't mind making a mess in the kitchen. Gnocchi has such a unique flavour that I don't think it should ever be served with anything but a simple tomato and basil sauce. Always ensure you serve it with plenty of freshly grated Parmesan cheese on top and, if you make it for a large number of people, place in a baking tray with the tomato sauce, sprinkle over the cheese and bake in the oven at 220°C/425°F/gas mark 7 for 10 minutes.

Place the potatoes in a large saucepan, cover with salted water and bring to the boil. Cook for 15–20 minutes until tender and drain.

Peel the hot potatoes and tip into a large bowl. Mash quickly, then stir in the eggs and flour while the mash is still hot. Season with salt and pepper.

Use your hands to work the mixture on a floured surface for about 3 minutes to create a soft dough texture. Take a handful of the potato mixture and roll into a long thin sausage shape about 1.5cm thick. Cut into pieces, each about 1.5cm long. Continue in this way until all the potato mixture has been turned into small dumplings.

With your thumb roll each gnocchi against a fork to form ridges on one side. Place the gnocchi on a well-floured tray and set aside.

To prepare the sauce, heat the olive oil in a large frying pan and fry the onion over a medium heat for 8 minutes or until golden. Add the passata and the basil, season with salt and pepper and cook, uncovered, over a low heat for about 10 minutes.

Bring a large saucepan of salted water to the boil. Cook the gnocchi, in batches if necessary, by lowering them into the water. As soon as they rise to the surface, use a wire scoop to transfer them to the pan with the tomato sauce. Gently stir the gnocchi into the sauce and cook over a low heat for a further 2 minutes. Serve immediately, sprinkled with plenty of Parmesan.

Baked Aubergines with Spinach and Pecorino

Serves 4

2 aubergines (about 200g each)

4 tablespoons olive oil, plus extra for greasing

150g frozen spinach, thawed and chopped

3 tablespoons chopped flat-leaf parsley

80g freshly grated Pecorino cheese

5 tablespoons toasted pine nuts

400g tinned chopped tomatoes

2 Mozzarella balls, drained and sliced

1 ciabatta loaf, cut into 2cm slices

2 garlic cloves

Salt and pepper

I learnt this recipe in a restaurant in Roma as I was filming 'La Prova del Cuoco', an Italian cookery show. I remember how as I was eating, it I felt such an explosion of flavours and texture in my mouth. Of course, I had to have a chat with the chef and he told me that this dish was the most popular in the restaurant. I managed to convince him to give me his secret recipe and after adding a few of my touches, I think I've probably got the best aubergine recipe. Ensure your aubergines are nice and fat, as you will need plenty of space for filling them. You can substitute pine nuts for walnuts or pistachio nuts and if you don't want to use Mozzarella, you can use any melting cheese.

Preheat the oven to 180°C/350°F/gas mark 4.

Halve the aubergines lengthways and place on a greased baking tray, skin-side down. Score the flesh with a sharp knife and bake in the oven for 25 minutes. Remove from the oven and set aside to cool.

Use a tablespoon to gently scoop out the flesh of the aubergines, keeping the skin intact. Place the flesh on a board, roughly chop, then transfer to a large bowl. Add in the spinach, parsley, Pecorino cheese, pine nuts and chopped tomatoes. Season with salt and pepper, 2 tablespoons of the olive oil and mix well.

Use the mixture to fill the cavity in the reserved aubergine skins, then return to the baking tray skin-side down. Lay the Mozzarella slices on top, drizzle with the remaining olive oil and return to the oven and bake for about 15 minutes until they are golden and the cheese has melted.

Meanwhile, toast the ciabatta, then rub the garlic all over the slices.

Once the aubergines are cooked, leave to rest for 2 minutes and serve with the warm garlic ciabatta.

Moroccan-style Pasta

PAPPARDELLE ALLA MAROCCHINA

Serves 4

6 tablespoons olive oil

1 onion, finely sliced

8 medium tomatoes, chopped, skin and seeds included

1 teaspoon ground cinnamon

1 teaspoon ground cumin

120g tinned chickpeas, drained

120g flaked almonds, toasted

500g pappardelle

3 tablespoons chopped flat-leaf parsley

2 tablespoons chopped fresh coriander

Salt and pepper

In the summer of 1995, I was working as a head chef in the famous Mambo King restaurant in Puerto Banus when I met a great Moroccan chef who also knew a lot about Italian cuisine. I can clearly remember his versions of many Italian classic dishes such as pastas, stews and even desserts, but the one that stood out was this dish. Even today, I still find its combination of flavours and spices really appealing. The greatest thing about this recipe is that you can use any shape of pasta that you fancy, and if you don't want to use coriander, you can use chopped parsley. Reserve a few herbs and flaked almonds to garnish the finished dish.

Heat the olive oil in a large frying pan and fry the onion for about 8 minutes until soft and light brown. Add in the tomatoes and spices and cook, uncovered, over a medium heat for 15 minutes until the tomatoes break down. Stir occasionally. Season with salt and pepper, add in the chickpeas and almonds and cook for a further 5 minutes.

Meanwhile, cook the pasta in a large pan of boiling salted water until al dente. Drain and add to the frying pan. Stir the pasta into the sauce over a medium heat for 1 minute, then add the herbs and continue to stir for a further minute. Serve immediately with a cold beer.

Italian Tortilla with Peppers and Parmesan

TORTILLA ALL'ITALIANA

Serves 4

10 tablespoons olive oil

250g onions, thinly sliced

650g baking potatoes, peeled

2 red peppers, deseeded and sliced

6 medium eggs

3 tablespoons chopped flat-leaf parsley

50g freshly shaved Parmesan cheese

Salt and pepper

If you want to cook something that you can eat the same night and then again for lunch the next day, this is definitely the one you should try. I love these kinds of recipes, where all the ingredients used are mainly simple ingredients that you would probably find lying around in your kitchen. A great dish if you don't want to do a lot of washing up and, served with a nice salad, it becomes an extremely satisfying and comforting meal. Try to avoid using green peppers for this recipe, as they are very bitter and you can easily substitute Parmesan cheese for Cheddar cheese.

Heat 5 tablespoons of the olive oil in a large frying pan and gently fry the onions over a medium heat for about 10 minutes or until golden and softened.

Meanwhile, thinly slice the potatoes (use a mandolin, if possible), then add to the onion together with the peppers and cook for a further 10 minutes, stirring frequently. Leave to cool and transfer to a large bowl.

Whisk the eggs with the parsley in a separate bowl, season with salt and pepper and add to the bowl with the potatoes. Mix well to combine and leave to rest for 2 minutes.

Meanwhile, preheat the grill. Use some kitchen paper to clean the frying pan and heat the remaining olive oil. Add the potato mixture to the hot frying pan, pressing it down gently. Cook, uncovered, over a medium heat for 8 minutes or until the base is golden brown.

Sprinkle the top with the Parmesan and place under the hot grill for about 4 minutes until the top sets and the cheese crisps up. (Remember to protect the pan handle with foil if necessary.)

Enjoy the tortilla either warm or cold with your favourite salad.

Sour Cream Potato Bake with Aubergines and Taleggio

TORTA DI PATATE

Serves 4

5 tablespoons olive oil

300g aubergines, cut into 2cm cubes

650g onions, finely sliced

1 tablespoon soft brown sugar

950g Jersey royal potatoes, peeled

220g sour cream

1 tablespoon finely chopped thyme

Butter, for greasing

250g Taleggio cheese, chopped into small pieces

300ml vegetable stock

Salt and white pepper

If I ever decide to become a vegetarian, I would definitely choose this recipe as one of my regular dishes. This recipe was really a mistake, that came together when I threw together everything I had in the cupboard and fridge. Believe me when I say that this is probably the best mistake I have ever made. I've tried Cheddar cheese instead of Taleggio and it still works beautifully. A great dish to prepare in the afternoon, ready to be baked later the same evening.

Heat the olive oil in a large frying pan and fry the aubergines over a medium heat for about 15 minutes until golden and crispy. Transfer using a slotted spoon to a plate.

Reduce the heat to moderate and cook the onions with the sugar in the frying pan for about 20 minutes until soft and caramelised. Stir occasionally.

Meanwhile, put the potatoes in a large saucepan and cover with cold salted water. Bring to the boil, cook for about 10 minutes, then drain. Preheat the oven to 220°C/425°F/gas mark 7.

Once the potatoes are cool enough to handle, cut into 1cm-thick slices. Place in a large bowl and gently mix with the sour cream and thyme. Season with salt and pepper.

Butter a shallow 2-litre ovenproof dish and cover the base with half the potatoes. Sprinkle with the onions, aubergines and two thirds of the chopped Taleggio.

Cover evenly with the remaining potatoes and pour over the vegetable stock. Sprinkle the remaining cheese on top and cook in the centre of the oven for about 40 minutes or until golden brown. Remove from the oven and leave to rest for 5 minutes.

Serve immediately with a crisp green salad.

A good side dish is a crucial part of your main course, but it is often treated with not as much respect as it deserves. I feel that the selection I have chosen is a good balance for the main courses featured in this book. Many of these recipes can also be used as a vegetarian option – for example, the Peperonata (page 131).

The secret of choosing a good side dish is simple – you need to try to complement the flavour. For instance, if you have a very delicate fish course, do not choose a side dish that will overpower the flavour of the fish – my recommendation for fish would be something as simple as Spinaci all'Arrabbiata (page 133).

Cooking tips

1. Do not choose a cheesy side dish if you are having fish
2. Do not choose a fishy side dish if you are having meat
3. Always try to make at least two side dishes
4. Never serve your side dish on the same plate as your main course (I don't think the flavours should be mixed on the same plate)
5. Try to have a good balance of colour between a side dish and the main course
6. Make your own bread such as the Schiacciata Toscana (page 137) and I guarantee that your guests will be impressed
7. To make a mash with a lovely texture and without any lumps, use a potato ricer, which looks like a large garlic crusher, instead of a masher.

Celery Gratin

SEDANI GRATINATI

Serves 6

2 heads celery

3 bay leaves

250g sour cream

1 teaspoon paprika

3 tablespoons chopped flat-leaf parsley

60g toasted fine breadcrumbs (see page 8)

60g freshly grated Parmesan cheese

Salt

Celery is unfortunately not a vegetable that many people would choose to use as a side dish. To me, this is a great shame because, cooked in the right way, it makes a great side dish to accompany most meals but especially meat. Because I've used Parmesan cheese for this dish, try to avoid serving it with fish — remember my rule is never serve fish with cheese. You can replace the parsley with chives or fresh basil and the sour cream with crème fraîche.

Preheat the oven to 200°C/400°F/gas mark 6. Trim the celery, discarding any tough outer stalks and cut into 6cm lengths. Reserve all the inner leaves.

Bring a large saucepan of salted water to the boil and cook the celery with the bay leaves for 8 minutes until al dente. Drain, discard the bay leaves and transfer to a gratin dish.

Finely chop the reserved celery leaves and place in a large bowl. Add the sour cream, the paprika and parsley, season with salt and mix well.

Pour the cream mixture over the celery, sprinkle with the breadcrumbs and Parmesan and bake in the oven for about 30 minutes or until the top is crisp and golden brown.

Cauliflower with Capers and Olives

CAVOLFIORE ALLA CONTADINA

Serves 6

500g cauliflower, cut into florets

4 tablespoons extra virgin olive oil

2 garlic cloves, finely sliced

60g anchovy fillets in olive oil

2 tablespoons capers in salt, rinsed

40g pitted Kalamata olives, chopped

3 tablespoons chopped flat-leaf parsley

Salt

It wasn't until I came to England that I came across cauliflower regularly. For me, it can be a little bland, so here I've added some stronger flavours.

Bring a large saucepan of salted water to the boil and cook the cauliflower for 6 minutes until al dente.

Meanwhile, heat the oil in a small saucepan and gently fry the garlic and anchovies over a medium heat for 1 minute, stirring frequently. Add the capers, olives and parsley, mix and transfer to a large bowl.

Drain the cauliflower and place in the bowl with the garlic and anchovy mixture. Toss gently to avoid breaking up the cauliflower.

Serve hot as an accompaniment to fish or meat – it's good with lamb.

Roasted Peppers with Olives, Capers and Garlic

PEPERONATA

Serves 6

2 whole green peppers

2 whole red peppers

2 whole yellow peppers

3 tablespoons olive oil

1 garlic clove, finely sliced

1 tablespoon capers in salt, rinsed

100g pitted Kalamata olives

1 tablespoon chopped flat-leaf parsley

Salt and pepper

This is a recipe that comes from the mountains of Avellino, a town near Napoli where they are mad about roasted peppers.

Preheat the oven to 200°C/400°F/gas mark 6. Place the peppers on a baking tray and roast for about 20 minutes. Transfer the hot peppers to a large bowl, cover with clingfilm and leave to cool. Once cooled, peel off the skin, halve the peppers lengthways and discard the seeds and stalks. Cut into 1 cm slices. Set aside on a chopping board.

Heat the olive oil in a medium saucepan and fry the garlic over a medium heat until golden. Add in the peppers, capers and olives. Season with salt and pepper and add the parsley. Mix well and cook, uncovered, over a low heat for 20 minutes, stirring occasionally.

Serve hot with your favourite fish or meat dish, or cold on top of some crusty bread or bruschetta.

Roast Potatoes with Garlic and Rosemary

PATATE ARROSTO

Serves 4

1kg small floury potatoes, unpeeled

6 tablespoons olive oil

1 tablespoon walnut oil

15 garlic cloves, unpeeled

5 tablespoons fresh rosemary, stripped from stalks

Sea salt and pepper

Whenever I cook a roast dinner at home, this is the dish I choose to accompany it. I strongly believe that there is nothing better than garlic and fresh rosemary with a good roast potato, and the touch of walnut oil makes it perfect.

Put the potatoes in a large saucepan, cover with cold water and bring to the boil. Cook for 3 minutes and drain.

Preheat the oven to 200°C/400°F/gas mark 6. Pour both oils into a roasting tin and place in the oven to get really hot.

Tip the potatoes into the hot oil with the garlic and rosemary. Season, mix well and roast in the oven for 35–40 minutes, basting occasionally. Serve with a few cloves of roasted garlic on each portion.

Spicy Spinach with Garlic and Chillies

SPINACI ALL'ARRABBIATA

Serves 6

6 tablespoons olive oil

2 garlic cloves, finely sliced

2 small red chillies, deseeded and finely sliced

500g spinach, drained

Freshly squeezed lemon juice

Salt

I have to agree with Popeye; there is nothing healthier or tastier than a good plate of spinach. The combination of the garlic and the chilli works beautifully with the sweetness of the spinach and, of course not only do you need one saucepan to cook it, but it only takes a few minutes to prepare.

Heat the olive oil in a large saucepan and fry the garlic and chillies over a medium heat for 1 minute. Add the spinach, season with salt and mix.

Continue to cook, uncovered, over a medium heat for about 10 minutes until all the water from the spinach has evaporated, stirring occasionally.

Serve hot or cold with a squeeze of lemon juice.

Italian-style Broccoli Stir-fry

BROCCOLI SALTATI

Serves 6

5 tablespoons olive oil

2 tablespoons runny honey

1 tablespoon light soy sauce

2 tablespoons balsamic vinegar

1 garlic clove, finely sliced

1 small red chilli, deseeded and finely sliced

3 tablespoons sliced fresh basil leaves

60g pine nuts

700g broccoli, cut into florets

Salt and pepper

Everybody in my family loves broccoli and we always have it in the house. One day I thought I would experiment with a few oriental ingredients. This is what came out of that day and I must say that I was so excited about the flavours that I decided to put it in this book.

Mix together 1 tablespoon of the olive oil, the honey, soy sauce, balsamic vinegar, garlic, chilli, basil and pine nuts in a large bowl.

Bring a large saucepan of salted water to the boil and cook the broccoli for 3 minutes until al dente. Drain the broccoli and place in the bowl with the dressing. Toss gently to avoid breaking up the broccoli.

Heat the remaining olive oil in a wok and fry the broccoli with the dressing for 4 minutes until piping hot, stirring frequently.

Check the seasoning and serve hot as an accompaniment to fish or meat.

The Ultimate Cheesy Mash

PURÉ DI PATATE

Serves 4

1kg potatoes (King Edward are best), peeled

150ml full-fat milk

100g freshly grated Parmesan cheese

50g freshly grated Cheddar cheese

100g salted butter

Salt and white pepper

There is nothing I hate more than a boring, tasteless, lumpy mash. This side dish goes perfectly with any kind of meat, especially with sausages and steak.

Put the potatoes in a large saucepan, cover with cold water and bring to the boil. Cook until tender. Drain and mash in the saucepan.

Return the pan to a low heat and use a wooden spoon to stir in the milk and beat to a creamy texture. Add in the cheeses, the butter, season with salt and pepper and continue to stir for a further 3 minutes over a low heat until the cheeses are completely melted. Serve immediately.

Deep-fried Polenta with Sage and Pancetta

POLENTA FRITTA CON PANCETTA

Serves 4

300g quick-cook polenta

5 tablespoons olive oil

2 onions, finely sliced

6 sage leaves, finely sliced

100g pancetta, finely diced

100g freshly grated Pecorino cheese

1 litre oil for frying, e.g. vegetable or sunflower oil

Butter, for greasing

Salt and pepper

If you like chunky chips, try this. It goes well with fish and meat, and if you make a big batch, you can reheat in the oven.

Bring a saucepan of salted water to the boil and cook the polenta until it thickens (follow the instructions on the packet).

Meanwhile, heat the olive oil in a medium frying pan and fry the onions, sage and the pancetta for 8 minutes until golden, stirring frequently.

Add the onion mixture to the polenta, along with the Pecorino. Season with salt and pepper and mix well using a wooden spoon.

Pour the mixture into a buttered dish about 20cm square and 3cm deep and leave to cool.

Once cooled and firm, tip the polenta onto a chopping board. Cut into slices about the size of a fish finger and deep-fry in hot oil for about 1 minute until crisp and golden. Drain on kitchen paper and serve.

Baked Polenta Topped with Four Cheeses

POLENTA AI QUATTRO FORMAGGI

Serves 4

300g quick-cook polenta

Butter, for greasing

4 large plum tomatoes, sliced

100g Gorgonzola cheese, 100g Taleggio cheese, 100g strong Cheddar cheese, all at room temperature

100g grated Parmesan cheese

Salt and pepper

This is a northern Italian recipe which I came across when I was working in Bologna, and it is a brilliant alternative to potatoes or rice.

Bring a saucepan of salted water to the boil and cook the polenta until it thickens (follow the instructions on the packet). Season and pour the mixture into a buttered dish about 20 x 25cm and leave to cool.

Meanwhile, preheat the oven to 180°C/350°F/gas mark 4. Once the polenta is cooled and firm, place the tomatoes on top. Break the Gorgonzola, Taleggio and Cheddar into small pieces into a large bowl. Mix together, add the Parmesan and continue to mix. Sprinkle over the tomatoes. Bake in the centre of the oven for about 8 minutes until the cheeses are melted and lightly browned.

Tuscan-style Bread with Rosemary and Extra Virgin Olive Oil

Serves 4

450g strong plain white flour, plus extra for dusting

1 teaspoon fast-action dried yeast

130ml extra virgin olive oil, plus extra for greasing

2 tablespoons fresh rosemary, stripped from stalks

Coarse sea salt, for sprinkling

No Italian meal would be authentic if it wasn't served with a good-quality bread. Personally, I would not be able to eat any starter or main course if not accompanied with some kind of bread on the side. I chose this bread, because it is easy to make and it goes well with any kind of dish. Of course, I don't suggest that you should bake your own bread all the time, but I do believe everybody should experience the satisfaction of doing so if only once. Make sure that you always, always use fresh rosemary because the flavour is much better and, of course, a good-quality extra virgin olive oil, preferably Italian – the smell and the colour is just fantastico.

Mix together the flour and yeast in a large bowl. Make a well in the centre and pour in 300ml of warm water with 6 tablespoons of the olive oil. Mix well to make a soft dough.

Turn out the dough onto a floured surface and knead for 10 minutes until smooth and elastic. Place in an oiled bowl, cover with a tea-towel and leave in a warm place to rise for 1 hour until it has doubled in size.

Turn out onto a floured surface again and knead the dough for a further 2 minutes, then roll out to a large rectangle about 2cm thick.

Transfer the dough onto an oiled baking tray, cover with oiled clingfilm and leave to rise again for about 25 minutes. Meanwhile, preheat the oven to 220°/425°F/gas mark 7.

Remove the clingfilm and prick the risen dough all over with a fork. Brush the dough with half the remaining oil and sprinkle with the rosemary and sea salt.

Bake in the centre of the oven for 30–35 minutes until golden and brown. Remove from the baking tray and transfer to a wire rack. As it cools, brush with the remaining oil to soften the crust.

Potatoes, Peppers and Shallots Roasted with Rosemary and Thyme

PATATE ALL'ORTOLANA

Serves 4

600g small floury potatoes, unpeeled

8 tablespoons olive oil

2 sweet yellow peppers

15 shallots

2 thyme sprigs

3 tablespoons fresh rosemary, stripped from stalks

15 cherry tomatoes, on the vine

Sea salt and pepper

Whenever my mother had guests over for dinner, this would be the recipe she would choose to accompany the main meal. I remember my sister and I used to love it when we knew this was on the menu and always begged her to make twice as much. The combination of the roasted peppers with the shallots and the fresh cherry tomatoes is an unbelievable experience that everybody should try. You can substitute yellow peppers with green peppers, and if you don't have shallots, you can use a normal white onion.

Put the potatoes in a large saucepan, cover with cold water and bring to the boil. Cook for 3 minutes and drain.

Preheat the oven to 200°C/400°F/gas mark 6. Pour the oil into a large roasting tin and place in the oven to get really hot.

Meanwhile, trim and deseed the peppers and cut into large chunks. Peel the shallots, allowing them to fall into their natural segments.

Once the vegetables are prepared, tip into the hot oil with the thyme and rosemary. Season with salt and pepper, mix well and roast for 30 minutes, basting occasionally.

Add the cherry tomatoes, roast for a further 10 minutes, and serve immediately.

SWEET THINGS

I think that a good meal should always be followed by a good dessert. The ones I have chosen for this chapter are in my opinion Italy's finest and, of course, I have added a couple of traditional English recipes with a Gino twist.

If you are on a diet you have two options: either choose the Bellini in Gelatina (page 143) or go for a ten-mile run and then choose whatever you want!

Cooking tips

1. There aren't any rules for desserts - you should have the ones you fancy
2. If you are having fish as a main course, the Torta al Limoncello (page 152) would be my recommendation as it will remove any fishy aftertaste
3. I think it is worth spending time making a really good dessert, as it is the one dish that your guests will remember
4. If you are making the Biscotti (page 154), make sure you serve a good-quality coffee with them
5. If you are having a lot of guests, the last thing you want to serve is Zabaglione (page 144) — too time consuming
6. If you want to impress, go for the Double Chocolate Mousse with Pistachio and Chilli (page 146)
7. Serve your desserts at least 20 minutes after the main course is finished
8. Forget cappuccinos and cafe lattes. After a big meal, the only thing to serve is an espresso, as milky coffee hinders digestion

Fresh Blackberry and Prosecco Jelly

Serves 6

130g caster sugar

Zest and juice of 1 unwaxed lemon

4 teaspoons powdered gelatine

50g strawberry purée

450ml Prosecco

180g blackberries

This has to be the most stylish and yet easy dessert that you will ever make. Not only can you use this dish as a dessert, but you can also serve it as a great aperitif. You can substitute the Prosecco for a good Champagne and if you don't want to use blackberries, you can use fresh strawberries. If you want to make fresh strawberry purée, just blitz 50g of fresh strawberries with 1 tablespoon of cold water and 1 teaspoon of honey into a smooth purée. Once the dessert is ready, you can decorate the jellies with a touch of whipped cream on top.

Put the sugar in a medium saucepan with 300ml of water and the lemon zest. Heat gently until the sugar has dissolved. Remove from the heat, leave to cool and discard the lemon zest.

Put the lemon juice in a small bowl and sprinkle in the powdered gelatine. Leave to soak for 3–4 minutes. Place the bowl over a pan of gently simmering water, ensuring that the base of the bowl does not touch the water, for a couple of minutes until the gelatine has completely dissolved.

Stir the gelatine into the sugar syrup together with the strawberry purée and the Prosecco. Mix well.

Meanwhile, share out three quarters of the blackberries among six Champagne glasses and carefully pour over enough of the liquid jelly to cover the fruit and chill until set. When the jelly has set, pour over the remaining liquid jelly to the top of the glass and refrigerate for 5 hours until completely set.

Decorate with the reserved blackberries and serve.

Zabaglione

Serves 4

5 really fresh egg yolks

120g caster sugar

8 tablespoons Marsala wine

4 tablespoons toasted hazelnuts, crushed

8 savoiardi biscuits (sponge fingers)

There is a rumour that zabaglione was used to give a man stamina before a night of passion. I don't believe everything I read but on this occasion, I can confirm that this is true.

Place the egg yolks, sugar and Marsala in a large heatproof bowl and set over a pan of simmering water, ensuring that the base of the bowl does not touch the water. (You also need to ensure that the bowl does not get too hot or the eggs will cook too fast and scramble.) Whisk continuously to achieve a smooth and foamy texture. When the mixture has tripled in volume, pour the hot zabaglione into four large wine glasses.

Decorate with crushed toasted hazelnuts on top and serve immediately with 1–2 savoiardi biscuits.

Tiramisu

Serves 4

300ml cold strong black coffee, preferably espresso

6 tablespoons Amaretto liqueur or a good Marsala wine

2 medium eggs, separated

3 tablespoons caster sugar

250g mascarpone cheese

250ml double cream, whipped

About 30 savoiardi biscuits (sponge fingers)

Cocoa powder, for dusting

Some people still believe that tiramisu is French in origin but that's rubbish. Tiramisu is the ultimate Italian dessert.

Pour the coffee into a large bowl, mix in 3 tablespoons of the Amaretto and set aside.

Beat the egg yolks and sugar in another large bowl for about 5 minutes until thick and pale. Add the mascarpone cheese and beat thoroughly to mix. Use a metal spoon to gently fold in the whipped cream.

Beat the egg whites in a third large bowl until soft peaks form. Fold them quickly, but gently, into the cream mixture, then add the remaining liqueur, trying not to lose the volume.

Dip each biscuit into the coffee for just 2 seconds and no longer, otherwise the biscuits will go soggy. Drain and use to cover the bottom of a glass dessert bowl about 8cm across (or four small ones). Spread some of the cream mixture over the biscuits, then repeat the process. Smooth the surface, cover with clingfilm and chill for about 2 hours to allow the flavours to develop. Just before serving (and not before or the cocoa powder will go bitter), remove the clingfilm and dust with cocoa powder.

Strawberry, Pistachio and Ricotta Soufflé

COPPETTE DI FRAGOLE

Serves 4

200g strawberries, sliced

3 tablespoons Amaretto liqueur

4 medium eggs, separated

130g caster sugar

325g ricotta cheese

1 tablespoon vanilla extract

30g pistachio nuts, finely chopped

Zest and juice of 1 unwaxed lemon

Butter, for greasing

Icing sugar, for dusting

This is the kind of dessert that will always put a smile on people's faces. I guess it must be because everybody thinks you put a lot of effort into making such a beautiful-looking and tasty dish. Well, let me tell you, it is definitely full of flavour, but it needs minimum effort to put it together. The only difficulty is that you need to be quite precise on the cooking time, so allow a good 30 minutes between the end of your main course and the beginning of your dessert. If strawberries are not in season, you can use any berries of your choice.

Preheat the oven to 180°C/350°F/gas mark 4. Place the strawberries in a small saucepan with the Amaretto and gently simmer for about 8 minutes until soft. Remove from the heat and leave to cool.

Beat together the egg yolks and the sugar in a large bowl until thick and pale. Add the ricotta, vanilla extract, pistachios, lemon zest and juice and mix thoroughly.

In a second large bowl, whisk the egg whites until stiff. Very gently fold into the ricotta mix.

Grease 4 ramekins and share out the strawberries and their juices between the dishes.

Spoon the ricotta mixture over the strawberries, level the tops, and bake in the centre of the oven for 30–35 minutes until puffed and lightly browned.

Dust with icing sugar and serve immediately.

Double Chocolate Mousse with Pistachio and Chilli

MOUSE DI CIOCCOLATO CON PISTACCHIO E PEPERONCINO

Serves 4

150g good-quality dark chocolate, chopped

100g good-quality white chocolate, chopped

3 medium eggs, separated

2 tablespoons caster sugar

8 tablespoons pistachio nuts, crushed, reserving a few to decorate

1 small red chilli (medium–hot), deseeded and finely sliced

2 tablespoons Grand Marnier

250ml double cream, softly whipped

I think you will agree with me that nearly everybody likes chocolate mousse and if you are one of these people, you will absolutely love this recipe. I came across the combination of chilli and chocolate in Mexico, when I was filming my series 'An Italian in Mexico' and since then, I realised that the spiciness of the chilli with the sweetness of the chocolate is a match made in heaven. You can substitute the pistachio nuts for hazelnuts and please make sure that when you melt the chocolate, the glass bowl doesn't touch the simmering water, otherwise it will become bitter. Make sure you allow at least half an hour between the end of your main course and this fabulous dessert.

Melt all the chocolate together in a heatproof bowl over a pan of simmering water, ensuring that the base of the bowl does not touch the water. Set aside to cool, but not to harden.

Beat the egg yolks and sugar together in a large bowl until thick and pale.

Whisk the egg whites in a second large dry, clean bowl until stiff.

Use a metal spoon to fold the chocolate into the egg yolk mixture. Add the pistachios, chilli and Grand Marnier. Mix well and fold in the whipped cream. Lastly, gently fold in the egg whites, mixing the ingredients together.

Pour the mixture into four dessert glasses (each about 250ml), cover with clingfilm and chill for 3 hours until set.

Just before serving, remove the clingfilm and decorate with crushed pistachio nuts.

Panettone and Butter Pudding

Serves 4

800ml full-fat milk

Zest of 1 unwaxed lemon, finely grated

50g salted butter, at room temperature

6 slices Panettone, about 3cm thick

50g flaked almonds

3 medium eggs

45g caster sugar

3 tablespoons Cointreau

30g soft brown sugar

Icing sugar, for dusting

One of my favourite British recipes has to be a good bread and butter pudding. The simplicity of the flavours and the warm sensation it gives you is brilliant. I chose Panettone because after Christmas I always have too much left over and I wanted to create something else with it rather than just eat it with a cup of tea. The lightness of the Panettone is much better than normal bread and gives this dish a fantastic twist. My only tip for this recipe is to ensure that the Panettone is soaked into the milk mixture for at least 30 minutes, which will allow the pudding to grow in the oven like a soufflé.

Preheat the oven to 180°C/350°F/gas mark 4. Heat the milk with the lemon zest in a medium saucepan and bring to the boil. Remove from the heat and set aside.

Meanwhile, butter the Panettone and cut each slice into triangles.

Sprinkle half the almonds over the base of an ovenproof dish measuring about 25cm long and at least 8cm deep. Neatly overlap the Panettone over the almonds.

Beat together the eggs, sugar and Cointreau in a large bowl. Slowly add the milk and mix well. Spoon the mixture over the Panettone and leave to soak for about 30 minutes. Use your fingers to gently push the Panettone down into the mixture.

Sprinkle the top with brown sugar and place in a roasting tin. Pour in enough hot water to come halfway up the sides of the dish. Bake in the centre of the oven for 50–55 minutes until the custard is lightly set and the top is golden brown. Sprinkle the remaining almonds on top for the last 10 minutes of cooking.

Dust with icing sugar and serve immediately.

Fresh Fruit Pavlova

CESTO DI FRUTTA

Serves 8

3 medium egg whites

180g caster sugar

1 teaspoon white wine vinegar

1 teaspoon cornflour

1 teaspoon vanilla extract

FOR THE FILLING

300ml double cream

2 kiwi fruit, peeled and sliced

100g strawberries, halved

3 passionfruit (cut in half and scoop out the pulp and seeds)

250g fresh pineapple, peeled, cored and cut into chunks

1 papaya, peeled, deseeded and sliced

3 tablespoons Limoncello liqueur

This is definitely one of those desserts that everybody should just tuck into and choose how much they want to eat. Simple to prepare and yet still has the wow factor. Every time I cook it for my friends or family, I hope to enjoy the leftovers with a cup of coffee in the morning, but I'm always disappointed as there is never any left. This dessert goes well after a long, heavy meal because of the fresh fruits and lightness of the meringue. My tip is to ensure that once you put the cream and the fruits into the meringue, you serve it within an hour, otherwise the meringue will start to get soggy in the middle.

Preheat the oven to 120°C/250°F/gas mark ½.

Whisk the egg whites in a large, clean, dry bowl until stiff. Whisk in the sugar a little at a time until stiff and very shiny. Whisk in the vinegar, the cornflour and the vanilla extract.

Draw a 20cm circle on a sheet of non-stick baking paper, and pour the meringue onto it, spreading it out to ensure that there is a substantial hollow in the centre.

Bake in the centre of the oven for 90 minutes or until light brown and dry. Press it gently with a finger to check that it is a little soft in the centre. Leave to cool on a rack, then peel away the baking paper.

In a large bowl, whisk the double cream until soft peaks form. In a separate bowl, mix together all the fruits with the Limoncello.

Spoon the whipped cream into the centre of the pavlova and top with the fruits.

Italian Chocolate and Nut Cake

Serves 4

250g good-quality dark chocolate

3 medium egg whites

50g candied peel

200g ground almonds

100g walnuts, crushed

50g hazelnuts, crushed

200g icing sugar

4 tablespoons Amaretto liqueur

FOR THE TOPPING

100g good-quality dark chocolate

70g icing sugar, plus extra for dusting

This is a traditional northern Italian recipe that comes from Siena. While I was at catering school, I came across hundreds of recipes on how to make a good Panforte and ten years ago, I decided that this would be the recipe that I was going to stick with. Historically, this dessert was used by the monks like a coin (hence the round shape), so they could trade for things they needed in the monastery. Please, please, please ensure that you use a good-quality dark chocolate, at least 70 per cent cocoa. This cake is also great for afternoon tea.

Melt the chocolate in a large heatproof bowl over a pan of simmering water, ensuring that the base of the bowl does not touch the water.

Use a fork to beat the egg whites in a large bowl for 2 minutes. Add in the peel, ground almonds, the nuts, icing sugar and Amaretto. Mix well, then very gently fold in the melted chocolate.

Line a circular flan dish measuring about 18cm across and 3cm deep with clingfilm. Pour in the mixture and set aside for 2 hours.

To make the topping, melt the chocolate in a heatproof bowl over a pan of simmering water, ensuring that the base of the bowl does not touch the water.

Melt the icing sugar and 2 tablespoons of water in a small saucepan over a low heat. Stir to check the sugar has melted, then add the chocolate to make a syrup.

Turn out the cake onto a plate and peel off the clingfilm. Use a spatula to cover the surface with the chocolate syrup. Set aside for 1 hour until the chocolate has hardened.

Serve in slices, dusted with icing sugar, with a cup of your favourite tea.

Limoncello and Plum Tart

TORTA AL LIMONCELLO

Serves 8

Zest and juice of 2 unwaxed
lemons

4 tablespoons double cream

100g ground almonds

200g caster sugar

5 medium eggs

120g butter, melted

10 tablespoons Limoncello
liqueur

6 plums, cut into wedges

Icing sugar, for dusting

FOR THE PASTRY

190g plain flour, plus extra for
dusting

100g chilled unsalted butter, plus
extra for greasing

This recipe comes from the beautiful town of Sorrento where Limoncello is used in nearly every dessert. In the south of Italy, we serve it after a big meal as a digestive served in a cold shot glass. If you don't fancy making the shortcrust pastry, feel free to use ready made – no one will know!

To make the pastry, sift the flour into a large bowl and use your fingertips to rub in the butter until the mixture resembles breadcrumbs. Add 2–3 tablespoons of cold water and mix to a dough. Bring together into a ball, wrap in clingfilm and chill for 20 minutes.

Roll out the pastry on a floured surface to fit a 25cm loose-based flan tin. Grease the tin with a little butter, then line it with the pastry. Leave to rest in the fridge for at least 2 hours.

Preheat the oven to 180°C/350°F/gas mark 4. Line the pastry with grease-proof paper, fill with baking beans and bake blind for 15 minutes. Remove from the oven and leave to cool before removing the beans and paper.

Put the lemon zest and juice in a large bowl. Add the cream, almonds, sugar, eggs and butter and mix together to a smooth paste using a hand blender. Stir in the Limoncello.

Arrange the plums on the base of the pastry case and pour the lemon mixture on top. Bake in the centre of the oven for 20 minutes. Turn off the oven and leave the tart to cool in the oven. To serve, decorate with a thick layer of icing sugar.

Apple and Pine Nut Cake
with Honeyed Mascarpone

Serves 6

100g raisins

5 tablespoons Marsala wine

5 tablespoons honey

250g mascarpone cheese

1.2kg Cox apples, peeled, cored,
and cut into chunks

100g soft brown sugar

100g pine nuts

3 medium eggs

200g caster sugar

200g salted butter, at room
temperature

200g ground almonds

5 tablespoons flaked almonds

There are three things that my mother-in-law gave me: number one her daughter, number two wisdom and love, and number three (most importantly) this recipe! I can't remember when, but one day she told me that she had an old recipe that was passed down from generations and she wanted to give it to me. Of course, being the good son-in-law I am, I tried it and absolutely loved it. Out of respect, I decided not to change anything about this dessert and am sure you will agree that it is fantastico.

Preheat the oven to 180°C/350°F/gas mark 4. Put the raisins in the Marsala and set aside to soak. Combine the honey and mascarpone in a small bowl, cover with clingfilm and chill until ready for serving.

Put the apples in a medium saucepan with the brown sugar and cook over a low heat until soft. Once ready, mix in the soaked raisins and pine nuts and set aside.

Cream the eggs and sugar in a large bowl. Add the butter and ground almonds and combine to give a smooth paste.

Place the apples in an oval baking dish measuring about 25cm long and 8cm deep. Spread the creamed mixture over the top.

Cook in the centre of the oven for about 30 minutes until golden brown. Sprinkle over the flaked almonds and cook for a further 10 minutes.

Serve hot, with a dollop of mascarpone cream on the side.

Italian-style Biscuits

BISCOTTI

Serves 4

2 whole medium eggs

3 medium egg yolks

150g caster sugar

300g plain flour, plus extra for dusting

100g hazelnuts, chopped

'Biscotti' means cooked twice, but I chose not to use the traditional method, because I found a way of simplifying the process while retaining a fantastic texture and flavour. The biscuits can be preserved in a sealed plastic container.

Preheat the oven to 160°C/325°F/gas mark 3 and line a baking tray with greaseproof paper.

Beat together the whole eggs and egg yolks in a large bowl. Use a wooden spoon to gently mix the sugar and the flour into the eggs. Add the hazelnuts and use your hands to fold in gently until you have a doughy mixture.

Turn out the dough onto a well-floured surface and roll into a sausage shape. Slice into diagonal strips each about 1.5cm thick.

Place the biscotti on the lined baking tray and bake for 17 minutes in the centre of the oven until golden. Turn out and cool on a rack until very firm.

Best with Italian coffee or vanilla ice cream.

Almond Biscuits

AMARETTI

Serves 4

Butter, for greasing

4 medium egg whites

350g caster sugar

350g ground almonds

30ml Amaretto liqueur

Preheat the oven to 180°C/350°F/gas mark 4 and line a baking tray with greaseproof paper. Lightly grease with the butter.

Whisk the egg whites in a large, clean, dry bowl until stiff and firm. Gently mix in the sugar and almonds. Pour in the Amaretto and fold in carefully to make a smooth paste.

Use a teaspoon to place small heaps of the mixture on the lined tray, spaced about 3cm apart to allow for expansion during cooking. Bake in the centre of the oven for about 15 minutes until golden brown.

Enjoy warm or dry the biscuits on a rack until crisp and firm.

Best served with coffee or ice cream.

Sometimes I find myself in situations where I can't quite find the words to express my feelings – and believe me for a man, that happens quite often.

I know that this is going to be the most popular chapter in the book, because I believe that the language of food is understood by everyone. Therefore, you have no more excuses not to tell your loved ones how you feel.

Cooking tips

1. This is the one instance when presentation is very important, so make an effort to ensure your food looks really fantastico
2. Make sure you have rehearsed this recipe at least once before so you won't feel too stressed on the night
3. A good bottle of wine or a cold glass of Champagne always goes down well

Sausage, Bean and Olive Casserole

SALSICCE E FAGIOLI

Serves 4

6 tablespoons olive oil

350g onions, chopped

2 carrots, chopped

400g pancetta, diced

1kg pork sausages, cut into chunks about 3cm thick

2 tablespoons plain flour

2 glasses red wine

80g tomato paste

400ml beef stock

150g pitted black olives

400g tinned cannellini beans, drained

200g button mushrooms, quartered

5 bay leaves

Salt and pepper

I always make this casserole for my best friend. A northern Italian classic, it is usually made with lard and pork belly, but I have updated it by replacing them with olive oil, sausages and pancetta. This way you get the strong flavour of the pork, but less cooking time. The combination of olives and pork is one that you will find in Italian restaurants now, and I love it. Try also replacing the sausages with small ribs. Leave the casserole to rest for about 10 minutes — you don't want to serve it scorching hot. It will be even better reheated the next day (just add a little water).

Preheat the oven to 200°C/400°F/gas mark 6. Heat the olive oil in a large flameproof casserole dish and fry the onions and carrots over a high heat for 2 minutes until golden.

Add in the pancetta and the sausages and cook for about 3 minutes, stirring with a wooden spoon. Mix in the flour and cook for a further minute, stirring continuously.

Add in the wine and cook for about 2 minutes to allow the alcohol to evaporate. Stir in the tomato paste, add in the beef stock, the olives, the cannellini beans and the mushrooms. Add the bay leaves, season with salt and pepper, and bring to the boil. Cover the pan and cook in the oven for 30 minutes until the sausages are tender and the sauce has thickened.

Serve with your favourite crusty bread.

'one for the boys'

Lamb Cutlets with Herb Crust and Warm Cannellini Bean and Fennel Salad

COSTOLETTE DI AGNELLO CON CROSTA

Serves 2

6 slices white bread

2 tablespoons finely chopped rosemary

2 tablespoons finely chopped sage

150g salted butter, melted

4 tablespoons olive oil

8 lamb cutlets

4 tablespoons Dijon mustard

FOR THE SALAD

300g tinned cannellini beans, drained

2 small fennel bulbs, thinly sliced

3 tablespoons extra virgin olive oil

1 tablespoon white wine vinegar

1 tablespoon chopped flat-leaf parsley

If I had to choose one meat, I would choose lamb – it's such a male meat with strong flavour. Served with a crust of sage and rosemary, the flavours are ten times better. I decided to serve my lamb cutlets with a warm fennel salad to give the dish a rustic look with plenty of colours and flavours. Of course, you can serve this dish with your favourite potatoes and use chops instead of cutlets. If the fennel is not in season, try French beans or pak choi.

Remove the crusts from the bread and blitz in a food-processor to form breadcrumbs. Place the crumbs in a large bowl and mix in the rosemary, sage and butter with your fingers. Season with salt and pepper and set aside. Preheat the oven to 200°C/400°F/gas mark 6.

Heat the olive oil in a large frying pan and seal the cutlets for 1 minute on each side to brown. (Work in batches, if necessary.) Transfer to a baking tray. Gently brush one side of the cutlets with the mustard and place 2 tablespoons of the breadcrumb mixture on top of each one.

Roast in the oven for about 10 minutes until the lamb is tender and the breadcrumbs are golden brown.

Meanwhile, place the beans and the fennel in a medium frying pan with 2 tablespoons of water. Cook over a high heat for about 5 minutes, stir in the extra virgin olive oil, the vinegar and the parsley. Season.

To serve, divide the warm salad between two plates and arrange four lamb cutlets around it.

Grind over some black pepper and serve immediately.

'for my husband'

Chicken in Marsala and Dill Sauce

Serves 2

2 skinless, boneless chicken breasts

Plain flour, for dusting

100ml olive oil

4 tablespoons Marsala wine

150ml double cream

1 tablespoon chopped dill

2 medium potatoes, unpeeled and par-boiled

2 garlic cloves, halved

2 tablespoons fresh rosemary, stripped from stalks

Salt and pepper

Every man at some point asks himself, 'what should I do to impress my girlfriend or wife?'. Of course, a diamond ring would be the first option, but for those who, like me, believe in 'minimum effort, maximum satisfaction', I would suggest that they get cooking. Trust me when I say that there is no woman on this planet who would not be seduced by this dish. The sweetness of the Marsala wine touching the cream and coating the chicken breast is amazing. Served with tasty sauté potatoes makes it perfect.

With a meat mallet, beat the chicken breasts between two sheets of clingfilm on a board until the breasts are 1cm thin. Lightly dust the breasts with flour.

Heat 2 tablespoons of the olive oil in a medium frying pan and fry the chicken for about 1 minute on each side. Add the Marsala and flame for about 15 seconds, allowing the alcohol to evaporate.

Add the cream and the dill, season with salt and pepper and cook, uncovered, over a low heat for about 4 minutes to allow the sauce to thicken.

Meanwhile, slice the potatoes about 1cm thick. Heat the remaining oil in a second frying pan, fry the garlic and rosemary for 1 minute, then add the potatoes. Season with salt and pepper and cook over a medium heat for 5 minutes or until golden on both sides.

Place a chicken breast on each plate and surround with sautéed potatoes. Drizzle some of the sauce over the chicken and serve immediately.

'for my beautiful wife'

Pasta with Lobster and Cherry Tomatoes

LINGUINE ALL'ARAGOSTA

Serves 2

1 whole live lobster (or a ready-cooked one, if you prefer)

4 tablespoons olive oil

1 garlic clove, finely sliced

1 small red chilli, deseeded and finely sliced

½ glass dry white wine

1 tablespoon freshly chopped flat-leaf parsley

10 cherry tomatoes, halved

250g linguine

Salt

I decided to write this recipe for one reason only: to prove to everybody that sometimes it's easier to cook a meal for someone than actually say 'I love you' to them. People need to be reminded how much somebody loves them and what better way to do so than this. I can understand that this recipe has an expensive ingredient, but don't worry, you can always replace it with large king prawns. Remember once the pasta is coated with the sauce, it needs to be served and eaten immediately, otherwise it will go dry and sticky.

Bring a large saucepan of water to the boil and cook the lobster for 10 minutes. Drain and leave to cool.

Twist off the claws and pincers. Using the back of a large, heavy knife, crack open the large claws. Use a skewer to carefully remove all the meat from the claws and cut into small chunks.

Place the lobster, back uppermost, on a flat surface and cut the lobster in half lengthways. Remove the meat from the body and cut into small chunks. Clean the shell under cold running water and set aside.

Heat the olive oil in a large frying pan and fry the garlic and the chilli for about 30 seconds over a medium heat, then add in the lobster meat and cook for about 1 minute. Add in the white wine, parsley, tomatoes, season with salt and continue to cook for about 5 minutes, uncovered, stirring occasionally.

Meanwhile, cook the pasta in a large pan of boiling salted water until al dente. Drain and add to the lobster sauce. Mix well over a low heat for 1 minute to allow the pasta to absorb the flavours of the lobster sauce.

To serve, spoon the pasta into the cleaned lobster shell, pour over any remaining sauce and enjoy immediately.

'I love you'

Duck Breasts in Limoncello Sauce

PETTO D'ANATRA AL LIMONCELLO

Serves 6

6 duck breast fillets (about 180g each)

4 tablespoons olive oil

Handful of fresh mint leaves, to garnish

FOR THE SAUCE

120g salted butter

2 tablespoons mixed peppercorns

200ml Limoncello

Zest and juice of 1 unwaxed lemon

300ml chicken stock

Salt and pepper

I have to admit that I don't often cook duck at home. One of the reasons is that I always save it for when I'm out in some friend's restaurant, but if I have to cook it, I would only use this recipe. The flavour of the Limoncello sauce works beautifully with duck breasts, and it doesn't take long to cook. Remember to rest the duck before slicing to allow the meat to relax. If you really don't fancy duck, you can use a good steak. Why for the girls? Because they love Limoncello.

Place the duck breasts in a large bowl and use your hands to rub in the olive oil with some salt and pepper.

Preheat the oven to 200°C/400°F/gas mark 6 and set a dry griddle pan to heat on the hob. Place the oiled breasts on the hot griddle, skin-side down first, and seal for about 2 minutes on each side. Transfer to a roasting tin and roast in the oven for about 10 minutes until it is crisp on the outside but pink in the middle. Remove from the oven and leave to rest for 1 minute before slicing each breast on the diagonal into four.

Meanwhile, prepare the sauce. Melt half the butter in a large frying pan, add the peppercorns and cook over a medium heat for 1 minute. Add in the Limoncello with the lemon zest and juice and simmer, uncovered, until reduced by half. Add the chicken stock, season with salt and pepper and continue to cook for about 8 minutes until the sauce is again reduced by half. Add the remaining butter to the sauce and stir with a wooden spoon until you create a creamy texture.

Place the sliced duck in the middle of a serving plate. Drizzle over the sauce, garnish with fresh mint leaves and serve immediately.

'something for the girls'

Chicken and Mediterranean Vegetable Pie

TORTA DI POLLO E VEGETALI

Serves 4

300g potatoes, peeled and cut into 2cm chunks

300g leeks, cut into 2cm chunks

2 carrots, peeled and cut into 2cm chunks

100g parsnips, cut into 1cm chunks

1 chicken stock cube

50g salted butter

1 garlic clove, chopped

3 skinless, boneless chicken breasts, cut into 2cm chunks

50g plain flour

100g Dolcelatte cheese

2 courgettes, finely sliced

2 tablespoons chopped fresh chives

1 medium egg, beaten

Salt and pepper

FOR THE PASTRY

300g plain flour, plus extra for dusting

120g salted butter, at room temperature

70g freshly grated Parmesan cheese

1 medium egg

I have never been a big fan of pies, but things changed when I came to live in England. I started to appreciate them so, of course, I've had to design one with my own signature.

To make the pastry, mix the flour with a pinch of salt in a large bowl and rub in the butter with your fingers to create a breadcrumb texture. Mix in the Parmesan and make a well in the centre. Add the egg and about 2 tablespoons of cold water. Knead until firm, wrap in clingfilm and chill in the fridge for about 30 minutes.

Cook the potatoes, leeks, carrots and parsnips in about 600ml of boiling salted water for 10 minutes until softened. Drain, reserving the liquid and mix with the stock cube and more water to give 600ml of stock.

Melt the butter in a saucepan and fry the garlic for about 30 seconds. Add the chicken and cook over a medium heat for about 3 minutes, stirring, until golden on all sides. Remove the pan from the heat and mix in the flour with a wooden spoon. Return the pan to the hob and continue to cook over a medium heat for about 2 minutes. Slowly add the stock, bring to the boil and cook for a further 3 minutes.

Add in the Dolcelatte, courgettes, the cooked vegetables, the chives, then season and stir well. Spoon the mixture into a 1.5-litre pie dish.

Preheat the oven to 180°C/350°F/gas mark 4. Roll out the pastry on a floured surface and mark out a round or oval shape to fit the top of your dish. Moisten the rim of the dish with water and place the pastry on top. Press the edges to seal and trim away any excess pastry. Garnish with some leaf shapes made from the pastry trimmings and brush beaten egg over the entire pie.

Bake in the centre of the oven for about 40 minutes or until the pastry crust is a lovely golden brown colour. Serve immediately.

'for my special family'

Sticky Banana and Chocolate Tart

Serves 6

50g salted butter

120g golden caster sugar

6 firm large bananas, peeled

100g chocolate chips

250g ready-to-roll puff pastry

Plain flour, for dusting

1 tub good-quality vanilla ice cream, to serve

What a fantastic way to end a meal. So far, I don't think I've met anyone, especially children, who doesn't like this recipe. I promise you that once you've made this dish and realise how easy it is to do, it will become a favourite. My tip would be to make sure that you bake the tart in the middle of a preheated oven to avoid the pastry burning. If you have to, you can replace the bananas for firm large pears, peeled and cut in half.

Melt the butter with the sugar in a deep-sided, heavy-based frying pan that can be used in the oven. Cook over a medium heat for about 5 minutes until it turns into golden caramel. Remove from the heat and set aside to cool slightly. Preheat the oven to 200°C/400°F/gas mark 6.

Place the whole bananas in the pan creating a circle, breaking as necessary, ensuring that the entire base is covered. Sprinkle over the chocolate chips.

Meanwhile, unroll the puff pastry onto a floured surface and cut a disc shape about 25cm diameter, or about 5cm bigger than the top of your pan.

Lay the pastry over the bananas and tuck the overlap down inside the pan with your fingers.

Bake the tart for 20–25 minutes or until the pastry is golden brown. Remove from the oven and set aside to cool for about 5 minutes.

Take a large circular plate and place face down on top of the pan. Quickly invert the pan to turn the tart upside down. Remove the pan, leaving the bananas facing upwards.

Serve generous portions with vanilla ice cream.

'for my children'

Chicken Breasts in Pizza Sauce with Mozzarella

POLLO ALLA PIZZAIOLA

Serves 4

8 tablespoons olive oil

3 garlic cloves, finely sliced

4 large skinless, boneless chicken breasts

800g tinned chopped tomatoes

1 teaspoon dried oregano

2 Mozzarella balls, drained and finely sliced

Salt and pepper

Being Neapolitan, it was easy for me to design a recipe with chicken and the same flavours as a pizza margherita. This is definitely a winner when you have your best friend over for dinner and is also very quick to prepare leaving plenty of time for chatting. My tip would be not to buy buffalo Mozzarella, because it contains too much water – just buy normal cow's milk Mozzarella. Make sure you have plenty of warm crusty bread to soak up the sauce.

Heat the olive oil in a large frying pan and fry the garlic and the chicken over a medium heat for 2 minutes on each side until golden.

Add in the tomatoes and oregano and season with salt and pepper. Cook, uncovered, over a medium heat for about 10 minutes until some of the water from the tomatoes has evaporated. Meanwhile, preheat the grill.

Remove the pan from the heat and place the sliced Mozzarella on top of the chicken breasts. Grind over some black pepper and place the pan under the grill for about 2 minutes or until the cheese starts to melt. (Protect the handle of the frying pan with foil, if necessary.)

To serve, pour some of the sauce in the middle of a each plate, place a breast of chicken on top and enjoy with warm crusty bread.

'for my best friend'

Saffron Risotto with Courgettes and Pork

RISOTTO ALLO ZAFFERANO

Serves 4

20g vegetable stock cube

5 tablespoons olive oil

1 onion, finely chopped

2 courgettes, cut into ½cm cubes

1 teaspoon finely chopped fresh rosemary

200g minced pork

400g Arborio rice

½ teaspoon powdered saffron

200ml dry white wine

80g salted butter

100g freshly grated Parmesan cheese

Salt and pepper

Saffron is a very popular ingredient in Italy especially in a risotto recipe. This dish comes from the northern part of Italy and is a classic to which I've added my own twist. A warm and comforting dish that will leave you truly satisfied. I never had the chance to cook this dish for my grandfather, but I'm sure he would have loved it.

Make up hot stock by dissolving the vegetable stock cube in 1.2 litres of boiling water. Pour into a jug and set aside.

Heat the olive oil in a large saucepan and fry the onion over a medium heat for about 2 minutes until softened. Add in the courgettes, rosemary and pork and keep cooking for a further 3 minutes, stirring continuously with a wooden spoon. Add the rice and keep stirring for 3 minutes, allowing the rice to toast in the olive oil and start to absorb all the flavours.

Add in the saffron, then the wine and continue to cook for a further 3 minutes to allow the alcohol to evaporate.

Start to add the warm stock a little at a time, season well and cook gently, stirring occasionally until the stock is absorbed. Continue adding more stock as each addition is absorbed. If necessary, add a little more hot water to the stock.

When most of the stock has been absorbed (about 20 minutes), taste the rice and make sure it is al dente. Remove the saucepan from the heat and add the butter to the risotto. At this point, it is very important that you stir the butter very fast into the rice for at least 1 minute – this creates a fantastic creamy texture.

Stir in the Parmesan and serve immediately.

'for my fantastic grandparents'

Chicken in Breadcrumbs with Tomato Salsa and Spicy Spinach

Serves 2

8 tablespoons olive oil

250g spinach leaves

1 garlic clove, sliced

½ teaspoon crushed dried chilli

2 large skinless, boneless chicken breasts

Plain flour, for dusting

2 medium eggs, seasoned and beaten

70g toasted fine breadcrumbs (see page 8)

Salt and pepper

FOR THE SALSA

3 large fresh plum tomatoes, chopped, seeds and skin included

2 tablespoons pitted black olives, sliced

5 fresh basil leaves, chopped

2 tablespoons extra virgin olive oil

I dedicate this recipe to all the dads for two reasons: firstly because my own father loves this dish, but also because this is my all-time favourite and I would love my boys to cook it for me one day. The combination of the crispy coated chicken with the spicy spinach is absolutely fantastic. Ensure that the topping for the chicken marinates for at least half an hour and try to get good-quality tomatoes. You can substitute chicken for veal or pork.

For the salsa, mix the tomatoes, olives and basil in a large bowl, drizzle with the extra virgin olive oil and season with salt and pepper. Mix well and allow to rest.

Heat 2 tablespoons of olive oil in a large frying pan and fry the spinach with the garlic and chilli. Season with salt and cook over a medium heat for about 4 minutes until softened. Keep stirring with a wooden spoon.

With a meat mallet, beat the chicken breasts between two sheets of clingfilm on a board until the breasts are 1cm thin. Lightly dust the breasts with flour, dip in the beaten eggs and finally coat in the breadcrumbs.

Heat the remaining olive oil in a large frying pan and gently fry the chicken over a medium heat for about 3 minutes on each side until golden and crisp. Transfer to kitchen paper to allow the excess oil to drain.

Place a chicken breast in the centre of each plate, spread 3 tablespoons of the tomato salsa on top and serve immediately with the spicy spinach.

'I love you, Daddy'

Conversion chart

WEIGHT (SOLIDS)

7g	¼oz
10g	½oz
20g	¾oz
25g	1oz
40g	1½oz
50g	2oz
60g	2½oz
75g	3oz
100g	3½oz
110g	4oz (¼lb)
125g	4½oz
150g	5½oz
175g	6oz
200g	7oz
225g	8oz (½lb)
250g	9oz
275g	10oz
300g	10½oz
310g	11oz
325g	11½oz
350g	12oz (¾lb)
375g	13oz
400g	14oz
425g	15oz
450g	1lb
500g (½kg)	18oz
600g	1¼lb
700g	1½lb
750g	1lb 10oz
900g	2lb
1kg	2¼lb
1.1kg	2½lb
1.2kg	2lb 12oz
1.3kg	3lb
1.5kg	3lb 5oz
1.6kg	3½lb
1.8kg	4lb
2kg	4lb 8oz
2.25kg	5lb
2.5kg	5lb 8oz
3kg	6lb 8oz

VOLUME (LIQUIDS)

5ml	1 teaspoon
10ml	1 dessertspoon
15ml	1 tablespoon or ½fl oz
30ml	1fl oz
40ml	1½fl oz
50ml	2fl oz
60ml	2½fl oz
75ml	3fl oz
100ml	3½fl oz
125ml	4fl oz
150ml	5fl oz (¼ pint)
160ml	5½fl oz
175ml	6fl oz
200ml	7fl oz
225ml	8fl oz
250ml (0.25 litre)	9fl oz
300ml	10fl oz (½ pint)
325ml	11fl oz
350ml	12fl oz
370ml	13fl oz
400ml	14fl oz
425ml	15fl oz (¾ pint)
450ml	16fl oz
500ml (0.5 litre)	18fl oz
550ml	19fl oz
600ml	20fl oz (1 pint)
700ml	1¼ pints
850ml	1½ pints
1 litre	1¾ pints
1.2 litres	2 pints
1.5 litres	2½ pints
1.8 litres	3 pints
2 litres	3½ pints

LENGTH

5mm	¼ inch
1cm	½ inch
2cm	¾ inch
2.5cm	1 inch
3cm	1¼ inches
4cm	1½ inches
5cm	2 inches
7.5cm	3 inches
10cm	4 inches
15cm	6 inches
18cm	7 inches
20cm	8 inches
24cm	10 inches
28cm	11 inches
30cm	12 inches

Index

175

Acknowledgements

It would have been impossible to write this book without the help of my wife Jessie, who spent many nights translating my ideas and feelings onto paper. And of course, thank you to my two boys Luciano and Rocco, who spent many nights sleeping so I could actually write this book, Vi amo.

A big thank you to everybody at Kyle Cathie who made my dream come true. It's been a pleasure working with you – you made the ride easy and fun. Also thanks to Kate for the fantastic pictures, making me look half decent after many a late night.

A special grazie goes to everybody at Bontà Italia for the continuing support and understanding, Marco, you are the best!

A big kiss to Ali, who spent many days in the kitchen testing out my recipes, and to her family who were forced to eat them.

This is probably my only chance to really express my gratitude to my fellow colleagues who have supported and helped me in my television career: Jeni Barnett – I love you, Ainsley Harriott – a true friend, Antony Worrall Thompson – you are my wisdom and dictionary and finally, the guys at Prospect Pictures for giving me a chance. (Barry – my Pozzo di Scienza – auto-cue is now mastered).

Last, but not least, a huge thank you to the Don (ladies and gentlemen – Mr Jeremy Hicks) who continues to guide me in the right direction and believed in me from day one. You are not just my agent, you are someone I respect, admire and love like a father.

Grazie, grazie, grazie to all of you for choosing my book – Buon Appetito!